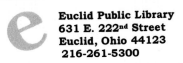

Poland Betrayed

Campaign Chronicles

Poland Betrayed

The Nazi-Soviet Invasions 1939

David G. Williamson

Campaign Chronicles
Series Editor

Christopher Summerville

Pen & Sword
MILITARY

To Alex and Sarah

First published in Great Britain in 2009 by
Pen & Sword Military
an imprint of
Pen & Sword Books Ltd
47 Church Street
Barnsley
South Yorkshire
S70 2AS

Copyright © text David G. Williamson 2009
Copyright © maps Christopher Summerville 2009

ISBN 978 1 84415 926 0

A CIP catalogue record for this book is
available from the British Library.

Typeset in Sabon
by Phoenix Typesetting, Auldgirth, Dumfriesshire

Printed and bound in England
by the MPG Books Group

Pen & Sword Books Ltd incorporates the imprints of Pen & Sword Aviation, Pen &
Sword Family History, Pen & Sword Maritime,
Pen & Sword Military, Wharncliffe Local History, Pen & Sword Select, Pen & Sword
Military Classics, Leo Cooper, Remember When,
Seaforth Publishing and Frontline Publishing.

For a complete list of Pen & Sword titles please contact
PEN & SWORD BOOKS LIMITED
47 Church Street, Barnsley, South Yorkshire, S70 2AS, England
E-mail: enquiries@pen-and-sword.co.uk
Website: www.pen-and-sword.co.uk

Contents

Poland Betrayed

Contents

Maps and Illustrations

Maps and Illustrations

Acknowledgements

———————◆◦◆———————

Sincerest thanks are due to Teresa Glazer, Irena Haniewicz, Jan K. Siedlecki, Walery Choroszewski, Adam Lasocki, Władzia Tański, Louise McCall, Christopher Muszkowski and Mr Naharnowicz – all of whom found time to talk to me about their experiences of the September Campaign.

Dr Andrzej Suchcitz, at the Polish Institute and Sikorski Museum, Chris Summerville, my editor, Pamela Covey, my proofreader, as well as the staff at the National Archives and in the Reading Room of the Imperial War Museum, were unfailingly helpful whenever I approached them.

The author would also like to thank Ewa Haren, Taisa Kiczkajło and Jerzy Chodyrew for help with sources and Polish spellings, and the following for granting him permission to use copyright material: Teresa Glazer, Irena Haniewicz, Jan K. Siedlecki, Walery Choroszewski and Louise McCall, all of whom lent him copies of unpublished manuscripts. He would also like to thank the owners of the following papers in the Imperial War Museum, London: B.M. Poloniecki, R. Zolski, Wiktor Jackiewicz, Peter Fleming (P.Z. Tarczynski), B.J. Solak, F. Kornicki, M.A. Rymaszewski, R. Smorczewski, S. Kurylak, W. Krey, A. Golebiowski and S. Goldberg. Special thanks are also due to the Taylor Library for the use of images.

Finally, the author would like to acknowledge his debt to S.J. Zaloga's and V. Madej's book, *The Polish Campaign 1939*, which greatly assisted in technical matters associated with the September Campaign.

Every effort has been made to trace copyright holders and the author and the Imperial War Museum would be grateful for any information which might help to trace those whose identities or addresses are not currently known.

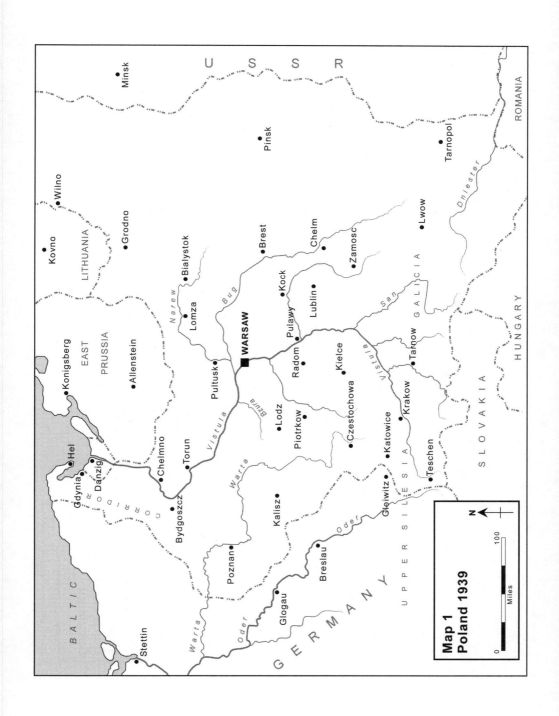

Map 1
Poland 1939

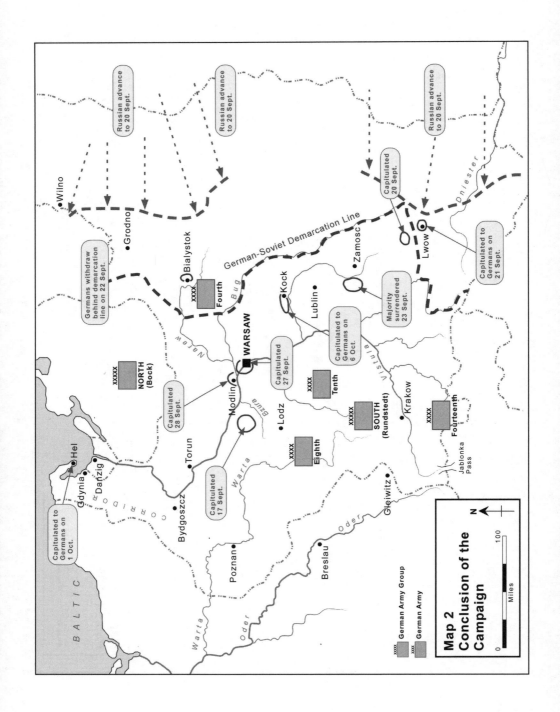

Map 2
Conclusion of the
Campaign

Background

Poland: The Crucified Nation

Historian Norman Davies described Poland as a 'country on wheels both in regard to its geographical location and also to its exits and entrances on the political stage'. For 200 years, from the 16th to the 18th centuries, after the union of Poland with Lithuania, the Polish-Lithuanian Commonwealth formed one of the largest political entities in Europe. Yet, as a result of internal political instability it became increasingly vulnerable to its neighbours, Russia, Prussia and Austria, who, in the partitions of 1772, 1793 and 1795, effectively divided up this once proud state amongst themselves. Although the Poles several times revolted against the partitioning powers, the re-establishment of an independent Poland was to depend on the simultaneous defeat of the three great Eastern European powers, Prussia, Austria and Russia. This occurred in the early 19th Century when Napoleon destroyed the military capabilities of first Austria, then Prussia and Russia. He then created a Polish satellite state, the Grand Duchy of Warsaw, but once France was defeated in 1814 by the victorious Anglo-Russian, Prussian and Austrian coalition, Poland was again partitioned by the three Eastern powers. For a short time Tsar Alexander of Russia granted Russian Poland – or Congress Poland as it was called – a constitution, but this was soon abrogated.

The Polish poet, Zygmunt Krasiński, in his epic poem of 1843, *The Moment Before Dawn*, depicted the partition and suffering of Poland as a sacrifice for the sins of the world, but he was also convinced that, as a result of this sacrifice, Poland was destined to emerge spiritually strengthened as a great world leader. In effect,

1

he saw Poland as a Christ amongst nations. Such sentiments as these, as well as tenacious attempts to preserve Polish culture and language, helped keep the spirit of Polish nationalism alive. There were two revolts in the Nineteenth Century, the insurrections of 1830–31 and 1863–4, but as long as Prussian Germany and the Austrian and Russian empires had an interest in continuing partition, there was no hope of re-establishing a united Polish state. In 1914, however, with the outbreak of the First World War, for the first time for nearly 150 years St Petersburg was at war with Berlin and Vienna, creating a window of opportunity for resurrecting the Polish state in some shape or other. All three empires attempted to appeal to Polish nationalism by promising to form some sort of Polish state after the war. The Austrians also allowed a Polish Legion to be formed for service on the Eastern Front, commanded by the charismatic nationalist, Joseph Piłsudski. In the West, the Polish National Committee was set up in Paris, in an attempt to win over the Western powers to the cause of Polish independence, but for fear of offending their allies, the Russians, neither France nor Britain would initially commit themselves to backing an independent Poland.

In 1917 the situation did, however, dramatically change with the outbreak of revolution in Russia and the entry of America into the war. On 31 March 1917 the new Provisional Government in Petrograd issued a proclamation of Polish independence, while President Wilson, in his Fourteen Points of January 1918, established national determination as the main principle on which the future peace settlement with the Central Powers was to be based. These programmes could not immediately be put into effect as the Germans had occupied Russian Poland and set up a puppet state there. The Polish Legion was now transferred to German control and when Piłsudski and several other officers refused to swear loyalty to the German Kaiser, they were arrested and imprisoned in the fortress of Magdeburg.

Emergence of the New Poland 1918–20

In the autumn of 1918 both the Austrian and German empires were defeated and a vacuum of power subsequently opened up in Eastern Europe, which created the preconditions for a restored

Polish Forces in the First World War

Traditionally, dating from the Napoleonic era, the Polish Army had a close link with the French. In 1915 Polish units were formed as part of the French Foreign Legion. These were expanded under the command of General Haller by recruiting Polish prisoners of war who had been serving in the Austrian and German armies. To these were added another 25,000 Polish-American volunteers who were at first trained in Canada, as the USA remained neutral until April 1917.

The Russian Government had also created a Polish Legion (the Puławy Legion), but it was disbanded due to fears of growing Polish nationalism. In 1917, however, the more liberal Kerensky Government allowed the formation of the 1st Polish Eastern Corps, which was then transferred to the front in Byelorussia. When the Germans advanced into this area, Polish units were disbanded and sent back to German-occupied Poland, where they formed an important reservoir of manpower for the future Polish state.

The Austrian Polish Legion was smaller but had according to the military historians Zaloga and Madej a 'disproportionate influence on the later Polish Government'. Two brigades were formed under the command of Józef Piłsudski, the nucleus of which were the paramilitary sporting and rifle clubs, which had already existed before the war in Austrian Poland. They were disbanded when they refused to swear an oath of allegiance to the new Austro-German dominated Kingdom of Poland, and replaced by the German-controlled Royal Polish Army, which was contemptuously nicknamed *die Polnische Wehrmacht*.

Poland. The Austrian Empire collapsed and the Germans withdrew from Russian Poland. They also released Piłsudski from the Magdeburg fortress and sent him to Warsaw (Warszawa) in a sealed train, in the hope that he would be able to set up a pro-German Poland. On 11 November 1918 he was appointed Commander-in-Chief of Polish forces by the Regency Council and given the task of creating an independent National Government.

The Polish state re-emerged, but its borders were as yet unfixed. Piłsudski, however, was not prepared to wait for the interminable delays of a peace conference, and, as early as November 1918, Polish militia units invaded and occupied eastern Galicia, on the grounds that it was militarily important to secure the frontier with Romania in case of a joint German-Bolshevik attack on the new Poland.

Neither did the Poles in the German provinces of Posen (Poznań) and Upper Silesia passively await the decisions of the Peace Conference. In Posen, on Boxing Day, Polish Nationalists launched a revolt against the German authorities that escalated into a bitter guerrilla war. In the south there were also disputes with Czechoslovakia regarding Teschen, formerly part of the Austrian Empire. The Poles took the initiative and sent in troops, who clashed with an advancing Czech force. Further confrontation was prevented by the dispatch of an inter-Allied commission to report to Paris on the situation, and a year later the Poles grudgingly agreed to Teschen's partition.

The Treaty of Versailles did not lead immediately to the fixing of Poland's frontiers. On the one hand the outline of the new state was clear. It comprised former Russian or Congress Poland with Warsaw as its capital; in the west, the German province of Posen was awarded to Poland; in the north, access to the Baltic was achieved by driving a corridor through German territory; while in the south, most of Austrian Galicia was added. On the other hand, the eastern frontier with Ukraine was still undeliniated, and, largely as a result of British pressure, plebiscites were to be held in Upper Silesia and Marienwerder and Allenstein (Olsztyn) in the Polish Corridor.

In Upper Silesia, where there was a concentration of coal mines and iron and steel industries second only to the Ruhr, the Poles, with French support, attempted to seize the initiative and pre-empt the plebiscites. In turn, German *Freikorps* volunteers poured in to defend the province, and in May 1921, before Allied troops managed to restore a semblance of order, won an epic victory by

Background

storming the ancient convent of St Anna, which commanded the hills along the right bank of the Oder. The storming of the Annaberg was regularly celebrated by the Nazis of Hitler's Third Reich.

Although some 60 per cent of the population voted to remain German, under French pressure, the League of Nations ruled in favour of Polish claims in October 1921. The fighting in Upper Silesia left a lasting legacy of bitterness between Germans and Poles that was to erupt with ferocity in September 1939 and lead to a series of atrocities on both sides.

Poland's eastern frontiers with the USSR were the result of war and were forged independently of the Allied powers in Paris. Piłsudski rejected Britain's attempt to limit Poland's expansion eastwards, and instead sought security from the USSR by annexing Byelorussia and the Ukraine. Polish forces penetrated as far as Kiev by May 1920, but then, with the defeat of the anti-revolutionary White forces in Russia, the Red Army was able not only to expel the Poles from Ukraine but also to advance deep into Poland. By August 1920 Warsaw was threatened by five Soviet armies. Once again it seemed that Poland was on the brink of partition. Leon Trotsky, Commander of the Red Army, proposed carving up Poland with Germany, in what would have been an early version of the Ribbentrop-Molotov pact of August 1939 (see pp. 58–9), but, however attractive this proposal might have been, the presence of French occupying troops in the Rhineland ensured that Germany remained neutral.

Unexpectedly, the threat to Poland's existence was removed by a daring counter-offensive launched by Piłsudski, which destroyed three of the five Soviet armies just outside Warsaw. The fourth had to seek safety by withdrawing into East Prussia, while the fifth suffered immense losses a few weeks later at the Battle of Komarów, near Zamość. Polish victory was finally secured at the Battle of the River Niemen in September 1920, and her frontiers with the USSR were formalized by the subsequent Treaty of Riga, by which Poland annexed considerable areas of Byelorussia and Ukraine.

The defeat of the Bolsheviks also enabled the Poles to seize Wilno from the Lithuanians in October 1920 and defy pressure from the League of Nations to return it. All in all, the victory did much to boost Polish morale. It avenged the brutal Russian suppression of the revolts of 1830–31 and 1863–64 and gave Poland the crucial self-confidence to grapple with the daunting domestic problems that faced her. Strategically, the Soviet defeat stopped the forces of revolutionary Bolshevism and gave Poland security on her eastern frontier until September 1939. It also strengthened the Versailles settlement, of which Poland was a major prop.

Enemies of the New Polish State

But victory came at a price. The resurrection of Poland was a consequence of the simultaneous defeat of Russia, Germany and Austria. The Austrian empire was shattered beyond repair, but Russia, which historically regarded eastern and central Poland as part of its sphere of interest, was deeply embittered by its defeat in 1920, and had every intention of seizing back the territories lost to Poland at the first opportunity. In short, in the words of Léon Noël, the French Ambassador to Poland in 1939, the acquisition of these territories, which were inhabited by only a minority of Poles, was, in many ways, a 'running sore' to Russia. Tension remained high along the borderlands, and bands of Ukrainians frequently crossed the frontier to attack isolated Polish farms. In 1924 the Border Patrol Corps (KOP) was established by the Polish Government in an attempt to control the situation.

Germany, too, was determined to regain not just Danzig (Gdańsk) and the Corridor, but also the industrially valuable area of Upper Silesia and the agricultural regions of Pomerania, which she had lost to Poland. To do this she was ready to cooperate with the USSR and agree to a new partition, whenever the opportunity might arrive. In 1922 General Hans von Seeckt, the Commander-in-Chief of the German Army encapsulated this view in a frank comment:

Poland's existence is intolerable, at variance with the survival of Germany. It must disappear, and it will disappear through its own internal weakness and through Russia – with our assistance. For Russia, Poland is even

6

Background

more intolerable than for us; no Russian can allow Poland
to exist [. . .] the creation of the broad common frontier
between Russia and Germany is the precondition for the
regaining of strength of both countries.

Throughout the 1920s Germany exploited every opportunity to
weaken Poland. In 1922 it signed the Treaty of Rapallo with the
USSR, which prepared the way for German-Soviet military cooperation. In 1925 Foreign Minister, Gustav Stresemann
specifically excluded Germany's eastern frontiers from the
Locarno treaties that guaranteed Germany's western borders, and
viewed cooperation between Germany and Russia as a precondition for territorial revision in the east.

The mere existence of Poland was a challenge to Russia and
Germany, but Poland had also alienated both Czechoslovakia and
Lithuania, which were potentially allies. Ultimately, in the 1920s,
Poland's only effective ally was France. In 1921 both states
signed a defensive alliance. Britain was more interested in re-
establishing a balance of power on the Continent. To do this she
needed to restrain France and build up German economic power.
Consequently, the Germans attempted to use Britain to put
pressure on Poland to agree to frontier adjustments – perhaps
even the return of Danzig – in the interests of general peace. To
bring that about both German politicians and diplomats were
agreed that 'an understanding with Poland is neither possible nor
desired. The tension with Poland must be maintained if only for
the reason that the world will not lose interest in a revision of the
German Polish frontiers'.

When Hitler came to power in 1933, Piłsudski initially
proposed joint Franco-Polish intervention to remove him, but
such action was rejected by the French. For his part, Hitler – far
from intensifying the pressure on Poland – initially needed time to
consolidate his grip on Germany and to build up the German war
machine: he was therefore ready to defuse the tension with Poland
and negotiate a non-aggression treaty with Warsaw. He told
representatives of the Nazi Party in June 1933 that Germany's
aims could not be realized in 'a few days or weeks' and that it was
consequently vital to 'avoid anything that might give the world

cause for suspicion'. Piłsudski, disillusioned with the French, was ready to try to improve relations with the Germans, and on 26 January 1934 the Polish-German Non-aggression Pact was signed in Berlin. For a period of ten years it pledged both countries to seek to reach a direct understanding on matters of dispute and not to 'proceed to use force in order to settle such disputes'. Nevertheless, to Hermann Rauschning, President of the Danzig Senate, Hitler described the agreement as having 'a purely temporary significance'. He added: 'I have no intention of maintaining a serious friendship.'

Development of Poland 1919–38

Polish arms had extended and consolidated the new state, but its domestic problems remained daunting. The new Poland was an amalgamation of three different zones, each with their own legal and administrative structures as well as their separate currencies. It was also far from a homogenous state: some 30 per cent of its population was Ukrainian, Byelorussian, German or Jewish, most of whom were reluctant citizens of the new state.

Economically, Poland also faced enormous problems. It had been fought over during the war and in its immediate aftermath. Millions of farms and cottages had to be rebuilt. Agriculture was backward and based predominantly on small peasant holdings, the transport infrastructure was poor and industry limited to a few enclaves such as Upper Silesia, Łódź and the industrial region around Warsaw. Poland was not in a position to survive a war against an economically stronger power. It also lacked a modern fiscal system with a central bank and an effective means of tax collection. As historian Peter Stachura observed, 'the overall economic position of the country could not have been more unpropitious, or the challenge of reconstruction more demanding'.

Political stability was also lacking. Few Poles had any parliamentary experience, while the electorate was politically inexperienced and fragmented. In 1922, when the first national elections were held, there were ninety-two different parties, seventeen of which won seats in the *Sejm* (Parliament). Inevitably, this led to a series of shortlived coalition governments – between 1918

8

Background

and 1926 there were fourteen of them. It was no wonder that many observers in both Germany and the West wrote Poland off. In Britain, for instance, the great economist, J.M. Keynes, observed that Poland was 'an economic impossibility whose only industry is Jew baiting', while Lloyd George, the British Prime Minister from 1916–1922, had no doubts that the fledgling state was an 'historic failure'. Yet, against all expectations, the Polish Second Republic managed to survive until Nazi-Soviet military force destroyed it in September 1939.

Perhaps as important as the Battle of Warsaw for the survival of Poland were the economic reforms of 1924–26 and Piłsudski's coup of 1926. The economic reforms introduced by Władysław Grabski ended hyperinflation and introduced the new *złoty* currency, which was backed by gold. This allowed the budget to be balanced and in 1927 to attract an important stabilization loan from the USA. This led to increased investment in industry and such ambitious schemes as the construction of Gdynia, Poland's new port and naval base on the Baltic coast. While Grabski's economic reforms stabilized Poland economically, Piłsudski's coup, although more controversial, did the same thing politically. Concerned about Poland's economic and political weakness and the implications of the Locarno Pact for its future security, as well as rumours that the Government was threatening to reduce the size of the Army to a mere 144,000 men, Piłsudski seized power in May 1926. He exercised authority through the Army but allowed the *Sejm* to continue to sit, albeit with diminished powers. The coup was bitterly criticized by democrats but arguably it stabilized Poland and gave a firm direction in defending the national interest.

The Great Depression of 1929–33 dealt Poland a savage blow, bringing massive unemployment and acute poverty, which was made worse by the Government's refusal to devalue the *złoty*. This inevitably exacerbated ethnic tension, and in the eastern provinces Ukrainian nationalists attacked Government buildings and assassinated officials and police. By 1935 the Polish economy had recovered, and the Government was able to launch a four-year investment plan, an important part of which was the construction of the 'industrial triangle' in the Warsaw–Kraków–Lwów area, combined with state-directed investment into the defence industries.

Piłsudski died in 1935, and from 1935–39 Poland was ruled by his former legionaries, of whom Colonel Józef Beck was the most prominent. They established an increasingly authoritarian and nationalist regime, which until the end of 1938 was both anti-Czech and pro-German.

The Re-Emergence of Germany and Russia as Major Military Powers

In the 1920s, as a result of the restrictions imposed by the Treaty of Versailles on Germany's Armed Forces after her defeat in 1918 and the decisive rout of the Red Army in August 1920, Poland enjoyed over a decade of security. Until 1933 the Polish Army, for all its deficiencies, was far larger than the *Reichswehr*, which was limited to 100,000 men and forbidden to build tanks or armoured vehicles. The Red Army was numerically larger but after the turmoil of the revolution, the defeats of 1920 and the peasant revolt of 1921, the Soviet Government was in no mood to risk large-scale intervention in Poland and retreated into the fortress of 'socialism in one country'. Nevertheless, as Piłsudski realized, this interlude of relative security would not last forever and both Germany and the USSR were developing their Armed Forces as fast as was practical.

Germany Rearms

Throughout the 1920s Germany evaded with some success the restrictions imposed by the Treaty of Versailles. Thanks to the Rapallo Treaty of 1922 her aircrews were able to train as pilots, navigators and technicians in the USSR, and her Army, too, was able to conduct manoeuvres in modern mechanized and chemical warfare. Between 1927 and 1933 detailed plans were drawn up for creating the infrastructure for a much larger mechanized force. Between 1933–36 these installations became a key pre-condition for the rapid and relatively smooth progress of German rearmament.

The coming to power of Hitler's National Socialists and the paralysis of the western world as a result of the Great Depression

10

Background

created what one German historian calls 'extraordinarily favourable conditions' for rearmament. Hitler lost little time telling his generals that he was aiming to increase 'Germany's military determination by every means'. Essentially, the whole nation and its economy were to be organized for war. On 18 December 1933 the Defence Ministry announced a new programme, which envisaged a peacetime army of 300,000 men or twenty-one divisions, and, on the assumption that conscription would soon be introduced, a field army of 600,000. Further increases followed, and the union (*Anschluss*) with Austria, the annexation of the Sudetenland and Bohemia and the destruction of Czechoslovakia produced yet more men and equipment. This was backed from 1935–39 onwards with a series of massive annual defence budgets. By 1 September 1939 the strength of the Wehrmacht had risen to 2,758,000 men, organized into 103 divisions.

In many ways, the German Army of the 1920s was a new army unencumbered with past traditions. In defeat, German planners had been able to jettison much of the baggage of the old Imperial Army and digest the strategic lessons of the First World War much more effectively than their opponents. For instance, the part that Allied tank formations played in the German defeat in 1918 persuaded the *Herresamt*, which was the old General Staff in disguise, to study tank tactics in depth and develop a new strategy for attack. In the army manoeuvres of the 1920s extensive experimentation was carried out with cars and lorries playing the role of armour. Thanks, too, to the Rapallo Pact, Germany was able to establish a training centre for the use of armoured vehicles near Kazan in the USSR.

In 1935 Germany began building a formidable Panzer force. By 1939 the Wehrmacht had six Panzer divisions and four light divisions, unlike most contemporary European armies. German armoured experts, such as General Heinz Guderian, argued that tanks should be organized in their own divisions rather than being attached to infantry battalions for close support. At a demonstration of new weapons organized by the army ordnance office at the military training area of Kummersdorf on 11 July 1935, Guderian was able to show off his Panzer prototypes to Hitler. Hitler enthusiastically endorsed mechanization and a month later, in extensive manoeuvres attended by the Commander-in–Chief, Guderian proved that tanks could restore mobility to the battlefield.

The Panzer divisions were mixed formations of tanks, motorized infantry and artillery. The Germans were also ahead in their use of radio control. No other European army used radio so effectively. A large percentage of German Panzers deployed radios, and unit commanders operated from a radio-equipped tank called a *Befehlspanzer* (command Panzer). However, German tanks were not the formidable machines that were used later in the war. The great majority, such as the PzKpfwI and the PzKpfwII, were lightly armed with machine guns. The Germans were initially convinced that a machine-gun armament would be perfectly adequate for most battlefield situations, but in Spain the experience of the German Condor Legion showed that the enemy tank threat could not be ignored. The PzKpfwII was thus given greater firepower. With its 20mm gun it was able to destroy the opposing Polish tanks in September 1939, but it was vulnerable to anti-tank gunfire and troops protected by field fortifications. The PzKpfwI and II were supported by a new generation of tank, the PzKpfw III and PzKpfwIV. The former was armed with a 37mm gun, which would dominate the battlefields in 1940–42, but there were only ninety-eight of these in service in 1939. The latter was specifically designed to provide fire support for light tanks and was armed with a 75mm gun, but in September 1939 there were still only 211 in service.

As with the Army, the rapid expansion of the German Navy rested on carefully thought out plans drawn up in the Weimar Republic. In 1933 contracts for four destroyers were awarded, and preparations for submarine construction were accelerated. This already broke the tonnage limit stipulated by the Versailles Treaty, but in 1935 under the Anglo-German Naval Treaty, instead of the 144,000 tons allowed by Versailles the Germans could now legally build up to a tonnage of 520,000. By 1939 the German Navy could dominate the Baltic, but, as Admiral Raeder said: 'the surface ships are so few and weak compared with the British fleet, that even if fully committed, they would be able to show that they knew how to be able to die with honour'.

It was different with the Luftwaffe. In the words of a German

Background

historian, its 'development was spectacular and aroused the boundless imagination as well as the dark forebodings of contemporaries'. As with the army, basic plans for future development had been laid during the Weimar Republic. By training pilots, navigation officers, observers and technicians at Lipsk in the USSR, and by cooperating closely with such civil enterprises as Lufthansa, the fledgling German Air Force was able to keep abreast of the latest air technology and developments. In July 1933 the decision was taken to create an independent Luftwaffe, although steps were still taken to camouflage its existence. It was to consist of twenty-seven squadrons, ten of which were bombers. A year later, the July Programme was unveiled, which envisaged the construction of 17,015 planes. Of these only 6,671 were combat planes consisting of:

- Fighters 2,225
- Bombers 2,188
- Dive-Bombers 699
- Reconnaissance aircraft 1,559

The rest were training planes aimed to familiarize future pilots with flying, so that the Luftwaffe could be greatly increased in size in the near future. The most effective school for the Luftwaffe was the Spanish Civil War, where both its fighters and bombers could be assessed and future tactics developed. It was in Spain where *die Rotte*, which was to become the characteristic Luftwaffe dual air formation was introduced. It consisted of a flight of two pairs of planes (*die Rotte*), and within each pair one of the pilots acted as the attacking unit and the second as the covering unit.

By August 1939 the Luftwaffe had a total of 302 combat ready squadrons at their disposal or 4,093 front-line aircraft. It was also supported by 21 regiments of flak artillery with 2,600 heavy anti-aircraft guns. Its build-up was achieved in a surprisingly short time, which was a consequence of both German technology, and economic rationalization, as well as the injection of a massive amount of money – the equivalent of 4 billion US dollars. A series of new aircraft had been constructed – the Ju (Junkers) 87, the He

(Heinkel) 111 and Do (Dornier) 17 bombers, and the Me (Messerschmitt) 109 fighter. In 1937 the task of producing and equipping the next generation of planes, the Messerschmitt Bf 110 and the Ju 88 bomber, began although the latter only entered squadron service with a mere twelve aircraft on the first day of the attack on Poland in 1939.

At the commanders' conference following the opening of the Ministry of Aviation in 1933, General Blomberg stressed that the flying officer corps should be an 'elite corps' filled 'with an intensely aggressive spirit'. Göring and the OKL (the Supreme Command of the Luftwaffe) devised what became known as the Blitzkrieg doctrine. The role of aircraft was to cooperate with ground forces while destroying the enemy's air capability by bombing aerodromes and communications. This was to be used with deadly effect in Poland.

Development of Soviet Armed Forces
The roots of the Red Army lay in an egalitarian militia formed in early 1918 to defend the revolution, but during the course of the Russian Civil War it was to expand to a force of 3 million. It had a dual leadership composed of the professional army officers, many of whom had served in the old Russian Imperial Army and the political commissars, whose duty was to ensure loyalty to the Communist Party. In 1920 it experienced both victory and defeat. It trounced the anti-Bolshevik Whites but in its attempt to destroy Poland and open up central Europe to Communism, it suffered a grievous defeat at the hands of Piłsudski outside Warsaw.

The failure before Warsaw put an end to dreams of world revolution, in which the Red Army would be the principal instrument. It had now to consider the more mundane task of defending the USSR against a possible hostile capitalist alliance. Its main potential enemy appeared to be an alliance formed between Poland, Romania, the Baltic States and Finland, which, it was calculated, could field armies amounting to a total of 572,000 men. Mikhail Frunze, who commanded the southern front during the Civil War and became Chief of Staff in 1924, argued for a relatively small cadre army, which could be expanded in wartime, and backed by a territorial force that would enable the civil popu-

14

Background

lation to receive some military training. Essentially, his arguments were accepted in 1922 and determined the shape of the Red Army until 1936.

Over the next fourteen years the Red Army developed into an effective modern force. A French military historian, Michel Garder, wrote in 1959 (arguably with some exaggeration) that: 'what can be stated without any reservation is that in 1937 the Red Army was superior to any western force at that time in almost all fields'. Frunze paid considerable attention to the creation of an effective officer corps, as it was vital to re-educate and improve the cadres developed in the Civil War and at the same provide intellectual and physical training for young men who wanted to make the Red Army their career. This was achieved by setting up military schools and academies. The most promising Russian officers were sent on courses to Germany.

In 1930 the Soviet Army was, to quote historian John Erickson, flung into a 'permanent technical revolution which marked its history throughout the 1930s'. In 1929, V. Triandafillov, the Deputy Chief of the Red Army Staff produced a ground-breaking study of the impact of motorization. He argued that modern mass armies must make every possible use of motor transport and mechanical warfare. In other areas, too, the Soviet Army experimented with new techniques. Parachute detachments were created and close contact formed between air power and mechanized forces. By 1935 Germany's General Heinz Guderian estimated that the USSR had about 100,000 army lorries. He also reckoned that a third of its corps artillery had been motorized, as well as half of the anti-aircraft artillery and the heavy artillery of the Main Reserve. Three rifle divisions were also motorized. The first serious Soviet military study of tanks and their use in war began in 1928, and throughout 1930–31 extensive tests were carried out: but it was only in 1932 – after the USSR had built up its own tractor and automobile industry – that the Red Army received tanks in any number. In May 1930 the first 'mechanized brigade' was set up. The British Vickers models and the American Christie designs formed the basis of the early prototypes, the T26 and 26A, which were to outperform German tanks in the Spanish Civil War.

Poland Betrayed

In the manoeuvres of 1936, which were attended by foreign observers, the Russians displayed their skills in tank handling and air-ground cooperation. But British observer, Lieutenant General Martel, was unimpressed, describing the event as 'more like a tattoo than manoeuvres'. The mechanized formations took part in a 'spectacular battle' but little handling skill was, as yet, demonstrated. In conclusion, Martel reckoned that the Red Army was not unlike its Imperial predecessor: it remained a bludgeon with 'armoured spikes on its head, but the danger was that a more tactically effective force might be able to dodge the blow'. He also noted that Soviet armour made little use of radio and that the tactical training of junior officers was unimpressive. Tukhachevsky attempted to address the latter problem in the new Provisional Field Service Regulations, but Stalin purges of 1937 delivered a massive blow to the Soviet Army. Of an officer corps numbering 75,000–80,000 about 20,000–25,000 officers were 'purged'.

In the Civil War of 1918–20, both the naval and air arms had played a relatively minor role. After the Kronstadt uprising the Navy was initially viewed as politically unreliable. It was only in 1923 that the first effective command organization and policy decisions were made freeing the Air Force and Navy from subordination to the Army. Both arms benefited from the Rapallo Treaty and close cooperation with the Germans. Junkers, for instance, set up a factory near Moscow, manufacturing metal aircraft, spares, and aircraft engines. In 1925 the Soviet Navy contacted the German *Marineleitung* to request the dispatch of a mission to advise on the construction of submarines. For the Navy the Baltic remained the chief theatre, as the Soviets feared a naval attack by an alliance of the Baltic States and Poland, supported materially by Britain and France. The construction of the Baltic–White Sea canal enabled the Navy to defend Leningrad more effectively, and in 1933 the Northern Fleet was created. The Soviet Naval command basically preferred to maintain a relatively small force with a preponderance of submarines. But this was rejected by Stalin, who insisted the Navy should be equipped with powerful surface ships capable of taking the war into enemy waters.

Background

In the immediate years after the Civil War, Russian air capability was a shambles: it was supplied with thirty-two types of different aircraft, its personnel were both badly trained and ill disciplined, and it was considerably understrength. In 1923, a big shake up effectively created a proper Soviet Air Force, consisting of a strategic force and corps aviation. The strategic force was further divided into fighter-bomber and reconnaissance units, while corps aviation had the task of army cooperation, tactical reconnaissance and artillery observation. By the mid-1930s the Soviet Air Force was being rapidly expanded. The Second Five-Year Plan envisaged the creation of sixty-two air regiments and the capacity to put some 500 machines into front-line service. In 1936 the strategic bombing Air Force was developed, consisting of the TB and ANT bombers, while new fighters, the I-15 and I-16 were simultaneously introduced.

By 1939 the Soviet armed services were, on paper at least, very formidable. The Spanish Civil War had shown the effectiveness of Soviet tanks and the bomber fleet enjoyed a fearsome reputation. But the purges hit all three services and did immense damage. For example, in 1938 10,000 officer cadets were forced out of military academies before they had fully trained to make good the losses suffered by officer corps during the purges.

Rebirth of Poland's Armed Forces 1919–39

In February 1919 the newly created Polish parliament, the *Sejm*, passed the Army Law, which set up an official Polish defence force under Piłsudski. Inevitably, its core was composed of the former Polish legions, which Piłsudski himself had led, but it was strengthened in April 1919 by the arrival of Haller's Polish units from France. The role played by the Army in securing Poland's frontiers in 1919–20 ensured that it was, together with the Roman Catholic Church, one of the few national institutions that enjoyed the respect of the Polish ethnic population, thereby helping to cement national unity. However, in its early years, the Army was far from being a unified force in itself, as it inherited often conflicting traditions from Russia, Austria and Germany. Staff talks, for instance, were conducted in Polish, German and Russian. Meanwhile, units were poorly equipped and riven by ethnic tensions. In September 1921 a deserter from the 2nd Squadron, 15th Ułan (Lancer) Regiment in Poznań crossed the German border and told his German interrogators that:

> Clothing is very frugal. Each man has only a single pair of boots [. . .] the attitude of the troops in Posen is very divided, since there are many troops from Congress Poland. The Poznań troops all wish for union with Germany. In a war with Germany the Poznańian troops could not be used, since the larger part would desert [. . .] the number of German soldiers who commit suicide is very high. [Source: R.M. Citino, p. 101.]

The French for whom Poland was a vital pillar of the Treaty of Versailles played a key role in the first half of the 1920s in supplying equipment and officers to the Polish Army. In 1925 the German Ambassador in Warsaw reported that, thanks to the efforts of the French Military Mission, 'the Polish Army has been transformed in the last several years from something out of an operetta to a factor in European strategy'. Considerable efforts were made to train technical troops, and a start had been made to equip the cavalry with a limited number of tanks. The infantry, too, was being trained according to modern military concepts. Nevertheless, the Army still had serious faults, most notably that leadership on all levels was poor and inexperienced in modern war.

By the end of 1925 the Polish Army was in a state of crisis. As a result of financial pressures, the Government was faced with having to make swingeing cuts, which would have reduced the Army to a mere 144,000 men. This threat propelled Piłsudski to seize power in May 1926. With a force of some 2,000 men he marched on Warsaw. There he met armed opposition from a company of cadets and regular cavalry units loyal to the Government. For two and a half days Poland hovered on the brink of civil war before Piłsudski triumphed. The German Ambassador witnessed the action and 'couldn't help but notice that the troops on both sides fought bravely and cleverly'.

Piłsudski immediately vetoed all talk of cuts and ignored

Background

the protests of the finance ministry. He restored the morale of the Army and accelerated the process of modernization, but his legacy was also negative. He was not a trained Staff Officer, although, of course, he had had plenty of battle experience. Accordingly, his patience for detailed organization was very limited, as was his understanding of the new military techniques pioneered in the Great War. He also ensured that only men who had a record of personal loyalty to him were in positions of responsibility. This inevitably excluded men like General Sikorski, the former Prime Minister and Minister of War, and many other able soldiers whose experience was to be sorely missed in September 1939.

To judge the success of Piłsudski and his successors, the colonels, in modernizing the Polish Armed Forces (PSZ – Polskie Siły Zbrojne), it is necessary to look at their development up to 1939. The Armed Forces consisted not only of the Army, of which the Air Force formed a part, but also the Navy and the Frontier Defence Corps (KOP), whose task was to defend the Russian and Czech frontiers. This was set up in 1924 and was constantly maintained at a high state of readiness in case of another Soviet invasion. It was composed of ethnic Poles only, so as to ensure loyalty to the state. In 1939, after the German occupation of Bohemia, it took over the control of the Slovak border.

There were also some 1½ million reservists, as well as the National Guard, which was formed in 1936 from volunteers. In 1937 the Guard was taken over by the Polish Infantry and integrated into the national training system. The National Guard was composed of eighty-two battalions and by 1939 amounted to 10 per cent of the fully mobilized armed forces. Altogether, when mobilized fully, the Poles could potentially field an armed force of some 2.5 million men in 1939.

Piłsudski's legacy can be judged by the curious way he had organized the PSZ into an ineffective two track system. In peacetime the Armed Forces were the responsibility of the War Minister, who was in turn responsible to the Council of Ministers. His task was to maintain military bases and provide the necessary supplies and equipment. To facilitate this, the country was divided into ten administrative regions, which, significantly, bore no relation to how the Polish Army would be organized in war.

Poland Betrayed

Planning for war and ensuring the necessary economic back-up for the Armed Forces, as well as the direction of the PSZ in war, was not the responsibility of the General Staff, as was the case in Germany, but of the General Inspectorate of the Armed Forces (the GISZ). This consisted of twelve inspectors, eleven of whom were amongst Piłsudski's most loyal supporters. These, rather than the corps commanders, would organize the forces in their own districts in wartime.

This division of power created bureaucratic problems, which made the modernization of the Armed Forces more difficult. In Germany, for example, the General Staff was able to ensure all officers were conversant with their thinking on, say, the expansion of armoured forces. In Poland, however, any new strategic studies had to be passed to the General Inspectorate first and then be coordinated with the Committee for the Defence of the Republic and the War Ministry. As Zaloga and Madej have observed, this 'complicated situation tended to delay tactical or technical innovation and stifled a number of attempts at Army modernization'. Both the Air Force and some Army officers, such as General Daniel Konarzewski, were urging cuts in the cavalry so that mechanization of the Army and the expansion of the Air Force could be accelerated. Their efforts were thwarted in 1929 by Inspector, General Gustav Orlicz-Dreszer, who also vetoed any reduction in the cavalry and managed to preserve the Warsaw Cavalry Division.

In 1939 the Armed Forces were organized into seven armies, one of which was a reserve army. The total force consisted of :

- 30 infantry divisions

- 11 cavalry brigades

- 1 mechanized brigade

- 2 engineer brigades

- 11 artillery regiments

- 1 air command of 4 bomber squadrons, 11 light bomber squadrons, 15 fighter squadrons, 11 reconnaissance/observation squadrons, as well as torpedo, training and transport squadrons.

Background

The infantry formed the core of the Polish Army and a much greater percentage of the whole than was the case in either the Russian or German armies. In March 1939, out of a total active force of 283,000 men, the infantry counted for 160,000. At a time of general mobilization this would be swollen by a further 700,000 men in the first month. An infantry division was, in many ways, an army in miniature with its own artillery, cavalry and transport. Compared, however, to its equivalent in the German Army, a Polish division had arguably only half its combat power, especially if one considers firepower and mobility.

Anachronistically, cavalry continued to play a major role in the Polish Army. Altogether it comprised 10 per cent of active military units. Proportionately, this was five times larger than the German cavalry and one-and-a-half times larger than either the Soviet or French cavalry. The Poles hung on to their mounted units because they were convinced that they still had a major role to play. Cavalry had been, after all, highly effective in the Russo-Polish War of 1919–20. It is, however, also true that the Polish Army was stuck with the cavalry because it lacked the money to mechanize extensively. The cavalry was divided into eleven brigades, which, while lacking firepower, enjoyed considerable mobility. In the September Campaign, as we shall see, they did not live up to the exaggerated expectations of pre-war cavalry advocates, but, to quote Zaloga and Madej, they were, nevertheless, 'valuable because of their mobility and durability; when an infantry unit lost a battle, it was usually overrun and destroyed, but the cavalry escaped to fight again and again'. Troopers were armed with anti-tank guns and heavy machine guns and usually fought dismounted. In the September war there were to be frequent occasions when German units, some of them armoured, were caught unawares by Polish cavalry units.

The Poles did, however, make limited progress in mechanization. In February 1927 Piłsudski reorganized armoured car units into armoured squadrons of ten to twelve units each. By 1932 the Polish Army had managed to assemble a force of 382 tanks. By 1937 eighteen scout tank or tankette companies were assigned to the infantry divisions. Each company was composed of thirteen tankettes, four lorries, four fuel trailers, seven motorcycles, a

21

radio car and staff car as well as a field kitchen. The personnel consisted of four officers and eighty-seven men.

Each cavalry brigade also possessed a small armoured group of eleven tankettes and seven armoured cars, backed up with a small number of motorcyclists and motorized transport. Two of the cavalry brigades had been mechanized and equipped with reconnaissance squadrons, which consisted of a light truck company and two motorized rifle regiments. Their actual tank force consisted of two battalions and a company of light tanks, an R-35 tank battalion and a further three companies of obsolete light tanks (M-17 FT) in reserve. Like the British and French, the Poles saw tanks essentially as an infantry and cavalry support force, rather than a means of rapidly outmanoeuvring the enemy. Consequently, Polish tanks were never employed as a concentrated force in the September Campaign.

There were, too, ten armoured trains, which were used to provide mobile artillery support for infantry and cavalry units. They were particularly useful in areas where few roads existed and the local transport system depended on rail. They carried tankettes, an infantry assault unit, machine guns and, most importantly, artillery cars.

Crucial to the success of an army is its firepower. Here again the Polish Army was inferior to those of the Germans and French. To remedy the shortage of artillery, Piłsudski bought howitzers from both Skoda and Schneider-Creusot, the French armaments firm, and in 1932 began purchasing heavy railroad guns from the Americans. He also began setting up a national arms industry within Poland, which could produce foreign artillery models under license. By 1939 approximately one-seventh of the Polish Army was composed of artillery troops, whereas the proportion was one-fifth in Germany. The artillery arm consisted of thirty-nine light artillery regiments, each armed with twenty-four semi-obsolete French 75mm guns, and twelve equipped with 100mm guns. There were thirty heavy artillery sections, a further eleven horse artillery detachments, and each of the two mechanized brigades had a motorized battery. Compared to the Germans in 1939 the Poles had less efficient ammunition, fewer modern artillery pieces and a vastly inferior fire-control system.

Background

The same can be said for both the engineer and communication branches. Despite the earlier efforts of the French, the sappers and pioneers had been neglected, their numbers steadily reduced by the Defence Ministry. Only in the last three years of peace were there belated attempts to reverse this. By 1939 both infantry and motorized regiments had a mere platoon of engineers each. At divisional level there were engineer battalions, while the cavalry regiments had a squad each.

The signals branch was, according to Zaloga and Madej, 'one of the most outdated branches of the Polish Armed Forces'. Only in 1931 did the Polish Defence Ministry begin developing this unit seriously, and it was as late as 1936 that divisions began to be equipped with adequate two-way radios. Three years later, only limited progress had been made and the Army remained dependent on the civilian telephone system, messengers and liaison aircraft, all of which were vulnerable to enemy action.

The supply system was also, for the most part, dependent on horse-drawn vehicles. In the event of war, the War Ministry hoped to be able to commandeer at least 1,500 lorries from civilian usage. In practice the Polish supply system had not really evolved appreciably since 1920.

Air Defence

Poland's Air Force was organizationally part of the Army, its major role being to support land forces. The great majority of the fighter and reconnaissance units were allocated to the field armies, although the High Command did retain an independent force of eight bomber squadrons. The Army failed to grasp the importance of air power, and indeed, according to Jerzy Cynk, historian of the Polish Air Force (PAF), some generals had a positively contemptuous attitude towards it. As the country's armaments budget – which only amounted to the equivalent of 140 million US dollars in 1935 and 180 million four years later – was divided according to the perceived importance attached to the various branches of the service, the PAF received slightly under one-tenth of the budget, while the cavalry received one-fifth. Altogether, in the five years preceding the war, the PAF received about 74.5 million US dollars – ninety-five times less than the Luftwaffe. The PAF's status as a branch of the Army also impeded its technological development. For instance, the key department of Aeronautics was subordinated to the Ministry of Military Affairs, while the Aviation Commander was subject to decisions from six different military and civil non-aviation authorities.

In response to the rapid rise of the German Luftwaffe, a modernization plan was launched in 1936. Its more ambitious aims were rapidly pruned back and the final expansion plan was worked out according to the directives of the General Staff, which originally aimed for completion by 1941 before extending the programme a further year. The General Staff set a target of seventy-eight combat squadrons with a total of 688 aircraft. The force was to be made up of the following units:

- 15 Fighter interceptor squadrons with 11 aircraft each
- 10 Fighter-bomber attack squadrons with 11 aircraft each
- 14 Army cooperation squadrons with ten aircraft each
- 21 Bomber squadrons with 7 aircraft each
- 18 Observation squadrons with 7 aircraft each

Unfortunately, if the Aviation Command's target dates were to be met, the development of new models should have been started in 1934–35. But in the winter of 1938–39 only the P-37 Łoś bomber was being manufactured, and supplies of new combat aircraft had virtually come to a halt in the autumn of 1937. Indeed, the number of war planes actually began to decrease. Not surprisingly, in November 1938, General Józef Zając, Inspector of Anti-Aircraft Defences of the State, observed in a devastating report that the operational readiness of the PAF in the years 1939–1941 would actually deteriorate.

Yet, when Zając succeeded Rayski as Aviation Commander in March 1939, he merely compounded the problem by stopping production of the P-37 Łoś bomber, 'coming', to quote Cynk, 'to the astonishing conclusion that Poland did not need bombers'. He also suspended the production of the P-50 Jastrząb fighter as a result of production difficulties, which threw the entire Polish air industry into chaos and confusion. Instead of bombers, Zając

24

decided to concentrate his efforts on fighter and cooperation aircraft and ordered as a stopgap the mass production of a modernized version of the P-11 fighter. In the summer of 1939 he allowed production to resume on a mere thirty P-50 Jastrząb aircraft, and then, in the last days of August, gave the go-ahead for the production of the new P-45 Sokół, a totally new and untested fighter. These were to be supplemented by the purchase of foreign planes.

All in all, the Polish Air Force in the late summer of 1939 had 1,900 machines but only a quarter were actually serviceable. There was a first line strength of only 397 aircraft, as opposed to the planned strength of 688. Bomber strength was only about 20 per cent of the projected numbers and observation planes only about two-thirds of the intended figure. Although the number of fighter planes was theoretically up to strength, many were obsolescent. In general, the Polish Air Force was not capable of an offensive role, but could potentially act quite effectively in a defensive mission 'in support of the Army'.

Aerial defence also included AA units. A shortage of these ensured that they were primarily deployed in western Poland, in the big cities such as Kraków, Warsaw and Łódź, and the coastal areas.

The Navy

The origin of the inter-war Polish Navy can be traced back to November 1918 when the Vistula (Wisła) river monitors and gun boats, which had previously belonged to the Austrians, were ordered to report to the new Polish authorities in Kraków. The new Polish Navy first saw action in 1920 when gunboat flotillas penetrated to the Dnieper and reached as far south as Kiev. With the Russian advance the boats had to be scuttled and crews evacuated to Modlin, near Warsaw, where they then fought as infantry.

The Treaty of Versailles gave the Poles access to the sea through the Corridor to the Baltic. This enabled them gradually to create a small naval force based at the new seaport of Gdynia. The first generation of ships were built in French, British and Dutch yards, but by 1939 Polish shipyards were capable of building warships themselves.

Poland Betrayed

The Navy faced a dual task: on the one hand, in a war against the USSR the role of the Navy would be to protect the coast, escort merchant ships from the west into Gdynia and Danzig (Gdańsk), and possibly even undertake a limited offensive against the USSR. On the other hand, in a war against Germany it needed the power to hinder hostile shipping movements between the German mainland and East Prussia. Essentially, this required a force of destroyers, mine-laying submarines and torpedo boats, which the Poles began slowly to assemble. By 1938 the Polish Navy consisted of four destroyers, five submarines, six mine-sweepers and one minelayer. The two destroyers built in British yards were specially strengthened for ice navigation and were amongst the largest and strongest in the world.

The Navy had some limited ground forces to defend the coastal area between around Gdynia and the German frontier. Besides a frontier-force battalion and two infantry companies, it also possessed two naval brigades, which were equipped with anti-aircraft and naval artillery and two improvised armoured trains.

Industrial Mobilization

On paper, Poland's Armed Forces were formidable, but the crucial question was whether Polish industry could sustain them in time of war. The Piłsudski regime began to develop 'the arms industry triangle' to the south of Warsaw, and by the early 1930s the Poles were even exporting arms to Greece, Bolivia, Brazil and Romania. During the inter-war period Poland had made considerable progress towards industrialization. One economic historian, J.J. Taylor, has even argued that her economic development was 'outstanding', yet even so, it hardly compared to the massive industrial build-up in both Germany and the USSR: to survive, Poland would need financial and economic assistance from Britain and France.

Good communications were vital to the Polish war effort. Under the Four Year Plan (1936–40) the Polish Government had concentrated the new armament industries in the Central Industrial District, but this was widely separated from the coal mines and steel plants in Upper Silesia, and was thus dependent on

Background

good road and rail links. Military garrisons were also widely distributed throughout Poland, and were again dependent on an efficient communications system if they were to be mobilized rapidly. Impressive progress had been made since 1919: 1,744 kilometres of railway were laid down, more than 20,000 kilometres of new roads constructed and 260 million *złoty* were invested in expanding the waterway system. The construction of the Tarnowskie Góry–Poreba and the Zory–Pszczyna railways facilitated connections between Upper Silesia, Warsaw and the Central Industrial District, and there were further plans to build a line bypassing Warsaw, which would relieve it of much congestion. Yet overall rail links with the vital industrial area were still inadequate. As far as the roads went, the main roads along the northern and eastern frontiers were metalled by 1939, but were very limited in number, and the lateral communications between them were confined to dirt tracks. Although much of the road system in southern Poland was in a poor condition, the roads in Upper Silesia were excellent and work in 1938–39 was under way connecting the region with Warsaw.

The main focus of the war industries was the Central Industrial District. The British Embassy observed in its annual report for 1938 that 'solid progress was made in the development of gas and oilfields, and a massive 40,000kw station had been built on the River San near Nisko to supply the power needs of the Central Industrial District, and further were planned for the future'. The potential of the Polish war effort was also strengthened by a series of new factories, the most important of which was the Starachowice works, which produced the 155mm Schneider howitzer, and the 105mm Schneider 'long gun', as well as field artillery and anti-aircraft guns, and above all, the Bofors guns. In 1938 the British Embassy commented that 'the Starachowice works and the Cegielski factory at Rzeszów, for example, are far better equipped for the manufacture of the Bofors type 40mm anti-aircraft gun than the corresponding works in Sweden'.

The Starachowice works were the jewel in the crown of Polish industry. In May 1939 the British Military Attaché, Lieutenant Colonel Sword, gave the following description of them:

27

Poland Betrayed

The total number of men employed here is said to be about 10,000, divided into two main shifts, though a certain number of machines, which would otherwise be bottle-necks in production, work in three shifts. They work seven days in the week, with a reduced staff at weekends.

They stock a six-month supply of coal, which comes chiefly from Silesia, though a small amount is obtained from the oil district. The coal is of bad coking quality. Iron ore comes from Sweden, Russia and locally. A six-month reserve is kept together with other essential reserves of alloys for the manufacturing of steel.

They are at present experiencing a distinct shortage of skilled labour but have short courses to fit men to carry out one job only.

Ore is melted in one blast furnace, which is sufficient for their needs. There is a foundry, chiefly used for civilian production, and a small rolling mill in which structured steel is made. The firm are about to build an additional Siemens furnace, fired with natural gas. The main machine works cover a large area, and has about four big shops of 210 by 40 yards. The firm made all their own tools and gauges, using machines of English, German and Swiss make. [Source: NA FO 317/23144.]

Armament production was also carried out at the Cegielski works at Rzeszów, which had been built in 1937. It was equipped with a modern rifling machine, which could cut four grooves as opposed to the two or three in Britain. Its main production was the 40mm anti-aircraft gun and the 37mm anti-tank Bofors guns. One of the greatest achievements of the Polish rearmament industry was the construction of the Stalowa Wola steel mills and rolling mills located near Sandomierz. As Lieutenant Colonel Sword said in a lecture to the Royal Military Academy at Sandhurst:

This is a remarkable achievement. The first tree was felled eighteen months ago, the installation of plant began last year, and the first gun did its test last November. It covers literally miles of country, and has the most modern plant

Background

possible, which is largely imported from Germany. Two technical experts from Woolwich arsenal did a tour of the Starachowice, Rzeszów and Stalowa Wola factories last December. They were most impressed with the high standard of work and plant. They said that Polish shops for the manufacture of Bofors equipment were far superior to those in Sweden, the home of the Bofors. One of these two officers admitted to me that the Stalowa Wola factory 'made his mouth water'.[Source: E. Turnbull and A. Suchcitz, p. 73.]

The problems of financing rearmament were exacerbated by a shortage of foreign exchange and the high value of the *złoty*. Poland was one of the very few countries not to have devalued during the Great Depression in 1931, and it therefore had to pursue a policy of vigorous deflation. This ensured that the credit policy of the National Bank was very tight and that there was a short-age of internal capital. The Poles had a reserve in foreign exchange amounting to £19 million (480 million *złoty*), but if they devalued, they could double or treble the value of these reserves. In this way, so the Bank of England argued, 'the National Bank would be in a position to give considerably more help for the purpose of both financing the budget and industrial production'. Of course, the high value of the *złoty* did have an advantage when it came to purchasing foreign goods.

The Poles attempted to mitigate this problem by setting up the National Defence Fund to supplement expenditure on armaments and vital raw materials. The Committee of the National Defence Fund was situated in the War Office, and in 1937 collected nearly 2,330,380 *złoty* in cash and 6,645 tons of scrap metal. It also enabled 36 aeroplanes, 615 heavy machine guns and 130 light machine guns to be purchased, as well as making many other donations, which, according to Sword, were 'too numerous to mention'. Pressure was brought to bear on institutions and individuals to contribute to the fund and deductions were made automatically from workers' and managers' pay throughout Poland. As Sword observed: 'the system is therefore voluntary rather in implication than in fact, and provides some indication of the direction and manner in which the authorities consider that shortages should be made good'.

In October 1934 a Presidential decree announced that all private property was liable to requisition in the event of war. This decree was further supplemented in 1938, when animals and vehicles were also rendered liable to requisition and agricultural production controlled by the state. The supply of raw materials was also subject to strict supervision and control by the state.

Agriculturally, Poland was self-sufficient but she was still dependent on imported raw materials. Despite considerable progress made, her war industry was not yet in a position to arm and equip an army up to the standards of a first-class military power, or withstand the requirements entailed by the wastage and expenditure of a major war. As a result of cash bottlenecks, modernization of the armed forces had, by the end of 1938, inevitably proceeded relatively slowly. For example, only one regiment in the Army was armed with Bofors guns, while the artillery was still almost entirely horse-drawn.

Poland's Triumph: Breaking the Nazi Codes

In equipment and resources the Poles militarily lagged far behind Germany and the other great European powers. However, in the development of the *Enigma* machines, which were able to crack the German cipher system, they were in advance of any other power.

The Germans pioneered the use of cipher machines for military purposes. The first *Enigma* machine was developed by a German firm and was essentially intended for commercial purposes. In 1930 a military version of the machine was constructed as part of Germany's rearmament plans. The Poles, aware of Germany's intention of regaining the territory lost at Versailles, set up a special German Branch in their military cipher department to work on deciphering the German codes. In 1929 the director of the Poznań Mathematics Institute recruited several brilliant young mathematicians to work closely with the cipher bureau. Initially, they only had a commercial *Enigma* machine to work on. This had been secretly taken one Friday from the Railway Customs

Background

Office where it awaited delivery to the German Embassy and was returned the following Monday after detailed analysis. Gradually, the cryptologists were able – with the help of intercepts from German codes – to reconstruct how the *Enigma* machines worked. By February 1933 the Polish General Staff was able to commission the construction of fifteen replicas. A year later they were able to pick up highly secret messages regarding the Night of the Long Knives (Hitler's murderous purge of former colleagues and political rivals).

As the German Armed Forces expanded, a new generation of *Enigma* machines was introduced. The Germans had a blind faith in their technical invincibility and consequently, at times, made careless mistakes, which the Poles were immediately able to capitalize on. In January 1938 the Poles found that they could read 75 per cent of the Wehrmacht's cable traffic. By the summer the Poles had an impressive new code centre in the Kabackie Woods near Warsaw. A French officer, Captain Bertrand, remembered: 'everything was in concrete bunkers, from the radio station to the cryptologists' offices: this was the brain centre of the organization where work went on day and night in silence'.

On 15 September 1938 the Germans suddenly changed the rules for enciphering message keys on over 20,000 *Enigma* machines then in use in the Reich. Most of the stream of information then dried up. This created an urgent need for further automation of decryptment, which resulted in the development of the *Bombe*, named after the *Bomba*, a popular Polish ice cream dessert. According to historians Władysław Kozaczuk and Jerzy Straszak, it

> was an electromechanical machine based on six Polish *Enigma*s, combined with additional devices and transmissions. An electrically driven system of rotors revolved automatically within the *bombe*, successfully generating, over a period of about two hours [. . .] 17,576 combinations. When the rotors aligned in the sought-for position, a light went on, the motor stopped automatically, and the cryptologist read the indications . . . [Source: W. Kozaczuk and J. Straszak, p. 24.]

Poland Betrayed

Almost at the same time, a new method was devised for breaking the double enciphered *Enigma* keys by using a special type of perforated paper sheet with a capacity of 51x51 holes, and for manipulating the sheets so that coincident places could be matched in this pre-programmed system.

Up to the outbreak of war in September 1939 the Poles continued to keep abreast of the latest technical changes in *Enigma*. Here they really were at the cutting-edge of technology and had a gift of immense value to present to Britain and France. In January and then again in July 1939 British and French cipher experts met with their Polish counterparts, and an *Enigma* machine was taken back to both London and Paris.

From the *Anschluss* to the Seizure of Teschen

The main guidelines of Polish foreign policy were laid down by Piłsudski and implemented by his foreign secretary, Józef Beck. Essentially, the key was that if Poland was to remain independent, she had to follow what Piłsudski called a policy of equilibrium between Germany and the USSR. This effectively meant that Poland needed to cultivate good relations with both powers. However, to avoid being sucked into their orbits, she should also cooperate closely with Romania and the Baltic States, which had similar interests, and continue to keep the door open to military cooperation with France in the advent of war against Germany. In 1932 and 1934 non-aggression treaties were signed first with the USSR and then with Germany. Piłsudski observed that this latter agreement 'removed Poland from Germany's hors d'oeuvre to her dessert'.

The Polish Government, however, never lost its mistrust of the USSR. It suspected with some justification that Moscow was merely biding its time to reassert its power in Eastern Europe. Consequently, Poland refused to join the Franco-Soviet Pact in 1935, earning the rebuke from the Soviet Vice-Commissar for foreign affairs that Poland was 'within the orbit of German policy'. Yet in 1936, when German troops marched into the Rhineland contrary to the terms of the Treaty of Versailles, Beck informed the French Ambassador in Warsaw, Léon Noël, that

Background

Poland was ready to fulfil her obligations to France should war break out.

Once the British Government under Chamberlain launched its ambitious policy aimed at appeasing Germany through concessions in Eastern Europe, Polish foreign policy became more complicated. Without alienating either Germany or the USSR it had to ensure that any agreement worked out between the Western powers and Germany was not negotiated at Poland's expense. On the other hand, should, unexpectedly, France and Britain decide to fight Germany, then the door for cooperation must be kept open. Hitler was in no doubt that Poland would attack Germany should a favourable opportunity arise. He was convinced that

> our agreements with Poland will remain valid as long as Germany's strength will remain unshakeable. Should Germany have any setbacks, then an attack by Poland against East Prussia perhaps also against Pomerania and Silesia, must be taken into account.

Hitler's *Anschluss* or 'connection' with Austria on 12 March 1938 (annexation, in effect) did not present an immediate challenge to Warsaw. Much of the Polish press and the Polish Government hoped that it would deflect Germany from demanding the return of Danzig and the Corridor, but General Sosnkowski, the former Polish War Minister, predicted accurately that the fall of Austria would lead to the destruction of Czechoslovakia, Poland and then France.

As soon as Austria was annexed, Hitler began exploiting the demands of the Sudeten Germans to be incorporated into the Reich, insisting on the cession of the Sudetenland to Germany, in the hope that a Czech refusal would give him the pretext to destroy the whole state. In that situation, if the Western Allies were not ready to fight, Poland was determined to sell its neutrality to Germany for a cast-iron guarantee of Danzig, and at the same time secure its interests in Czechoslovakia.

Throughout the Sudeten crisis Poland had to attempt to exploit each shift in direction by Britain, France and Germany. The

Poland Betrayed

American Ambassador, Drexel Biddle, remarked that 'for each move forward', Beck 'generally leaves himself two ways for retreat'. He had to resist pressure from Germany to join the Axis Pact, while at the same time trying to use Polish neutrality as a carrot to persuade the Germans to recognize the independent status of Danzig. Similarly, he had to keep the door open for cooperation with France and Britain in the event of them coming to Czechoslovakia's aid. If they abandoned Czechoslovakia, Beck had then to make sure that he could save something from the wreck for the benefit of Poland. Poland wanted above all a guarantee of the rights of the Polish minorities in Czechoslovakia, a common Polish-Hungarian frontier and the annexation of Teschen.

Once Chamberlain and the French Prime Minister Daladier had conceded at Berchtesgarden in September 1939 that the Sudetenland should, in principle, be awarded to Germany, Poland – with strong backing from Germany – formally laid claim to Teschen. By 24 September about 40,000 troops were concentrated in the Teschen area. At the same time the Trans-Olzan Volunteer Corps was formed, which was affiliated to the Polish League of Silesian Insurgents. 10,000 volunteers enrolled in Warsaw and another 15,000 in Łódź. The Czech Government attempted to be conciliatory and agreed in principle to the transfer of Teschen, but tried to avoid being tied down to a precise date.

On 30 September, the Munich Agreement confirmed the cession of the Sudetenland to Germany but made no definite decision concerning Poland's and Hungary's claims to Czechoslovakian border territory. This galvanized Poland into action, especially as there seemed to be evidence that the Germans were planning to seize the industrialized district of Teschen. Beck sent an ultimatum to Prague demanding the cession of Teschen within ten days. If a negative response was received by noon of 1 October, Poland would use force. This action was especially praised by Hermann Göring, who called it a 'very bold action performed in excellent style'. The Czechs, under pressure from Britain and France, had little option but to agree. Over the next few days Polish troops moved into Teschen. The British Military Attaché described their entry into Czech territory on 8 October:

Background

The authorities responsible for the reception of the troops had carefully marshalled the spectators into groups, including girl Sokol [a Czech youth group] members dressed in Ułan (Polish Lancer) uniform, and children armed with bouquets. These not unnaturally gave the most vociferous expression to their feelings, but a number of the male adult population in the background remained grimly silent. The enthusiasm of the crowd was not very evident during General Bortnowski's speech on arrival, though it certainly increased with occasional widespread cheering when the troops made their appearance.

The latter consisted of units from the 23rd Division (Katowice), and the organization was most varied, bearing little resemblance to estimated war establishments, certain units being noticeably short of personnel and equipment. Some thirty tanks attached to this division were driven past without incident, and were heavily garlanded and loudly cheered.

The infantry made a good impression so far as their appearance and bearing was concerned; the *parademarsch* was well carried out, and morale was obviously high. Maintenance of equipment and harness left much [to be desired], judging by English standards of 'spit and polish', though the standard may have been serviceable enough from a field operations point of view. [Source: NA FO 417/38.]

The solution of the Sudeten crisis did not, however, lead to a lasting improvement in Polish-German relations. There was a serious Polish-German dispute over Bohumin, an important railway junction, which was finally settled on 8 October, but as a result of German insistence, northern Frýdek and the industrial centre of Vitkovice remained Czech. The Germans also excluded the Poles from arbitrating on a Romanian-Hungarian dispute over Hungarian claims in Subcarpathian Ruthenia. The Poles hoped that a common Polish-Hungarian frontier could be created. Consequently, when the arbitration commission met in Vienna, Beck took parallel action and sent ultimatums to Prague and

Poland Betrayed

Bratislava, successfully demanding frontier rectifications in the most important Carpathian and Tatra passes, in particular the Jabłonka Pass, and in the districts of Spiš and Orava.

However, the arbitration Commission's decision was potentially ominous for Poland because it made Slovenia and Subcarpathian Ruthenia autonomous provinces. The Poles feared that this would awaken similar demands amongst the Ukrainian minority in Poland. Indeed, in December, Ukrainian deputies in the Polish *Sejm* began demanding autonomy for south-eastern Poland (former eastern Galicia) and Volynia. In November, Poland had actually sent as many as 3,000 irregular troops – or so it was estimated by the British Vice-Consul at Lwów – over the frontier into Ruthenia to combat Ukrainian nationalists. They were organized in squads of five, each under an NCO and armed with revolvers and grenades. They were operational for three weeks, and some who were captured were hanged by the Czechs. Eventually they were withdrawn as a result of German pressure.

Poland, Danzig and the British Guarantee

The greatest danger that threatened Poland after the Munich Conference was that she might become the next victim of a 'peaceful settlement' between the great powers. The key concessions Hitler wanted from Poland were the return of Danzig to the Reich and the construction of an extra-territorial motorway across the Polish Corridor to East Prussia. In return for this he was ready to contemplate some eventual compensation for Poland at the expense of the USSR in the Ukraine. Conversations between Beck and Joachim von Ribbentrop, the German Foreign Minister, took place in Warsaw at the end of January 1939, which were conducted in a conciliatory spirit. Ribbentrop brought up the subject of Danzig and the motorway, but linked these problems with a proposal for a joint Polish-German attack on Russia and the prospect of awarding Subcarpathian Ruthenia to Poland. Beck rejected any concessions on Danzig on the grounds that Poland could not 'part with tangible rights in exchange for mere guarantees'. At this stage an open break was avoided because the Germans were not yet ready to force the issue and Beck was always careful to state the Polish case in such a way as to avoid a rupture

Background

and to give the impression that further discussion was possible.

But Beck was aware that at any time the Germans might run out of patience. Consequently, it was vital to reinvigorate the alliance with France and strengthen it by securing British backing. Here he was helped by a changing mood in London and Paris. Confronted by Italian claims to Nice, Corsica and North Africa, there was in Paris a revival of interest in the possibility of creating a network of Eastern European alliances, and Bonnet, the French Foreign Minister, specifically reaffirmed the Polish alliance. In London, while Chamberlain was still reconciled to the return of Danzig and Memel to Germany, as well as the complete dismemberment of Czechoslovakia, Lord Halifax, the British Foreign Minister, began to see Poland's value as a check to German expansion in Eastern Europe.

On 15 March the Munich agreement was shattered by the German occupation of Bohemia and the creation of a protectorate over Slovakia. This put Poland in grave danger, as she might well be Germany's next victim. On 19 March Lithuania was told to hand over Memel 'graciously' to the Reich, and two days later Ribbentrop informed the Polish Ambassador in Berlin that Poland must realize that she could only remain a national state if she worked for a 'reasonable' relationship with Germany. He again raised his demands for Danzig and the extra-territorial motorway.

In this situation Beck received unexpected support from Britain. Chamberlain first warned Germany forcefully against further aggression, but it is possible that he would not have followed this up with any action had Berlin not, on 16 March, demanded a German monopoly of Romania's oil exports and a say in running her industry. This led to the British Government implementing a more active policy in Eastern Europe. The British now aimed to set up a bloc that would deter German expansion eastwards. On 21 March Anglo-French conversations opened in London. The French wanted Poland to give a guarantee of assistance to Romania, but Lord Halifax argued that if the Western powers were asking Poland to aid Romania, then they should also give Poland a 'private undertaking that in return for such aid they would also help her', although, as such, there was to be no guarantee of Danzig.

Poland Betrayed

Tension rose on 22 March when the German occupation of Memel led to fears that Danzig might also be overrun. The Polish Government immediately warned that any coup would be met with armed force, and Polish troops concentrations were carried out in the Corridor. Poland also began a secret partial mobilization. The class of reservists released in 1938 were recalled, which enabled the Army to bring its cavalry brigades and some infantry divisions up to wartime strength. The Czech frontier was also reinforced, but care was taken to conceal this from the Germans. Hitler, however, was not yet ready to force a showdown with Poland, as he both wanted to give the Polish Government time to make concessions and to head off any agreement between London and Warsaw. Ribbentrop was entrusted with responsibility for the negotiations. He was instructed that 'for the present, the Führer does not intend to solve the Polish question. However, it must be worked on'. The ultimate fate of Poland was indeed 'grim': she was to be so 'beaten down' that she would not be a political factor for several decades. Eventually, the frontier of 1914 was to be restored and the Polish population in those regions evacuated and resettled in ethnic Polish areas.

On 31 March Chamberlain announced in the House of Commons that

> in the event of any action which clearly threatened Polish independence, and which the Polish Government accordingly considered it vital to resist with their national forces, His Majesty's Government would feel themselves bound at once to lend the Polish Government all support in their power. They have given the Polish Government an assurance to that effect.

He added for good measure: 'the French Government have authorized me to make it plain that they stand in the same position'.

The Poles had achieved something they had long worked for: the commitment of Great Britain to the maintenance of Polish independence. On the other hand, the guarantee was neither a firm commitment to Poland, nor did it necessarily imply any possibility of direct military aid. It was, as historian Anna

Background

Cienciala said, 'at best [. . .] a diplomatic deterrent'. In British and French eyes it did not rule out an orderly handover of Danzig to the Germans. Also, because it was unilateral, it could be revoked at any stage. Chamberlain himself wrote privately that 'what we are concerned with is not the boundaries of states, but attacks on their independence'. The British, certainly at this stage, had no intention of giving financial or military assistance to the Poles. In fact, both the French and British Chiefs of Staff agreed that 'there was nothing that either of us could do to save Poland'.

But the guarantee, however vague, put Poland and Germany on a collision course. The Polish Government feared a German coup in Danzig. If this occurred, Poland would initially treat it as a diplomatic incident and protest to Berlin about the irresponsibility of the local Danzig Germans. This would be backed up by the cancellation of through German traffic in the Corridor and partial mobilization. However, any German ultimatum on Danzig would be rejected and treated as a declaration of war.

Colonel Beck, the Polish Foreign Minister, visited London on 2 April with the hope of converting the British guarantee into an alliance or at the very least of defining it more precisely. He was quizzed by the British Government about the situation in Danzig, but did not mention the fact that Polish-German negotiations were in a state of deadlock, as he feared that this revelation might encourage the British to abandon their guarantee. Instead he stressed that Danzig had become 'a kind of symbol' for his nation, and outlined the Polish terms for a settlement: a bilateral German-Polish agreement guaranteeing free government for the local population and the safeguarding of Polish rights within the city.

Beck achieved a brilliant diplomatic success. He managed to persuade the British ministers of the advantage of a bilateral agreement between Poland and Britain. For the British the key point was that Beck promised that if the principle of permanent collaboration was reached, Poland would be willing to discuss an alliance with Romania and how she could assist Britain in the event of a German attack against Belgium, Holland or Switzerland. Crucially, it was left to the Polish Government to define when its independence was threatened by Germany. In the Summary of Conclusions embodying the agreement it was stated:

Poland Betrayed

His Majesty's Government in the United Kingdom have informed the Polish Government, and have stated publicly, that [. . .] in the event of any action which clearly threatened Polish independence, and which the Polish Government accordingly considered it vital to resist with their national forces, His Majesty's Government would feel themselves bound at once to lend the Polish Government all support in their power.

The German Response

Hitler was furious at the British guarantee, and realizing that the Poles were unlikely to make concessions over Danzig or move voluntarily into the German orbit to become a puppet state, ordered military preparations for an invasion of Poland aimed to begin at any time after 1 September. On 11 April the directive for *Fall Weiss* or 'Operation White' was issued:

The aim will then be to destroy Polish military strength and create in the east a situation which satisfies the requirements of national defence. The free state of Danzig will be proclaimed as part of the Reich territory at the outbreak of hostilities at the latest.

The political leaders consider it their task in this case to isolate Poland if possible, that is to say to limit the war to Poland only [. . .] The isolation of Poland will be all the more easily maintained, even after the outbreak of hostilities, if we succeed in starting the war with sudden heavy blows and in gaining rapid success [. . .] The task of the Wehrmacht is to destroy the Polish Armed Forces. To this end a surprise attack is to be aimed and prepared. Camouflaged or open mobilization will not be ordered earlier than the day before the attack and at the latest possible moment . . . [Source: J. Noakes and G. Pridham, Vol. 3, pp. 735–6.]

Some six weeks later, on 23 May, Hitler called a meeting of the twelve most senior German generals, as well as Admiral Raeder and Reichsmarschall Göring. Hitler fitted the Polish problem into the context of his overall strategy. Essentially, he argued that Germany's drive to gain living room in Russia would be faced with unrelenting hostility from Britain and France, and that Poland could not be relied upon as an ally against the USSR. Consequently, it was again stressed that it was vital 'to attack Poland at the first opportunity', but he warned that 'conflict with Poland – beginning with an attack on Poland – will only be successful if the West keeps out of the ring. If that is not possible, it is better to fall upon the West, and finish off Poland at the same time'. He also added, ominously, that Germany must prepare for a war of ten to fifteen years.

Too Little and Too Late

The British guarantee, however it was intended, strengthened Poland's resolve to fight. As Hitler recognized, it also ensured that any Polish-German conflict would lead to a European war rather than just a local conflict. By the same token, it was very much to the advantage of Poland that if war did break out, it should be a European or even global struggle against Nazism, as this would be likely to guarantee that the Polish question could not be over-looked at a future peace conference.

The next step was to pin down both Britain and France and see what aid they could offer. In May, the Polish Minister of War, Lieutenant General Tadeusz Kasprzycki went to Paris, where, on the 19th, he signed a military protocol committing France immediately in the event of a German attack on Poland. The French Army would begin limited action against the Germans within three days of mobilization and a major land operation some twelve days after that, which would entail an attack on Germany across the north-eastern French frontier with thirty-eight divisions.

This was music to the ears of the Poles, but there was one major drawback: the military convention was not to be signed until a political convention had been negotiated, which incorporated the British guarantees of March–April 1939 into the Polish-French alliance of 1921. The problem here was that the Poles demanded that the annexation of Danzig by Germany should be specifically regarded by France as a cause of war. Bonnet, the French Foreign

Poland Betrayed

Minister, refused to agree unless the British simultaneously pledged themselves to the city's defence, something Lord Halifax was reluctant to do. The political convention was only signed after hostilities actually broke out on 4 September 1939.

A week later, on 27 May, an Air Agreement was signed between representatives of the two Air Forces. The French Air Force agreed to 'act vigorously' as soon as hostilities broke out. Once Germany invaded Poland, the greater part of the French Air Force would attack Germany at the strategically appropriate moment. France also promised to deliver sixty bombers to Poland. In reality, however, the French had no intention of assisting the Poles. Group Captain Slessor, the Director of Plans at the Air Ministry minuted on 31 March that

> The French have no intention of attacking at all in the opening phase. They say their strategy will be to form a firm defensive flank and preserve the integrity of their territory. They will use their mass of manoeuvre to counter-attack any German forces advancing either through the Low Countries or Switzerland.
>
> The French Staff make no bones about distrusting their politicians, and say they tell them as little as possible; for this reason one must wonder how much the French Foreign Office know about the extent to which France could in fact support an ally in Eastern Europe [. . .] I hope that Beck will be left under no delusion as to the value of the assistance that could be afforded by Britain and France. The Poles would have to rely entirely on their own resources to defend their own territory. [Source: NA AIR 75/6.]

A British Military mission was sent to Poland at the end of May to discuss what aid could be given to Poland in the event of war. It was a low-level mission headed by Brigadier Clayton, a former Military Attaché in Warsaw, whom Sword called 'a rollicking old salt'. The talks were fairly non-conclusive. It was clear from the outset that there would be no British naval or military support. The only concrete agreements that emerged were that as soon as war broke out three Polish destroyers would

Background

sail straight away to Britain, as this would prevent them being sunk or interned in the Baltic. The Royal Navy itself would not enter the Baltic, although the possibility of submarine attacks on German shipping was not to be excluded. The RAF on the other hand, it was agreed, would launch attacks on German territory as soon as war broke out. At first these attacks would be limited to military targets but if Germany bombed civilian targets in Poland, then the RAF would be freed to concentrate on any target it liked.

A second series of discussions took place in July, when General Sir Edmund Ironside, the Inspector General of Overseas Forces, was sent to Poland to find out what the Poles would do in the event of a German attack, and to reassure them that Britain was ready to bolster their efforts with a loan and military material. As the Chargé d'Affaires at the British Embassy reported: 'the visit was [. . .] treated as a major political and military event by the press'. One paper, the *Kurjer Polski*, observed that the visit showed that 'Great Britain now realized that she could not evade her historical mission towards Europe and must part with isolationism once and for all'. Yet, in reality, Ironside's visit was little more than a political attempt to reassure the Poles. In practice, nothing was offered apart from a few crumbs.

Over the summer, the Air Ministry had given some consideration as to how it could help Poland in the event of war. A paper had been drawn up looking at the possibility of basing bombers in Poland. It considered the possibility of opening British bases there before hostilities broke out. The problem was the 'tenuous lines of communication'. Three options for supplying these bases in wartime were looked at:

a) By sea to Murmansk and rail via Leningrad.

b) Through the Suez Canal to Odessa and thence by rail via the USSR to Poland.

c) By sea to Basra and thence by rail through Turkey to the Black Sea and across the Black Sea to Odessa.

Despite the scepticism of Bomber Command, the Air Ministry did draw up plans for basing two Wellington bomber squadrons in

Poland Betrayed

Poland. After conducting operations against German targets these would operate a 'shuttle service' and land alternately in Poland and Britain, so that the stockpiling of supplies in Poland could be limited. On 3 August the Air Ministry was authorized

> to ask the Polish Defence authorities for their permission and assistance in preparing an advanced base in Poland, and in laying down stocks of material from which bombers of the British metropolitan bomber force could operate temporarily in the time of war. [Source: NA FO 371/23157.]

These included a supply of bombs, small arms ammunition, petrol and oil. It was, however, emphasized that this 'did not commit the Air Ministry, or rather the Air Force, to the operation of British aircraft from Polish bases'. Nevertheless, the British Government did give its assent, provided that 'the whole transaction [was] effected in a most secret manner in the guise of an apparent sale of the material and equipment concerned to the Polish Government'. The Poles would be required to provide one main base and a satellite aerodrome, ground defences and signals communications. The Polish Military and Air Attaché was actually told that 'as soon as the British Air Ministry receives the consent of the Polish defence authorities in principle to their request, they will take immediate measures to pack and ship the material, stores and equipment'.

By scraping the bottom of the barrel, the RAF was also able to offer at the end of August 100–150 Fairey Battles, which were single-engine light bombers built by the Fairey Aviation Company, for immediate dispatch, and a further 100, half of which were to be delivered between September and December and the remainder between April and May 1940. When General Rayski, the former Polish Aviation Commander, visited Britain in July, he asked for Spitfires and the most up-to-date metal-winged Hurricanes, but was told that none were yet available. Vickers was, however, given permission to negotiate the granting of a licence to Poland and to release the details and drawings of the Hurricane III.

Background

When discussing the British guarantee of Poland in April, much to the surprise of British economic and financial circles, the Poles did not raise the key question of finance. Apparently Beck, according to the British Ambassador in Warsaw, Sir Howard Kennard, 'was so gratified at Poland being accepted as an equal ally that he felt it would be undignified to ask directly for financial help'. Nevertheless, the need for financial assistance was urgent. Poland had only sufficient reserves of armaments to equip in the first instance about fifty-four infantry divisions, two cavalry divisions and a small number of mechanized formations. Once active operations started, Polish industry had only sufficient capacity to maintain about ten divisions in active operations. If Polish Silesia were lost, she would be dependent on deliveries from the Central Industrial District and deliveries would rapidly decline.

As an immediate step, Poland needed to build up her stocks of raw materials and ammunition as soon as possible within the Central Industrial District. But stockpiling would at best only defer the date at which Poland would become dependent upon imports for continuing her armed resistance. Consequently, loans were urgently needed to enable her to buy equipment, raw materials and enlarge her own industrial base. The sources of supply were inevitably more diverse, now that the armament industries in Bohemia and Moravia had been taken over by the Germans: Sweden, Norway, Belgium, France, the UK and the USA were possible alternatives. If war broke out, delivery too, would be a difficult and lengthy task. For instance, the importation by Poland of armaments from the USA via Murmansk would involve a port to port journey of about a month, besides a very long haul over more than 1,200 miles of the Soviet railway system.

The Franco-Polish military conversations in May led to recommendations that France should grant a financial loan to Poland, so that the country might purchase armaments and equipment in France. The French Military Attaché in Warsaw, General Musse, was only stating the obvious when he observed to his British colleague that 'providing Poland with maximum financial and material aid at the earliest possible moment [. . .] was so much cheaper than waiting until war broke out'. He went on to emphasize 'the moral and political effect on a Germany faced by Polish Armed forces known to be fully provided with modern equipment' (source: NA FO 371/23143). Sir Howard Kennard was positively apocalyptic in his tone when he advised his Government that it was of crucial importance to grant financial assistance to Poland as soon as possible. He cabled London on 22 April: 'If, as I believe to be the case, it is true that the British Empire will face for the next year or so a situation which will settle its fate and that of Europe for perhaps a century, ought we not to demonstrate our realization of what is at stake?'

However, initial approaches to London for a loan and financial assistance to purchase munitions and military equipment were turned down flat by the Treasury on the grounds that it would trigger requests from other states, such as Turkey and Greece. In June the Governor of the National Bank of Poland, Adam Koc came to London with a 'shopping list' for the following items:

Munitions . . . . £18 million

Raw materials . . . . . £18 million–£24 million

Industrial credits . . . £6.5 million

Cash loan . . . . £24 million

Initially the British Government's offer was parsimonious in the extreme: the Army was only ready to offer '£300,000 worth of uniforms, etc.'; the Navy nothing and the Air Force 100 Fairey Battle aircraft. Industrial equipment up to £3½ million, but no machine tools, was also offered, but the cash loan was turned down flat.

The Foreign Office was highly critical of the failure to provide generous help to the Poles. One senior official observed that 'it gives the impression that we are bankrupt. Surely we do not wish to do this at a moment when we are trying to induce foreign countries to join our camp?' Eventually, the Government did relent and together with the French granted a joint loan to Poland. But even then, the Treasury attempted to attach conditions to it: it wanted the *złoty* devalued, so that the loan would go further in grants to firms and would cut the price of exports. Similarly, it

Background

wanted the Poles to go back on their policy of denouncing the international Coal agreement. Again this met with criticism from the Foreign Office. One official minuted that 'it must be remembered [. . .] that our assistance to Poland is in its essence a military strategic matter [. . .] Therefore in the last resort, our decision to give help to Poland cannot be affected either by the question of the devaluation of the *złoty* nor by the coal difficulty'. The Treasury, however, argued that the overvaluation of the *złoty* weakened the Polish economy and that this in effect constituted, to quote the Treasury mandarin, Sir Leith Ross, 'a military danger'. It was not until 7 September that Britain finally gave Poland a cash advance of £5 million. It was no wonder that the Germans did not take the British guarantee of Poland seriously!

Polish Civil Defence Preparations 1938–39

As a result of the Sudeten crisis, steps began to be taken to prepare the civil population for war. On 29 September 1938 'Instructions on Air and Gas defence for the General Population' were issued by the Minister of the Interior. These contained a very comprehensive account of both public and individual duties during air raids. The education of the Polish public and the accumulation of the necessary equipment was carried out by the State Air Defence League (LOPP) and the Red Cross. The LOPP was responsible for training the necessary cadres to protect factories, institutions and private houses from the effects of air raids. The Red Cross was responsible for first aid and began to train teams for dealing with casualties. Moves were also afoot to get the universities to establish departments that would work specifically to coordinate medical research on the impact of gas attacks. Together, these two organizations were responsible for providing instructors for the various Air Raid Protection (ARP) training centres. Government officials and schoolteachers had to pass a course of training, as well as at least one person in every large house. Other voluntary organizations, such as the Women's Volunteer Corps and the Boy Scouts, were also being trained in the skills of air raid protection and first aid.

The first air raid precautions exercises in Warsaw in February 1939 were not entirely successful, but a British official was impressed by what he saw a month later:

During alarm periods all lights were extinguished, with the exception of those of vehicles on duty; pedestrians took cover or were forcibly removed as casualties of various kinds, cars were driven half onto pavements and abandoned, horses were unharnessed and tied up. Fires were well simulated, and various important buildings were partially enveloped in flames. Petards were exploded with realistic effect. Various forms of gas were emitted in the streets, and on one occasion a member of the Embassy staff was caught by tear gas, which was too realistic for comfort. [Source: NA FO 371/23144.]

Plans 'W' and 'Z'

Up to 1926 the Poles had planned for a two-front war against both the USSR and Germany, but then Piłsudski, as Director-General of the Armed Forces, ruled that, in reality, the main threat would come from the USSR, and accordingly 'Plan W' was drawn up. Concentration on this plan affected the shape of the Armed Forces and was a major factor in prolonging the retention of cavalry in the Polish Army, as the lack of roads in the Soviet-Polish borderlands limited the effective use of motor transport. The Poles had to rely on horses to give them tactical mobility.

In 1938 the General Staff began to modernize the Army's mobilization plans. The new updated Plan W was a general plan, applicable in the event of war breaking out with either Germany or the Soviet Union. The Army could be mobilized either conventionally by public announcement or by the dispatch of colour-coded cards, which would be sent by post and would bring conscripts into the Army in staggered waves. This would avoid the provocative impact of mobilization during an acute period of crisis. It was planned that the Army would be mobilized and concentrated within twelve to fourteen days.

Work on a strategic plan to deal with a German attack, 'Plan Z' ('Plan Zachód' or 'Plan West') had begun in 1935 with a team led by General Kutrzeba. An initial draft of Plan Z was presented to the GISZ in 1936. It called for the whole Polish Army to be

Background

committed to the German front, leaving the Soviet front covered by KOP units and a handful of eastern divisions. The Polish forces would be divided into four main armies, supported by a reserve:

- Army Warsaw, grouped just south of the East Prussian frontier.

- Army Pomorze, based in Toruń.

- Army Poznań, stationed just east of Poznań.

- Army Łódź-Częstochowa, concentrated on a line to the east of Łódź and Częstochowa.

- Reserve Army, grouped between Kutno and Warsaw.

This plan calculated that the main German attack would be from the north-west, while a supporting attack would come from Silesia and a minor thrust made towards Warsaw from East Prussia. The gist of the Polish response was for a pre-emptive Polish strike against East Prussia, while the main German attack would be contained by the Armies Pomorze and Poznań with the Reserve Army in support. A German thrust from Silesia was to be countered by the Łódź-Częstochowa Army.

Unfortunately, the German annexation of the Sudetenland and then the seizure of Bohemia and Moravia and the reduction of Slovakia to a puppet state seriously damaged Poland's defensive plans, and forced a radical revision of Plan Z. At first, the General Staff considered using the Rivers Niemen, Biebrza, Narew and San as their main defensive line. This would allow a smaller number of troops initially to hold off the Germans, and consequently enable Poland in the early stages of the war to dispose of larger reserves of armaments and equipment, thereby lengthening the time she could hold out against the Germans. But the General Staff feared that a German surprise attack would break through the lightly held frontier areas and interrupt the orderly mobilization of the Polish armies in their defensive positions. It would also mean surrendering a relatively large proportion of the Polish population and some key industrial areas, such as Upper Silesia, without firing a shot.

Poland Betrayed

The alternative, which was chosen by the GISZ, was to adapt the original Plan Z but to create another army to cover the Carpathians and act as a reinforcement for the Silesian front. This plan involved three different phases:

- The frontier forces would fight a delaying action along the borders, so that the bulk of the Army would have time to be mobilized.

- When this was completed the Germans would be confronted on the actual line of defence.

- The Reserve Army would be deployed in the sector that was most under threat.

It was hoped that this would suffice to hold the line until the French and British relieved the pressure in the west. The plan has at times been criticized for attempting to create a static, linear defence along the Polish frontier. In fact, this was far from the case. As Zaloga and Madej have pointed out, the plan 'envisaged the frontier armies as a screen permitting the completion of army mobilization, and a gradual retreat until French intervention'. It was, too, politically vital to defend from the very beginning of hostilities the whole of Polish territory, as western Poland was the richest part of the country containing the great industrial complex in Silesia. This does not mean, of course, that the plan did not have several serious flaws. It spread Polish forces too thinly along all the frontiers and committed them to initial defensive fighting where they had no value, instead of holding them in reserve for mobile counter-attacks. This was to prove fatal when the diluted and overstretched Polish Army was confronted by German armour backed with sufficient reserves, which could exert continuous pressure on the Polish divisions until they were either exhausted or annihilated.

On the day that Memel was annexed, Marshal Edward Rydz-Śmigły, the Inspector General of the Armed Forces, issued the western Army commanders with their orders for what was assumed would be the first stage of the battle:

- The northern front was to be defended by Operational Group Narew, under Major General Czesław Młot-Fijałkowski and Army

Background

Modlin, under Major General Krukowicz-Przedrzymirski. Their task was to stop German forces from East Prussia advancing to Warsaw. To the west of Army Modlin was Army Pomorze, under Lieutenant General Władysław Bortnowski. Together with Army Poznań, under Lieutenant General Tadeusz Kutrzeba, its task was to defend the north-western and western territories and ensure that they were not occupied unopposed. Army Pomorze had to prevent, for as long as possible, the conjunction of German forces on both sides of the Vistula.

- Army Poznań's initial duties were to protect the mobilization centres in Poznań and the flanks of the neighbouring armies.

- To the south lay Army Łódź, under General Juliusz Rómmel, which, at all costs, had to hold the Łódź and Piotrków regions. Its main line of defence was along the Warta and Widawka rivers, and it was to keep in contact with Army Kraków on its left flank.

- To the south was Army Kraków, under Major General Antoni Szylling. Its line of defence ran close to the German frontier. If a retreat to the Vistula became necessary, this Army would play a pivotal role. However, initially, it would lack two divisions, which would not be ready until the second stage of mobilization. This would inevitably deprive it of vital reserves. Szylling's right flank, defending the Częstochowa area, was also dangerously exposed. Between it and the Volynian cavalry brigade of Army Łódz there was a gap of about 25 kilometres, which would be vulnerable to a German Panzer break-through.

- Army Prusy, under Lieutenant General Stefan Dąb-Biernacki, was to act as the main reserve of the High Command. It was concentrated in the rear of the Łódź and Kraków Armies and was to be used to counter German attacks in the Piotrków–Radomsko direction.

- In July, Army Karpaty was formed, commanded by General Kazimierz Fabrycy, to defend the Central Industrial District, the flank and rears of Army Kraków, as well as protecting the route from Hungary to the vital Borysław oilfields from an anticipated attack by German and Slovak forces. Fabrycy was initially given only the 2nd and 3rd Mountain Brigades, together with some extra divisional units, as it was assumed that this attack would occur at a later stage in the campaign; but in case the attack was mounted earlier, Fabrycy was given a reserve of two divisions in the Tarnów area.

Poland Betrayed

Many of the structural and organizational problems facing the Army remained unresolved. Administration was still divided between the General Staff and the General Inspectorate. Rydz-Śmigły also created an impossible burden for himself by failing to delegate more control over the various fronts to the individual Army HQs. 'No general,' as Andrzej Suchcitz has observed, 'could possibly carry the burden of directly controlling eight armies, whilst also preparing and planning the future prosecution of the war.' The Army commanders were also handicapped by being given access to minimal information about their neighbouring armies in the interests of security. Thus none of the commanders had any idea of the overall plan of the campaign. The Army was further weakened by a shortage of NCOs and the poor education of the average conscript, while it could not rely on the loyalty of its Ukrainian troops, which had to be distributed as evenly as possible throughout the whole Army and kept away from the German frontier.

Polish Air and Naval Plans

The Air Force, too, was issued with an operational plan. The front-line elements were regrouped so they could deal with the anticipated combat demands of the Army High Command. Air assets were divided into the Dispositional Air Force, an independent tactical formation composed of two brigades: the Pursuit Brigade, which was composed of five fighter squadrons, whose role was to defend Warsaw, and the bomber brigade. This was composed of five Karaś light bomber and four Łoś medium bomber squadrons. Each Army also had squadrons attached to it for reconnaissance and protection operations.

The Navy and the Merchant Marine were also put into a state of 'heightened awareness'. In 1936 all Polish shipping companies were ordered to ensure that the decks of their ships were strengthened to accommodate artillery as well as heavy machine guns. On 30 March 1939 a law was passed by the *Sejm* requiring all shipowners to place their vessels at the disposition of the Government in the event of war. Then, in April, the Polish Naval Headquarters developed a special radio link for the Merchant Marine, which was used in late August to warn all ships to stay out of the Baltic,

Background

Plans for Intervention in Danzig

The Poles have been criticized by some military historians, such as Basil Liddell Hart, for their rash decision to defend the Corridor. Militarily there was, of course, no justification for such action, but politically the Polish Government could not tolerate a Nazi annexation of Danzig and the Corridor. Consequently, it was vital to ensure that the Germans would encounter some token opposition, which would activate the British and French guarantees. The Polish plan was to send in a Pomeranian cavalry brigade from the south, and from the north-west a further battalion of troops, while the Navy would give support from the sea.

This plan was valid until June, but then evidence multiplied that Danzig was turning into an armed camp. Fortifications were being built along the southern and western borders and German troops were being smuggled into the city disguised as tourists. Consequently, the decision was taken on 13 August to mobilize the Interventionary Corps, consisting of two infantry divisions. In the event of only local action in Danzig its goal was to seize the hills in the Emaus-Langfuhr region, to the south-west and west of the city, but if a general conflagration broke out, the Corps was to withdraw from the Corridor immediately. Initially, the Interventionary Corps was not going to be placed north of Bydgoszcz, but reluctantly the decision was taken to move forces nearer Danzig because otherwise it would take three or four days before they would be able to intervene in the city. When he took the decision to move the 27th Division deep into the Corridor, Rydz-Śmigły remarked to his Chief of Staff, that 'this is an operational absurdity, to which I have been forced by political motives'. On 31 August, once it was clear that large-scale hostilities were imminent, the troops were ordered to be withdrawn.

and to seek British, French, or neutral ports. From May onwards all ships returning to Gdynia were to have a minimum ten- to fifteen-day supply of bunker oil and food to allow a rapid departure for British waters, should war break out.

Both the Polish Destroyer and Submarine Divisions were put on a state of alert from March 1939 onwards. One destroyer was always on patrol in the Baltic observing German shipping. Anti-aircraft crews stood at action stations. In the event of war the destroyers were to head for British ports. The task of the submarines was to interdict the passage of German troopships and transports to East Prussia, while the three boats with mine-laying capacity were to lay mines in the Gulf of Danzig (Gdańsk).

Fall Weiss

In May, General Rundstedt and his Staff, who were responsible for planning the attack on Poland, attempted to forecast what the Polish plan of operations would be. They correctly assessed the Poles were unlikely to surrender their valuable border territories without a fight. What they most feared was that the bulk of the Polish Army would then be able to withdraw behind the Narew–Vistula–San line without having been decisively defeated, 'in the hope that behind this line with the material or military help of Russia, they will be able to hold their own until the economic or military intervention of the Western powers proves successful'. Given Poland's strategic position and the major threats of encirclement from the north and the south-west, Rundstedt's Staff reckoned that the flanks of the Polish Army would be strengthened at the cost of its centre.

The German plan for invading Poland was completed on 15 June 1939 and was primarily the work of Generals Halder, von Stulpnagel, the Chief of Operations, Colonel Hans von Greiffenberg, Head of Operations Section, and General Kurt von Tippelskirch, Chief of the Intelligence Section. It was simple and straightforward:

> The object of the operation is to destroy the Polish Armed Forces. The political leadership demands that the war should be begun by heavy surprise blows and lead to quick successes. The intention is to prevent a regular mobilization

Background

and concentration of the Polish Army by a surprise invasion of Polish territory, and to destroy the mass of the Polish Army west of the Vistula–Narew line by a concentric attack from Silesia on the one side and from Pomerania/East Prussia on the other. [Source: Absicht des Ob. D.H. und Aufträge, 15 June 1939, IWM 1448 (captured German documents, translated by the author).]

How was this to be achieved? The German forces were to be divided into two Army groups: North and South. The former was composed of two armies, the Third under von Küchler and the Fourth under von Bock, which came to 630,000 men. Sufficient bridging material was to be assembled in the course of the summer to construct four bridges over the Oder and the Vistula.

On the first day of hostilities – 'Y Tag' – the Army Group North was to bypass Danzig and restore the territorial link between East Prussia and the rest of the Reich. Polish forces in the Gdynia–Danzig area would be mopped up later. Danzig itself would be declared a part of the Reich and secured by local para-military forces, which would be made responsible to Army Group North. The great mass of the Third and Fourth Armies were to move eastwards to the Vistula and advance on Warsaw.

Army Group South was composed of three armies, the Eighth under Blaskowitz, the Tenth under Reichenau and the Fourteenth under List, in all totalling some 882,000 men under the overall command of von Rundstedt. The Tenth Army was to attack from Silesia between Zawiercie and Wieluń, in the general direction of Warsaw. As far as possible, the Upper Silesian industrial areas were to be spared from destruction. To achieve this, it was vital to eliminate as soon as possible, with the assistance of the Fourteenth Army, all Polish forces in the area up to the River Dunajec. The Fourteenth Army was to avoid being held up by the fortifications around Katowice and to break through Polish forces in the Kraków region and make for the River Dunajec as soon as possible. Slovakian territory could be exploited for strategic manoeuvring if necessary. The Eighth Army would protect the Tenth Army's northern flank and 'with all possible speed' advance on Łódź.

Poland Betrayed

What remained of the Polish Army would be destroyed in a pincer movement. Any large Polish forces still capable of putting up resistance would be prevented from escaping over the Vistula line and annihilated by two further offensives, one from the north and one from the south, which would be launched from behind the Vistula and its tributaries. In short, as the historian, M. Cooper, has observed: 'the Polish forces [. . .] would be caught in a grand double encirclement; destruction would be total'. This was not so much an example of the new *Blitzkrieg* tactics, but rather a throwback to the *Vernichtungsgedanke*, or strategy of destruction, as taught by the great master of the German General Staff at the beginning of the century, von Schlieffen, and indeed, before him, by Napoleon.

The roll of the Luftwaffe was primarily to destroy the Polish Air Force and its installations, to disrupt mobilization by attacking the recruitment centres and to prevent the concentration of troops by destroying the transport network. Parachute troops would also be held ready for giving immediate support where required. The Navy's part was limited to keeping open the sea links with East Prussia and to blockading Gdynia and the Gulf of Danzig.

Countdown to War
The German occupation of Bohemia and Moravia, the British guarantee and the partial Polish mobilization in March inevitably raised political tensions. The German Ambassador in Warsaw reported that amongst the population, 'the wildest of rumours were spreading'. For instance, that fighting had broken out between German and Polish troops along the frontier and that Minister Beck 'had been arrested'. This mood was further heightened by the Polish press, public meetings and public propaganda. It was claimed the Germans were decadent urban dwellers who would be no match for the Poles and that the glorious victory over the Red Army in 1920 would be repeated this time over the Wehrmacht. Anti-German pogroms broke out wherever there was a German minority. In Bydgoszcz, German children were attacked. And on 17 May, in Tomaszów, near Łódź, objections raised by ethnic German workmen to a resolution backed by their Polish colleagues in favour of a workers' contribution to the Air

Background

Defence loan, led to anti-German riots in which two Germans were seriously hurt.

Inevitably, this stoked up hatred amongst the Germans. Along the Upper Silesian frontier there were reports of men in 'coloured shorts and white stockings' engaged in SA drill, and in one small town the British Ambassador reported that 'a number of girls' were arrested 'for organizing a secret branch of the League of German Girls'. In Danzig there were also repeated incidents throughout the summer. On 20 July, for instance, a Polish frontier guard was killed when challenging a German officer and two SA men who were, in fact, on Polish territory.

Against this background both the Germans and the Poles prepared for war and attempted to perfect their mobilization plans. Fortifications were being expanded and strengthened in the west by the Poles and where possible extra divisions were being formed to fill dangerous gaps in the defences (see page 51).

All these measures were closely monitored by the Germans. While they were keenly aware of the vulnerable points in the Polish Armed Forces, an intelligence report observed in July that

> the switch of the armaments industry to a state of war seems to have worked. Even if a considerable amount of war material cannot be delivered in the short term, over the longer term it must be reckoned that a considerable increase in production will take place and this will probably enable more reserve divisions to be formed. [Source: IWM AL 1494 172/740–41 (translated by the author).]

In late June the *Oberkommando der Wehrmacht* (the German Military High Command) began to set a timetable for the mobilization and concentration of troops along the Polish borders. It stressed that, as far as possible, economic and military mobilization must be conducted with as much secrecy as possible. In July, all military power stations were to be supplied with sufficient coal, railway timetables for the movement of troops and equipment were also to be worked out, and in East Prussia the necessary stocks of war material were to be built up. By August inventories of key civilian personnel who were not to be called up were to be completed, ministries were to be put on round-the-clock alert, motor lorries requisitioned and civilian air raid protection measures put into operation. Troop movements were, as far as possible, to be disguised by claiming they were manoeuvres or else merely the transport of troops for the forthcoming ceremony to mark the 25th anniversary of the great German victory of Tannenberg over the Russians.

The Nazi-Soviet Pact

The key to the imminent conflict was the attitude of the USSR. The coming clash over Poland had made Soviet Russia a major player on the international scene. Stalin's ultimate aim was to extend the Soviet frontier westwards by eventually annexing the Baltic States, Finland, Bessarabia and eastern Poland. On 18 April he proposed a military alliance to both Britain and France. The offer was received with mixed feelings, as London did not trust the USSR and knew that the Poles would reject any request for Russian troops to cross the border into Poland. However, negotiations for a mutual defensive alliance started in May.

At the beginning of July detailed military talks began but they immediately ran up against a serious problem: the key question was whether the Poles would agree to the passage of Soviet troops through Poland. The Poles, fearful that this would be a preliminary to a permanent Soviet occupation rejected this. Beck himself informed his allies that he objected 'to the passage of Russian troops across Polish territory just as much as that of German troops'. The French and British Chiefs of Staff were highly critical of this attitude. An RAF Air Staff minute recorded that:

> Poland already has her back to the wall, and it will certainly be completely suicidal for her to break down the Anglo-Soviet agreement and eliminate the possibility of Russian support.
>
> The Polish General Staff are just as unreasonable. They say they see no benefit to be gained by the Soviet Government through Red troops operating in Poland against German land forces. The point is, not the benefit to be gained by the Soviet Government, but the benefit to be

Background

gained by the Polish Government, since the only direct support they can hope for is from Russia. [Source: NA AIR 75/6.]

In reality Beck was, of course, right. Stalin was using this demand as an excuse to bring the Anglo-French talks to an end. A victorious Red Army, as was seen in 1944, would never leave Poland. This was clearly recognized by Sir Howard Kennard, who observed a year earlier that once the Red Army entered Poland, it would take another war to oust it even if both Poland and the USSR were members of an anti-German coalition.

Essentially, an agreement with Germany would give Stalin all he needed without having to fight. It would also divide his potential enemies who, so it was presumed, would become bogged down in a war of attrition in the west. For Hitler, such an agreement would also make the destruction of Poland possible and destroy Britain's attempt to contain Nazi Germany. When the talks broke down on 17 August over the question of securing agreement to the passage of the Red Army through Poland and Romania, Stalin was ready to explore the German proposals for a non-aggression pact. On 23 August, Ribbentrop flew to Moscow and the pact was signed in the early hours of the 24th. It was also accompanied by a secret protocol outlining German and Russian spheres of interest in Eastern Europe: the Baltic States to the north of Lithuania and Besserabia would belong to the Soviet sphere, while

> in the event of a territorial and political transformation of the territories belonging to the Polish state, the spheres of interest of both Germany and the USSR shall be bounded approximately by the line of Rivers Narew, Vistula and San.
>
> The question of whether the interests of both parties make the maintenance of an independent Polish state appear desirable and how the frontiers of this state should be drawn can be definitely determined only in the course of further political developments. [Source: J. Noakes and G. Pridham, p. 744.]

Poland Betrayed

War Postponed for a Week

Hitler had originally planned to launch the invasion of Poland on 25 August, but the announcement of the ratification of the British guarantee of Poland, as well as Mussolini's reluctance to honour the Pact of Steel and support Germany, led Hitler to postpone the invasion in the hope that the Poles would agree to negotiations, or else that he would be able drive a wedge between them and their western Allies. Inevitably, news of this cancellation did not reach all the units and a small number of local attacks occurred. The most serious was in the Jabłonka Pass area, where a unit of German troops tried to seize a key railway station and tunnel. There was a rise in sabotage incidents in western Poland, as well as several border raids by *Abwehr* (counter-espionage) units.

Britain and France used the next few days to explore every possibility for avoiding war but in the final analysis they would not sacrifice Polish independence to do that. Germany in the meantime perfected her preparations for the coming invasion. As the French Air Staff's intelligence bulletin put it: 'while the latest manoeuvres to settle peacefully the question of Danzig and the Corridor are multiplying, Germany places her offensive forces in readiness for action against Poland'.

One young German private in an artillery regiment, Willi Krey, kept a campaign diary of the brief Polish war. On Tuesday, 29 August, his battalion left the barracks in Braunschweig in Central Germany at six o'clock in the evening:

> We drove past the Volkswagen factory at Fallersleben, thousands of Italian workers were in the street and waved and shouted Italian war cries. We stopped at Vorsfelde station because here we were going to load up the guns [. . .] A ban on alcohol had been ordered for the whole of the Wehrmacht. Since this work made us very thirsty, I crept into the station café and persuaded the landlady to give me a glass of beer. We waited for the departure signal until one o'clock in the morning . . .
>
> As the train moved off, I lay down and slept. I woke up in the early morning just outside Berlin. We went on then via Berlin to Frankfurt. We were given mugs of hot coffee

Background

by women voluntary workers. All the trains we met on the way were full of soldiers. We met every branch of the Army and shouted and waved at each other. Our destination was a few kilometres from Liefnitz – the small town of Maltsch. On all the larger factories, stations and bridges there were flak and railway guards. After unloading the guns, we were given coffee and fruit by girls of the BDM (The League of German Girls) and other women volunteers. Late afternoon we drove via Brieg to Kreuzberg. The population of the villages and little towns stood the whole night through on the streets and waved to us. Our only question though was: how far is it to the border? [Source: Krey, IWM 94/26/1.]

The Poles were handicapped in meeting the expected German attack by continued Allied attempts to secure a diplomatic solution to the Danzig problem. They had made considerable progress in mobilizing individual divisions and corps, although Anglo-French pressure prevented the implementation of general mobilization until the latest possible moment. From 23 August onwards call-up papers were being secretly dispatched by a variety of means to military personnel and conscripts throughout Poland. In Piorun, in eastern Poland, for instance, Walery Choroszewski, a sixth form student, volunteered to deliver them by bike so as to avoid any overt publicity. The young film director, Ryszard Zolski, was summoned into the studio office by his manager on 25 August, and, as he later recalled:

there was a policeman waiting for me. I was surprised, as I knew nothing the police could want me for; but the suspense was not for long. He asked me, 'Are you Mr Ryszard Zolski?' I replied, 'Yes.' Then he said, 'Please sign here that you have received this paper from me,' and added, 'I went to your place this morning.' Before signing I looked at the piece of the paper, even smaller than a normal letter page, and on it was printed: 'You will report to the barracks of 3rd Armoured Division stationed in Fort Bena, Wola, Warsaw at 12 noon.' [Source: R. Zolski, IWM 83/24/1.]

61

Poland Betrayed

Jan Siedlecki, who was a small boy in 1939, can still remember his father, who was a professional officer stationed in Pleszew near Poznań, riding off to war 'on a grey horse [. . .] down the avenue lined by old chestnut trees' on 24 August. Jan never saw his father again, as he was killed in the Battle of the Bzura.

By 31 August the situation was so threatening that the Poles at last announced general mobilization despite British and French objections. As a Foreign Office official minuted the day before on a dispatch from the British Ambassador in Warsaw:

> Personally I think the Poles are fully justified in mobilizing. The fact is that they have received information to show that German military preparations will be absolutely complete on the night of 30/31 August, viz. tomorrow. Polish military preparations are not complete, and it is unreasonable that the weaker power should have to bear this disability for fear of annoying a larger power who is admittedly out for their blood. [Source: NA FO 23153.]

On the same day the Polish Destroyer Division set sail from Gdynia at 14:00 hours for Leith in Scotland, to escape what would be inevitable destruction at the hands of a stronger German Navy in the Baltic, and PAF units were dispersed to their secret wartime bases.

Campaign
Chronicle

Preliminary Incidents

Britain and France had been concerned that the Germans would, through some incident on the frontier, provoke the Poles' retaliation, which would then give Berlin an excellent excuse to declare war. In fact, Hitler had indeed given this top priority. On 5 August 1939 the head of the SD (the Security Service of the SS), Reinhard Heydrich, entrusted the 28-year-old Alfred Naujoks with the task of creating just such an incident. Heydrich observed:

> There have been scores of irritating little incidents all along the frontier in the last few months [. . .] nothing serious, just an odd shot here and there, the usual diplomatic complaints. But nothing big enough, nothing manufactured on a large scale. Nothing, in fact, to set off the powder barrel. [Source: G. Peis, p. 115.]

In order to 'set off the powder barrel', Heydrich outlined a complex plan for blowing up the German radio station at Gleiwitz (Gliwice). A team of six commandos were to be dressed up as Polish soldiers and seize the radio station, taking its occupants prisoner. Then, a specially picked announcer who could speak Polish was to make a provocative speech, boasting of Poland's success in taking over the radio station. An engineer from Radio Berlin was to ensure that this was broadcast to the whole of Germany. To add a realistic detail to the operation, a Jewish concentration camp inmate was to be dressed up as a Polish soldier, shot dead, and left in front of the radio station.

On the night of 31 August the attack was successful, but the wireless expert panicked and could not find the correct landline switch, and thus was only able to broadcast on the local programme. Heydrich, however, was not bothered, as he had already leaked details of the incident to the Nazi paper, the *Völkischer Beobachter*. That night there were two other incidents. At 4 a.m. operation 'Agathe' was launched against a customs house in Hochlinden and a forester's house in Pitschau, by a group of German SS men disguised as drunken Polish pillagers.

Gleiwitz, and to a much lesser extent the other two incidents, enabled Hitler to claim that Germany was only going to war in self-defence when he broadcast his declaration of war to the German Army at 5.40 a.m.:

> The Polish state has refused the peaceful settlement of relations which I desired and has appealed to arms. Germans in Poland are persecuted with bloody terror and driven from their homes. A series of violations, intolerable to a great power, prove that Poland is no longer willing to respect the frontier of the Reich. In order to put an end to this lunacy I have no choice than to meet force with force; the German Army will fight for the honour and rights of a newborn Germany. [Source: N. Bethel, p. 2.]

31 August 1939: The Wehrmacht's Orders

The Wehrmacht was fully deployed for *Fall Weiss* by midnight on 31 August, and action was scheduled to start at 04:45 hours. The orders issued were simple: German forces were to encircle and destroy the Polish Army at the earliest possible moment, so that troops could then be transferred westwards to deal with the threat of a French invasion. Army Group North's aim was to move into the Polish Corridor and cut off Gdynia from the rest of Poland. Once the Corridor was occupied, the XIX Motorized and Panzer Corps would move east and, together with the Third Army, mount a southwards movement against Warsaw. In the south, the Tenth Army was to smash through the Polish border defences and advance rapidly on Warsaw, while the Fourteenth Army would shield its southern flank from the Polish Army Kraków and send Panzer and motorized forces deep into Poland to meet up with troops from Army Group North on the axis of Dęblin–Lublin–Chełm.

1–17 September: Fighting in Danzig, Westerplatte and the Coastal Regions

Within Danzig itself the bombardment by the old German battle-ship, the *Schleswig-Holstein*, of the arsenal at the Westerplatte, which was used as a transit base for munitions and other mate-rials for the Polish Army, at 04:45 hours, signalled the start of attempts by the SS Heimwehr (Home Defence) Danzig Division, supported by naval commandos and some paramilitary units, to occupy the small Polish outposts and official enclaves in the city. The Polish customs and railway offices, the Polish school and the students' hostel, as well the diplomatic mission, were all quickly occupied by SA and SS men. The Polish Post Office and the arsenal at Westerplatte, were, however, to cause the Germans considerable problems. The Post Office had originally been a German military hospital and in 1930 its structure had been considerably strengthened. All the personnel who worked in it were military reservists.

As soon as the first salvo of the *Schleswig-Holstein* was heard, armed police and SS men of the Heimwehr Danzig Division launched an attack against the Post Office, but it was easily beaten back. A second attack was attempted with the help of a police reconnaissance car but was again beaten back with heavy casual-ties. As Anton Winter, a member of the SS division, later recalled:

> It was simply impossible without a great number of casual-ties to climb over the walls and iron gate and penetrate into the building. After the attack with the armed reconnaissance car failed, there was a short pause in the fighting. Even after a heavy army howitzer opened up fire, the defenders could still not be forced to surrender. The Poles defended the Post Office with exceptional bravery in the belief that they would be rescued by the Polish cavalry, who, as we all know would

be in Berlin within seven days! [Source: R. Michaelis, p. 145 (translated by the author).]

Finally, late in the afternoon, a flame-thrower was brought up from Westerplatte and the Fire Brigade – protected by a barrage of fire – pumped petrol into the cellars and then set it on fire. This was successful and smoked out the thirty-eight defenders, who were later charged with war crimes, brought before a 'war tribunal' and shot.

A precondition of the German destruction of Polish land and naval forces in Gdynia and on the Hel Peninsula was the capture of the Westerplatte complex. The problem was that neither the commander of the German land forces in Danzig, Generalmajor Eberhardt, nor the captain of the battlecruiser, *Schleswig-Holstein*, Gustav Kleikamp, had an accurate picture of the defences of the arsenal. Optimistically it was assumed that after the Westerplatte had been softened up by a bombardment by the *Schleswig-Holstein* and by machine-gun fire from local police units, a naval commando force would successfully force it to surrender. In fact, the Germans faced a ring of fortified underground concrete bunkers and an elite force of 210 men under the command of Major Henryk Sucharski.

It was thus not surprising that the first German attack at 07:07 hours on 1 September was repulsed. A second attempt twelve hours later was again defeated, and the Germans had by now suffered eighty-two lost or wounded. The Poles, in contrast, lost only four men with a further four wounded, and were buoyed up with the feeling of having won their first skirmish. Kleikamp was consequently forced to rethink his tactics and reinforce his troops. Eberhardt was all for another assault as soon as possible but the news that the Poles had 'at least' twenty reinforced bunkers on the Westerplatte, persuaded him that caution was the better part of valour. The following day a battalion of sappers was sent by Army Group North and then between 18:05 and 18:45 hours the Westerplatte was bombarded by the Luftwaffe with devastating effect. Considerable damage was done and a further eight Poles were killed. Sucharski later conceded that if the Germans had followed this up quickly with a land attack, the Westerplatte would have fallen. The Germans, however, took their time and softened up the Westerplatte's defences with heavy mortar fire. By the night of 5/6 September the garrison was under great pressure. Lieutenant Kregielski briefly summed up the situation:

> the barracks after all the damage done to it are no longer recognizable. The soldiers [. . .] are exhausted and the wounded lie on stretchers. The only light comes from a candle [. . .] The hygienic situation is appalling and the air is terrible. [Source: B. Stjernfelt and K-R. Boehme, p. 113 (translated by the author).]

The soldiers were so exhausted that, in the words of Sergeant Gryczman, they were 'shooting at shadows' fearing that they were Germans. On the 7th, Sucharski decided to surrender. The news was received with disbelief by his men, but when they heard that the Germans had already driven deep into Poland, they realized that they had no other option. Such was the respect that the Germans gave Sucharski, that he was allowed to wear his sword into captivity.

Once the German troops had occupied the Corridor, Polish coastal and naval forces were isolated. The Naval Air Detachment force, which consisted of twenty-five obsolete planes, was rapidly destroyed by air raids. Poland's cruiser force had already sailed for Scotland, but left behind were the destroyer *Wicher*, the minelayer *Gryf*, a division of the ships of the *Jaskółka* class, which were capable of carrying out both minesweeping and minelaying operations, and a torpedo boat squadron. None survived the might of the Luftwaffe for long.

On 1 September the *Wicher* and *Gryf*, together with six minesweepers and two gunboats, left Gdynia to lay a minefield south-east of the tip of the Hel Peninsula. A reconnaissance aircraft spotted the *Gryf* and a force of thirty-three Junker Ju 87 (Stuka) dive-bombers took off within half an hour of hearing the news. They soon found not only the *Gryf* busy mine-laying, but the *Wicher*, six minesweepers and two gunboats sailing in a convoy. There followed then what Krzysztof Janowicz has called the first naval-air battle of the Second World War:

Poland Betrayed

The Junkers' pilots divided themselves into two groups and began the attack. Diving down they tried to locate precisely their bombs, but the ships were zigzagging and shooting massive fire at them. The sea was boiling with the explosions and machine-gun bursts, the skies were filled with streaks left by projectiles and with smoke. Polish ships concentrated in a loose group shooting at Stukas [Ju 87s] and forcing them to bomb from a higher altitude. [Source: K. Janowicz, *Luftflotte I*, p. 32.]

A German air attack killed the commanding officer of the *Gryf*, wounded twenty-nine of the crew, and severely damaged a minesweeper. The *Gryf* returned to Hel, but the *Wicher* continued on patrol. Unaware of the return to port of the *Gryf*, the *Wicher*'s captain let pass a unique opportunity of torpedoing a German convoy, as he was under strict orders not to risk the main mission of mine-laying. On 3 September, however, both ships, together with shore-based artillery, beat off a German attack on the Hel Peninsula, heavily damaging one of the German destroyers, but in the early afternoon the Polish vessels were sunk by yet another German air raid.

The shore batteries and coastal defence forces formed stubborn pockets of resistance. The Hel Peninsula was defended by about 2,800 troops, while there were a further 14,000 holding the defensive perimeter on the Oksywie Heights overlooking the Gulf of Danzig. These were composed of naval and artillery units as well as workers' militias. To eliminate these pockets the Germans assembled a corps of about 26,000 troops. Only the German 207th Infantry Division was composed of fully trained troops, while the rest were made up of various frontier or paramilitary units. After the fall of Westerplatte a further 12,000 troops under General Eberhardt became available.

Once the Luftwaffe had secured domination of the skies over Poland by 6 September, it was able to employ small groups of hydroplanes, Stukas and Heinkels to bombard and machine-gun Polish positions several times a day on both the Hel Peninsula and the Oksywie Heights. Captain Michał Pikula later described the effectiveness of their attacks on troops on the Oksywie Perimeter:

Campaign Chronicle

In the afternoon of 15 September our battalion was moved to [a] forest west of Suchy Dwór. At 5 p.m. the commander [. . .] organized a briefing in a country manor [. . .] Night was falling when we heard a hum of a hydroplane. After a while a bomb exploded in the garden, 30 feet away from our room. The explosion destroyed all the windows and we all fell on the floor. Some bigger shrapnel made a hole in the wall two foot thick and killed a beautiful Bernadine dog that was lying there. Having regained my consciousness I got up from the floor covered with glass and debris [. . .] From ten officers taking part in the briefing eight were more or less seriously wounded. [Source: Janowicz, p. 38.]

Two days later the remaining resistance on the Oksywie Heights was broken, and the Commander, Colonel Dąbek killed himself rather than surrender. The Germans then turned their attention to the Hel Peninsula, which managed to hold out until 1 October (see pp. 131–2).

1–6 September: Rout of the Polish Air Force

The German Air Force in eastern Germany on the eve of war consisted of two air fleets. In the north, Luftflotte 1, under General Albert Kesselring, which had 1,105 aircraft, including 526 bombers; and in the south, Luftflotte 4, under General Alexander Löhr, which possessed 729 aircraft including 303 bombers. To defend themselves from this armada, the Poles had effectively only 397 combat aircraft, of which 154 were medium bombers.

The senior officers of the Luftwaffe were disciples of the doctrine of the Italian air strategist, Giulio Douhet, who insisted that 'a decision in the air must precede a decision on the ground'. Consequently, the Luftwaffe was trained to destroy its enemies' air forces with the greatest rapidity. In a lecture on the Polish Campaign to the Military Attachés in Berlin on 24 November 1939, a German Air Force officer, Captain Kleb, observed that

The essential task of [the] Luftflotten was in the shortest possible time to gain mastery in the air over Polish territory, so that they might be free to support the advance of the Army

69

at full strength. Three consecutive phrases can be clearly distinguished:

- Achievement of mastery in the air.
- Support of the Army, which culminated in the attack on military objectives in Warsaw.
  [Source: NA AIR 40/1208.]

In fact it was not as clear cut as this. Luftflotten 1 and 4 during the first week pursued all three objectives concurrently. From the very beginning of the war the Luftwaffe worked in close cooperation with the troops on the ground.

On 1 September German plans to launch a massive attack against the PAF were upset by low cloud and fog. Consequently the planned attack disintegrated into a series of individual actions. Operation *Wasserkante*, the mass bombing of Warsaw, had to be cancelled. Luftflotte 1 was only able to carry out seven separate raids in the morning, five of which involved airfields. Only in the afternoon, when the clouds cleared, was Kesselring able to commit all his Luftwaffe units. In the south, where weather conditions were more favourable, most of the attacks were launched on time. The main attacks were directed against the airfields at Kraków, Częstochowa, Katowice, Krosno, Moderovka, Łódź, Kielce and Radom, but, repeatedly during the day, ground-attack sorties were made against troop concentrations.

The results achieved against ground targets were very effective and led to the disintegration of entire Polish units as the troops fled in panic. The Germans had not, however, yet succeeded in achieving their aim of destroying the Polish Air Force, even though they undoubtedly enjoyed air superiority. The Poles had been able to move their aircraft to emergency airstrips. The airfields that were attacked had been evacuated and only training aircraft were destroyed. Above all, the Luftwaffe had failed to find the Polish bomber force.

The Poles – outnumbered and flying inferior machines – conducted a heroic but ultimately doomed resistance. Over Warsaw, however, the Pursuit Brigade did manage to inflict serious losses on the German forces. It was helped by an effective early-warning system and was efficiently guided from a ground

Campaign Chronicle

command post. In the first five days the Germans repeatedly bombed Warsaw. On the early morning of 1 September, despite the cloud, formations of He 111s and Do 17s, escorted by Bf 110s were intercepted by some fifty fighters of the Pursuit Brigade. The Germans were forced to turn back and jettison most of their bombs over the countryside and a running fight ensued over a 20-mile area north-east of Warsaw. A good description of the battle from the Polish viewpoint was given by Lieutenant Jerzy Palusinski. He flew out from a bank of cloud and:

> there was a furious fight in front of us. Something around 200 planes in one place, at the same time [. . .] On my right I noticed three fat bombers heading south [. . .] from the distance of 400 feet I fired [at] the target with a long burst of fire. Manoeuvring my machine I aimed at the right engine and once again pulled the trigger. The Heinkel's engine was set [o]n fire and after a while [it] dropped off the formation and crashed to the ground with a twist [. . .] All of a sudden I heard a terrible rumble and a pull on my left arm. At my right a silhouette of a Bf 110 that was approaching an attack [*sic*] could be seen [. . .] I felt pain in my left arm and noticed a brown stain on my sleeve. I began to feel sleepy. I could not lose consciousness now! My controls were totally destroyed. Only the compass and timer were working. I took a look back. The upper section of my tail had disappeared and my wings were shattered . . . [Source: K. Janowicz, pp. 45–6.]

Fortunately Palusinski managed to land and was evacuated quickly to hospital.

That afternoon the bombers returned but the morning's fighting had already taken a heavy toll of the Pursuit Brigade. Four fighters had been lost and some twenty damaged. Consequently, only thirty were now able to intercept the waves of German bombers, but again they were able to beat them off without any major damage being inflicted on the armament factories or bridges over the Vistula. By the end of the day the Pursuit Brigade had lost ten fighters and achieved twelve confirmed air victories.

Poland Betrayed

This first day did much to bolster the self-confidence of the Pursuit Brigade's pilots. They believed – with considerable justification – that they were as good, if not better, than the German pilots (with the exception of those who had served with the Condor Legion in Spain) and only needed more planes and better equipment in order to defeat them. After the air campaign was virtually over, three young Polish pilots told the former British Vice-Consul in Lwów that

> while German equipment is absolutely first class, none of the [. . .] Polish pilots felt that the majority of the Germans were their equal in training or experience. The German fighters also lacked 'brio' and their freedom of action was perhaps hampered by too close wireless control from their leaders until the very moment of engagement. The bombers even when meeting with no interference were very inaccurate. None of these remarks, however, apply to the Condor Squadron, which was disastrously efficient. [Source: R.H. Hoare to Halifax, 3.10.39, NA FO 371/23093.]

They also reported that some of the younger German pilots, who were shot down, were apparently 'found in abnormally nervous condition. Some showed hypodermic needle marks on their arms and legs and they asked for ether injections if they were wounded'.

On 2 September a small formation of bombers confused the Polish observation posts around Warsaw by approaching at various heights and from different directions. They managed to penetrate the city's defences and inflict considerable damage. The following day they hit the PZL Okęcie plant and the fitting-out base for the Łoś bombers. This forced the Pursuit Brigade, on 5 September, to change their operational methods, and instead of relying on the early warning system, to fly patrols consisting of two to six machines. Again there were violent clashes with the Luftwaffe. Just before noon a squadron of Polish P-11s attacked fifteen Ju 87 dive-bombers escorted by Bf 109s, and managed to destroy two of the German fighters, but by the next morning the Pursuit Brigade had only twenty-one serviceable aircraft at its disposal.

Campaign Chronicle

Such was the attrition rate of the PAF elsewhere that the Pursuit Brigade was briefly, on 6 September, ordered to carry out a reconnaissance mission in the Łódź–Kielce region. Appalled by the signs of military rout, they then carried out two sweeps to the far south and west of Warsaw. They managed to intercept a large formation of Do 17s, which were only protected by a few Bf 109s and disperse them. In the confusion two German bombers collided and blew up.

That evening, what remained of the Pursuit Brigade was ordered to evacuate Warsaw for bases in the Lublin area behind the Vistula, where the Poles were hoping to regroup. The Brigade had fought heroically: it had destroyed forty-two German raiders at the cost of thirty-eight of its own machines. Now it was down to a mere sixteen fighters.

Rydz-Śmigły was uncertain how to use the Polish bomber brigade. Until 3 September the British and French urged him strongly not to use bombers on targets in Germany lest it 'provoke' Hitler even more! Light bombers, the Karaś, attached to Army Kraków, attacked enemy armour on 2 September. Crews of the light bomber group Karaś II/2, which was involved in reconnaissance of the Częstochowa region on 2 September, also, on their own initiative, loaded up with bombs to drop on opportune targets. The following day the Karaś squadron again attacked German armoured forces in the Radomsko region, north-east of Częstochowa. Captain Graf von Kielmansegg, who was on the receiving end of these attacks, observed in his diary that

> the 3 September – at least for us – was the great day of the Polish Air Force. One must give it to these Poles that they carry out their orders with an elegant skill [. . .] At times there were air attacks every half-hour. For the most part the Poles attack with units of three planes, sometimes, however with nine. Fortunately their aiming was for the most part poor. [Source: J. Piekalkiewicz, p. 81 (translated by the author).]

On 4, 5 and 6 September both Karaś and the heavy Łoś bombers repeatedly attacked German forces in the critical Piotrków sector (see p. 94) between the Army Łódź and Army Kraków, further west at Wieluń and in the north in the Pułtusk area. Von Höpner's XVI

Poland Betrayed

Armoured Corps in the Piotrków sector reported on 4 September that Polish air strikes had knocked out some 28 per cent of the 4th Armoured Division. Altogether, between 2 and 6 September, the bomber brigade had made 119 aircraft sorties. Out of a total force of 154 bombers they had lost 38.

Elsewhere along the front the Luftwaffe was opposed by small flights of or even single PZL fighters operating from hastily constructed ambush fields. Time and time again the Polish fighter pilots showed astonishing bravery, but essentially they could make little headway against the overwhelming strength of the Luftwaffe. This became painfully clear to Franciszek Kornicki of the 3rd Fighter Wing, which was attached to Army Łódź. On 2 September he was sent to the Observation Network Centre at Łódź to act as liaison officer with Wing HQ to help with the task of analyzing intelligence and advising on which enemy formations could be intercepted from the 3rd Fighter Wing's base. He rapidly grasped that

> in the air the Luftwaffe had complete superiority; reports of their actions poured in from dawn to dusk. It was impossible for III/6 Wing to have any serious impact on their air offensive, as I realized when I passed on reports of numerous large and medium-sized raids. I saw the end approaching fast . . . [Source: F. Kornicki, IWM 01/1/1.]

On the evening of 4 September he returned to base and there he experienced first-hand how desperate the situation was:

> On 3 September the Wing operated from both ambush fields and the main base. On 4 September three P-7s had returned to Widzew for refuelling and rearming after a sortie from their ambush field when German Do 17s appeared overhead. The readiness section took off and were almost immediately attacked by nine Me 109s. In this unequal fight one was wounded, attempted to land, was hit again, caught fire and crashed to his death. The other [pilot], wounded in his leg and with his engine damaged, managed to land on an adjacent field and leave the aircraft before it was shot up and

burned. The three helpless P-7s were hit on the ground and set on fire, as were another two P-7s damaged in previous fights and parked near a straw stook. By the end of the day III/6 had five serviceable aircraft left, and no replacements. [Source: F. Kornicki, IWM 01/1/1.]

Together with the Army the PAF had no option but to retreat and regroup. The fighter planes attached to Army Kraków had already been moved back to Dęblin, and late on 6 September all other fighters – and even trainer planes if they could be salvaged – were ordered to join the Pursuit Squadron in Lublin. B.J. Solak, who later became a squadron leader in the Polish Air Force in Britain, remembered vividly driving at night to some small airfield close to advancing Germans to pick up ten trainer aircraft:

Driving through small towns, burning after daylight bombing – sombre Jews in long black frocks standing motionless against the red glow of flames and smoke billowing from their destroyed houses. Then some airfield cratered by many bomb impacts, and a take-off with German planes high above flying to some other targets, us flying below the trees hiding in the shadows, avoiding crossroads and towns. [Source: B.J. Solak, IWM 90/11/1.]

From the first day onwards, the Luftwaffe provided the Wehrmacht with an increasing amount of tactical support by destroying railway communications, road arteries and bridges across the Rivers Narew, Vistula and Bug, so that the Polish Army would not be able to retreat and regroup. On 5 September, for example, Polish engineers were busy constructing as many as sixteen temporary bridges over the Vistula, but the following day these were all destroyed by aerial attack. Throughout the first week, attacks against the Polish railway system were carried out systematically. For instance, Polish forces on 5 September were forced to abandon rail transport in the areas of Radom and Kielce. The Germans rapidly learnt that the most effective way of disrupting rail traffic was to bomb railway stations rather than track, which could be quickly repaired. This was spelt out later by Captain Kleb in his Berlin lecture (see page 69), where he was reported as saying:

> Direct hits on congested stations had thrown everything into utter confusion and caused serious fires and explosions, so intimidating the railway personnel that no attempt was made to get the trains off since a large proportion of the railway workers had fled. [Source: NA AIR 40/1208.]

Operations against the Polish railroad system and transports en route to the front were based on detailed reconnaissance reports. On 3 September, for example, in the southern sector, German reconnaissance planes reported the following picture:*

- Krakau-Koenigshuette route   10 transport trains
- Konin rail depot   200 railcars
- Krakau–Tarnov route   4 transport trains
- Debicz   4 transport trains
- Trzbinia rail depot   900 railcars
- Auschwitz–Krakau–Przemyśl   Heavy traffic in both directions

Acting on this information planes of the 4th Bomber Wing of Luftflotte 1 made a number of attacks: the rail depot north of Rzeszów was destroyed, a troop rain south of Biel was attacked and the Tarnów–Dębica route was cut at several points, while the Kraków rail depot was set on fire. Similar action was carried out in the northern sector by the 77th Bomber Wing, which attacked troop trains in the depots of Kamienna, Kielce and Jędrzejów, destroying the depots in the process. Elsewhere an ammunition train was blown up and mineral oil and coal trains hit. Repeated attacks such at these over the first week led to a complete disorganization of Polish military movements.

*Place names given in the German version. [Source: General Spiegel, *The Luftwaffe in the Polish Campaign*, MLRS, 2006, p. 69.]

Campaign Chronicle

What was it like for those on the ground to be caught up in these attacks? R. Zolski, who was a company clerk in the newly formed Medical Company attached to the 3rd Armoured Division in Army Poznań, was in the process of transporting ambulances and equipment back by train from the front. He reached the outskirts of Sieradz, near Łódź:

> The train stopped on the siding so that the other trains could pass us by, and there were many of them in both directions. Some time in the afternoon we started rolling towards Zduńska-Wola and on this little line we were stuck: the line had been blown up. A small bunch of people were repairing the track, so there was some hope [. . .] There was never a dull moment in war, and to prove it a squadron of planes arrived, diving towards our train. On both sides of the track was a forest, so common sense told me to take cover in the woods away from the train. We ran to the forests with the planes after us. By sheer miscalculation, or lack of practice in bombing, all the bombs dropped on the forest where we took cover, at the side of the train. The whistling of the falling bombs is very penetrating and frightening. I had a quick look at the trees, but as there were no thick ones I dropped down, pressing my head to the ground and in seconds or so heard the PLONK, PLONK, PLONK, as though someone was dropping heavy stones. Then deadly silence . . . [Source: R. Zolski, IWM 83/24/1.]

Zolski was lucky. The bombs missed both him and the train. For the small boy, Jan Siedlecki, the experience was more traumatic:

> On the 9th day we reached our destination, Komarno in the south-east of Poland, and were unloaded onto a cobbled platform. Just then we observed a formation of German planes heading for Lwów. Before we could be taken to our quarters the planes were back, flying home, but with some bombs on board – presumably chased away from their target. This time they unloaded their bombs on us. I hid

amongst a huge pile of logs that were stacked on the side platform, and I could look through the gaps between them. Naturally the ground heaved with each explosion, but what drew my attention were the perfectly spherical balls like shot. Naturally nothing of the sort was subsequently found. In my fear I must have imagined it [. . .] Out of 300 women and children 116 were dead. And that was not my imagination. My mother shielded us from the sight of the children in the ditch with their guts spilling out. They were all buried in the local cemetery and when the priest mumbled prayers in deep baritone we scattered among the graves, taking it for the

The British Response to the German Bombing of Polish Civilians

On 1 September President Roosevelt appealed to all belligerents, 'publicly to affirm that [. . .] Armed Forces shall in no event and under no circumstances undertake bombardment from the air of the civil population'. The British and French agreed straight away, in the hope of averting large-scale bombing of their own cities. Hitler agreed, too, if only for propaganda reasons. Consequently, it is fair to say that London and Paris had a vested interest in underestimating the German attacks on the Polish civil population. It also gave them an excuse for not bombing western Germany. For as long as possible the British tried to play down German terror bombing in Poland. R.A. Butler, the Under-Secretary at the Foreign Office, stated in the Commons on 6 September that 'the best evidence showed that the German forces had not indulged in indiscriminate bombing of the civilian population'. This view was not easy to sustain. Next day, the British Military mission sent back a detailed analysis of several bombing raids showing that the Germans 'had gone beyond the strict limits of military objectives'. The report sound of another bomber. [Source: J. Siedlecki (unpublished MS).]

An important German aim of the first week of the air war was to destroy Poland's war industries. By 5 September the Polish air industry was virtually out of action. The PZL aircraft factory at Warsaw–Okęcie had been repeatedly dive-bombed. The British Air Attaché observed the attack from the roof of the Embassy, which was about 1½ miles away, and reported that the attack was preceded by a single reconnaissance aircraft, which placed a ring of smoke around the objective. The Ju 87s then followed, and in

initially convinced the Chief of the Air Staff, Cyril Newall, but by the time the Chiefs of Staff Subcommittee met to consider it, he had changed his mind. Incredibly, the Chiefs of Staff came to the conclusion that 'the Germans were making an honest effort to restrict their bombing to military objectives. The fact that they may have made mistakes was in the nature of the hazards of air warfare'. Over the next two weeks evidence of what was really happening in Poland continued to pile up in the press and from diplomatic and military sources. On 12 September Kennard informed the Foreign Office first-hand about the German attack on Krzemieniec, which was temporarily the home of the Polish Foreign Ministry and the diplomatic corps. He described it as an 'example of indiscriminate bombing [. . .] with many casualties'. This made the Chiefs of Staff revise their position somewhat, but they still stubbornly claimed 'all the evidence [. . .] so far emanates from interested parties'. Essentially, for tactical reasons, Britain needed to husband her strength for a long war and used the Roosevelt declaration as a moral excuse to do so, but it was, nevertheless, an example of rank hypocrisy to ignore what was happening in Poland.

his words, 'carried out what can best be described as converging bombing attacks from 3,000 feet on the lines of the Flycatcher* display at Hendon of past days'. The attack lasted no more than 3–4 minutes. Fires were started by petrol flowing from the damaged aircraft in the factory. The attack was then followed by a single aircraft photographing the results.

By the second week of the war the Luftwaffe dominated the skies over Poland. It harried refugees on the roads, interdicted rail traffic and prevented troop concentrations. For civilians and soldiers alike it was one of the dominant memories of the campaign. One veteran, Mr Naharnowicz, who was then a military policeman stationed on the Czech border, remembers how his men were so fearful of German attacks that a flight of storks sent them diving into a potato field!

1–7 September: The Land War

While the pockets of Polish forces in Danzig and along the Baltic were being isolated and the Luftwaffe was engaged in the destruction of the Polish Air Force, the German Army Groups North and South had crossed the frontiers and were probing the defences of the Polish armies opposing them.

Elimination of the Corridor

The immediate task of the German Fourth Army was to secure the Corridor so that a link-up with the Third Army in East Prussia could be achieved. It was therefore imperative to prevent the Poles from blowing up the Tczew bridge, which was a vital link carrying both rail and road traffic across the Vistula from Germany and Danzig. Consequently, in an attempt to destroy the detonators, which the Poles had already placed in readiness, Stukas made a pre-emptive strike at 04:30 hours on the morning of 1 September, even though the German invasion was planned to start at 04:45. The plan was to follow this up by sending troops across the frontier to secure the bridge. The bombs, however, managed only to discon-

*Fairey Flycatchers at the Hendon air displays of 1928 and 1929 impressed the audience by a manoeuvre where three Flycatchers attacked the same target simultaneously, diving from 2,000 feet from three different directions.

nect the wires that linked the detonators with the explosives, so that Polish troops were able very quickly to reconnect the wiring.

After this abortive raid the Germans had no alternative but to implement the next stage of their plan as quickly as possible. A Polish locomotive pulling empty trucks over the frontier from Danzig was seized and the driver and fireman replaced with German personnel disguised in Polish uniforms. The idea was that this train should cross the border and be followed immediately by an armoured train, which would destroy any Polish resistance and prevent destruction of the bridge. But the dispatch of the armoured train was delayed when Polish railwaymen in Simonsdorf managed to switch the points so that it ended up in the sidings. In the meantime, the goods train steamed onto the bridge but the Poles had closed the frontier gate across the line and the train had to halt. The German troops jumped out, but were pinned down by accurate machine-gun fire. As the train began reversing to Simonsdorf, the charges were detonated and the bridge destroyed. German frontier troops, backed by units of the SS Heimwehr Danzig, then attempted to seize Tczew. The Poles fought a stubborn rearguard action: they opened the sluice-gates and flooded the area, forcing the Germans to confine their advance to the road and rail tracks. The sole German armoured car was rapidly immobilized and SS troops were initially pinned to the ground by highly effective Polish fire. It was only after the Germans had called in artillery that the Poles were dislodged, and even then, they staged a successful counter-attack, but in the late afternoon of 1 September they were ordered to retreat southwards. In retaliation for the destruction of the bridge the Germans later executed nineteen Polish officials and railwaymen.

German troops crossed into the Corridor at five in the morning led by the 3rd Panzer Division. Oberleutnant von Cochenhausen, who was in command of a company of motorcyclists, recalled how:

We had to manoeuvre our cycles over potato and stubble fields. It was lucky that the tanks could grind along a firm surface. In the morning mist one could hardly see one's hand before one's eyes. There was no sign of the enemy anywhere. In Petzni, a German village, the inhabitants came out and gave us flowers and apples [. . .] We heard the first noise of battle 10 kilometres to the east, near Wiłkowo. Our armoured cars were engaged in an exchange of fire with an enemy force which had established itself in Gross Klonia. [Source: K. Bernhard, p. 11.]

The Polish Army Pomorze was essentially a trigger force, which was to act as a deterrent in case the Germans were only going to conduct limited operations against Danzig and the Corridor. Now that general hostilities had started, the northern elements of Army Pomorze – the Pomorska Cavalry Brigade and the 27th Infantry Division, covered by the 9th Infantry Division – began withdrawing southwards as quickly as possible to a more tenable position. The Poles had assumed that the Tuchola Forest would act as a barrier to German armoured forces and were surprised when they attacked through the forest with a Panzer division, two motorized divisions, plus three infantry divisions. Heavy fighting took place throughout the day, during which the Poles, despite severe losses, managed to hold the German infantry and in some places even push it back. Von Cochenhausen found progress through the wood heavy going: 'it was a desolate scene, dead Poles, and a pair of destroyed anti-tank guns lay in the forest breaks. Gunfire crackled from bushes and behind trees'. The crucial development of which the Poles were at first unaware was that the 3rd Panzer Division had made an unopposed crossing of the River Brda and would soon be in a position to threaten the Polish rear.

It was on this section of the front that an incident occurred that was misinterpreted by German propaganda to depict the Polish Army as a hopeless anachronism. After fighting the whole day of 1 September against the German 20th Motorized Infantry Division, Colonel Kazimierz Mastelarz, Commander of the 18th Regiment of Pomeranian Ułans (Lancers), who was refused permission to retreat to a more favourable position, decided to remount his two depleted line squadrons and outflank the Germans by attacking them from the rear. The Polish cavalrymen successfully broke up a battalion of German infantry, but were then surprised by a squadron of German armoured cars, which opened fire, killing some twenty men (including the regimental commander) before they could take cover. Italian journalists, who visited the battlefield the following day, were informed that the cavalrymen had been killed while charging tanks. In fact, from a military viewpoint, the manoeuvre was both unexpected and successful and temporarily halted the advance of a German motorized division. Far from charging tanks and armoured cars, Polish cavalry was trained to withdraw to cover and use their anti-tank guns.

These successes, however, were only fleeting. By 2 September, in the Corridor, Polish forces were under pressure from German troops advancing from the north, west and the south. The 3rd Panzer Division continued to exploit its breakthrough and was not far from Poledno, across the main branch of the Brda river, nearly behind the main Polish defensive positions. To the south, the Polish 22nd Infantry Division and the Koronowo National Guard Battalion managed to hold their ground, but the 32nd German Infantry Division was able to slip through a gap in the Polish lines and reach the Pruszcz railway station, which enabled it to cover the southern flank of the 3rd Panzer Division. The Polish 27th Division withdrew successfully southwards to the outskirts of Bydgoszcz by 3 September, but only remnants of the Pomorska Cavalry Brigade and the 9th Infantry Division managed to join them after breaking through encircling German forces.

The fighting on 3 September completed the defeat of Polish forces in the Corridor, and at 16:00 hours the surviving units were ordered to retreat beyond the Vistula, to where a new defensive line would be constructed. The Poles had lost some 10,000 casualties, and the Germans had succeeded in breaching the Corridor and linking up with East Prussia, although there still remained pockets of Polish resistance to be mopped up.

Massacres and Reprisals in Bydgoszcz

As news of the German advance spread to Bydgoszcz, the city's officials loaded files and their families onto three motor buses and quickly made their escape. Early on 3 September an outbreak of shooting and rumours of the approach of German tanks, triggered a mass exodus of refugees and marked the start of an attempt to seize control of the city by the *Volksdeutsche* (ethnic Germans), aided by German agents who had come over the border disguised as refugees. The plan was to secure control of the town before the German

Panzers entered at eleven o'clock, but this was to prove optimistic, as German troops did not arrive for another twenty-four hours. The District Officer and his colleagues managed to stop the flow of refugees and organize an effective resistance. As he recalled later:

> We ran from wagon to wagon, calling on the men to pull themselves together. Soon they became calm and ready to obey our commands. We left a driver in charge of each wagon and assembled the rest of the soldiers along the street. In this way we managed to collect some 200 men armed with rifles. Meanwhile, officers sent out by the Divisional Staff rode up on motorcycles, and a few police also arrived. The forces thus assembled were diverted into two detachments, and under command of two of the officers and two police commissioners they were marched to the bridge in order to suppress the 'diversionists'. [Source: F.B. Czarnowski, p. 79.]

Many of the 'diversionists' were armed with light machine guns, which they fired from the windows of the buildings. In the course of the struggle, probably about 1,000 *Volksdeutsche* were either shot or executed on the spot. By 6 p.m. the attempted putsch was over, but then, just as the town's officials felt sure that all thought of surrendering Bydgoszcz had been abandoned, they received the 'thunderbolt' that the Germans were advancing and that they should leave as quickly as possible.

The last Polish troops left Bydgoszcz in the night of 4/5 September. The defence of the city was now in the hands of a civilian defence committee, which managed to form a militia of some 2,200 railway workers, labourers, civil servants, boy scouts and students. Arms were distributed from the deserted military arsenals and two strongholds were established: one in the centre of the city, the other in Schwedenhoehe (Szwederowo) in the southern districts of the city. The Germans entered from the north and the west and immediately encountered concentrated rifle fire. Consistent to their instructions they responded by razing to the ground any buildings from which shots had come. By the afternoon of 5 September the militia men had surrendered, but isolated

84

attacks continued on German troops and the Headquarters of General Gablenz, the city commander. The Germans retaliated by a full-scale pacification of the city and the arrest of several thousand Poles, amongst whom the intelligentsia figured prominently. *Volksdeutsche* readily identified any Poles who had murdered ethnic Germans, and these were immediately shot. Local Jews were forced to bury them.

Despite these draconian measures, sniping on German troops and transports continued. The military authorities therefore decided to allow German troops and the Security Police to take the law into their own hands, and on 9 September nearly 400 Polish hostages were shot in the market square.

The German Advance From East Prussia

While the German Fourth Army was fighting its way across the Corridor, the Third Army, with which it was to link up and advance on Warsaw, launched on 1 September a two-pronged attack on the Polish defences manned by Army Modlin just over the east Prussian border. The key to these was the Mława stronghold, which was one of the few places where the Poles had constructed effective fortifications. The German 11th and 61st Infantry Divisions, supported by the Kempf Panzer Division, attempted to storm the pillboxes but were bloodily repulsed. Next day, after a heavy artillery bombardment, the 1st Infantry Division of the Wodrig Corps attacked the right flank of the Polish 20th Infantry Division, while the 12th Infantry Division and the 1st Cavalry Brigade attempted to winkle out the Mazowiecka Cavalry Brigade, which was positioned along the Ulatkowka river. This witnessed one of the last occurrences of a cavalry engagement in the Second World War. Although here the Poles were forced to retire, elsewhere the Germans made little progress.

Consequently, on 3 September, the decision was made to swing German forces around the right flank of the Mława pillboxes, either by cutting off the Polish 20th Division or forcing it to retreat. The majority of the Kempf Panzer Division was accordingly transferred to the Wodrig Corps. This manoeuvre worked well and the Kempf Division managed to advance through the gap opening up between two Polish infantry divisions and the Mazowiecka Cavalry

Brigade. By late afternoon of the 4th, the whole of Army Modlin began withdrawing to the main Vistula defence line. The Poles, however, had suffered such heavy casualties that they were to be incapable of holding the Germans along the Vistula.

In these operations the Luftwaffe played a crucial role in routing the Poles. In the Corridor, retreating Polish forces were harried in repeated attacks, which, to quote a post-war analysis of the campaign by General Spiedel, 'increased the existing confusion, panic, disintegration and disorderly retreat movements of the Polish troops in the entire Corridor area'. Luftwaffe pilots also enjoyed easy targets along the Vistula, where the Poles were already in disarray; but at Mława their task was more challenging, as they had to attack earthworks, bunker lines and fortified positions on the edge of villages. The Luftwaffe became, in effect, 'the extended arm of the artillery'.

To the east of Mława the front was quiet and Special Operation Group Narew was even able to tweak the lion's tail by sending over units of the Podlaska Cavalry across the East Prussian border. Apart from shooting up a few Home Guard units little was achieved but it did make good propaganda for home consumption!

By 5 September, Army Modlin had been pushed back to Modlin itself. And when the German Kempf Division routed the Polish 41st (Reserve) Infantry Division at Różan and managed to cross the River Narew, Warsaw was increasingly exposed to the threat of an attack from the north.

All Quiet in the Poznań Salient

To the south, along the salient held by Army Poznań, there was no large-scale fighting, but there were small-scale clashes across the frontier with German frontier and Home Guard formations, as well as attempts by local Germans to stage coups and diversionary tactics as they did in Bydgoszcz. Klemens Rudnicki of the 9th Ułan Regiment (Lancers), who was later to command the first Polish Armoured Division in 1945, unlike his comrades elsewhere, saw little fighting for the first three days of the war. His first task was to relieve a battalion of the National Defence Force some 9 miles north-west of Poznań. The city itself was full of foreboding for what was to come. Later he described its mood:

Campaign Chronicle

We passed Poznań before dawn. The streets were deserted, although nobody was asleep. Many people opened doors and windows, lured by the clatter of the hooves on the pavements. No lights were to be seen. If anybody asked a question it was in whispers – probably in order not to attract the enemy's Air Force! [Source: K.S. Rudnicki, p. 19.]

Two days later Rudnicki was ordered to retire eastwards to Gniezno to blow up the bridges over the Warta. As everywhere else, the roads were clogged with refugees and rumours of treason and German parachutists disguised as civilians were rife. Then further orders came through to retire to Sepolno to cover the regrouping of Armies Poznań and Pomorze.

As the Germans advanced south of Kalisz towards Łódź on 5 September, General Kutrzeba urged High Command in Warsaw to use the southern elements of his Army Pomorze together with Army Poznań to attack the German Eighth Army on its northern flank. This was dismissed as premature by Rydz-Śmigły, since he believed that it would merely lead to the destruction of both armies, but it was the germ of an idea that enabled Polish forces on the Bzura to seize the initiative – albeit temporarily – one week later.

The German Breakthrough in the South-west

The main thrust of the German offensive was in the south-west aimed at the hinge between the Armies Kraków and Łódź. It was here that the Germans had concentrated the greatest number of troops, Panzers and armoured units. Opposing the German Army Group South were the Polish Armies Kraków and Łódź. Army Kraków was the largest of the Polish armies in 1939 but it faced the most challenging task of defending the Upper Silesian industrial regions, and together with Army Karpaty, the mountainous regions of the Carpathians. Over the next few days of intense fighting the Poles initially managed to hold – or in places even inflict significant damage on – the advancing German forces, but in the end German armour managed to exploit weakness and gaps in the over-extended Polish line and outflank the defenders.

All along this area of the front at dawn on Friday, 1 September,

Poland Betrayed

the Germans launched a series of attacks. Claire Hollingworth, a *Daily Telegraph* journalist remembered that:

> As the first light of dawn pierced the sky over Katowice on 1 September, I was awakened by explosions. Distant gunfire created a noise like baying doom. Aircraft roared over the city. More heavy explosions. From my window – it was not even 5 a.m. – I saw the bombers riding high in the sky, and looking towards the German border less than 20 miles away I saw the flash of artillery fire. [Source: Claire Hollingworth, p. 15.]

On the southern edge of Army Poznań, R. Zolski, who had been for some five days waiting in a railway siding at Leśno, heard at the same time as Claire Hollingworth,

> an almighty roar in the sky and saw hundreds of planes flying towards Poland. On the ground there was still silence and no one knew what all that movement was about. In about fifteen or twenty minutes, when the planes had vanished, we heard a roar of tanks with firing guns. Soon after 5 a.m. the whole hell had opened. [Source: Zolski, IWM 83/24/1.]

The German Eighth and Tenth Armies launched a series of infantry attacks through the forested area along the frontier controlled by Army Łódź. The main Polish defence line was some 20 miles into Poland, but the Germans had to deal with a series of delaying actions, the most dramatic of which was the Battle of Mokra, a small village just north of Częstochowa, where the dismounted and entrenched Wołyńska Cavalry Brigade was protected by forests and a railway line from where an armoured train could provide effective covering fire. The cavalrymen dismounted and successfully fought off attacks with Bofors 37mm anti-tank guns and anti-tank rifles. The guns of the armoured train were also highly effective against the German Panzers, although they were vulnerable to Stuka attacks. The Germans, whose attacks showed a lack of coordination between infantry and armour, lost at least fifty armoured vehicles to Polish fire. However, the Wołyńska

Campaign Chronicle

Cavalry Brigade had suffered such heavy casualties that in the evening it had to withdraw, pursued by the 4th Panzer Division. Steven Zaloga, the military historian, has pointed out that Mokra was 'proof of the excellent training and morale of the cavalry' but 'it was also evidence of its shortcomings in contemporary conflict'.

Against Army Kraków in the south, the Germans achieved a significant success when the 1st Panzer Division opened up a gap between the Wołyńska Cavalry Brigade, which was defending Mokra, and the Polish 7th Division to the south. The Germans found the fortified zone around Katowice a harder nut to crack. Within the city, however, there was a mood of mounting panic by the evening of 1 September. The rich had already fled and trains packed with refugees were leaving for the east. There was also a threat from the German *Volksdeutsche*, who were ready to assist the Wehrmacht advance by seizing key buildings in the city. Claire Hollingworth remembered looking out of the window of the British consulate and seeing some forty men sporting Swastika armbands (the eldest of whom could not have been more than twenty) being marched under a double guard of Polish soldiers. When these young Nazi sympathizers first heard the sound of gunfire, they made the mistake of rushing onto the streets shouting 'Heil Hitler!' only to run into a group of Polish soldiers, who quickly disarmed them. They were later executed (Claire Hollingworth, p. 17).

On 3 September the 5th Panzer Division managed to break through the Polish defences near Oświęcim (Auschwitz), and Polish forces began to withdraw from Katowice. The remaining Polish resistance in and around Katowice was broken with great cruelty by the German 239th Infantry Division, Special Operational Groups and the Waffen SS *Standarte Germania*.

In eastern Silesia the advancing German Army met considerable opposition from Polish militia and civilians, who continued to harrass their rear echelons. The war diary of the German 45th Infantry Division noted that the enemy 'did not present a defensive front but rather was using hedgerows and underbrush to fight isolated actions against which advance battalions are foundering'. It added: 'Sniper fire is making the troops very uncomfortable and insecure.' Unsurprisingly, Willi Krey, the young German artillery reservist, confided in his diary that in the night of 1–2 September there is no chance of any sleep, we feel very insecure. Death lurks everywhere. From time to time a German battery fires. Red and green balls of light flash on the horizon. Suddenly we are being shot at by the civilian population [. . .] We return the fire immediately. We regroup as best we can and take cover behind garden fences and hedges. [Source: Krey, IWM 94/26/1.]

To counter Polish guerrilla activity, General Busch of the German VIII Corps in eastern Silesia deployed special *Einsatz* Commandos and SS units to guard communications behind the front. He also ordered that 'any guerrilla activity be dealt with severely using the harshest means available'. Further to the north, west of Łódź, on the afternoon of 2 September, Krey reported that the order had come through to his unit 'to burn down several villages'.

Advancing on 1 September across the difficult terrain of the Carpathians from the Slovak border against Army Kàrpaty, the Germans initially made little progress. For two days they were held along the Dunajec–Nida line by the 10th Mechanized Brigade, KOP troops and a regiment from the 6th Infantry Division. This prevented the Germans from encircling Kraków and driving a wedge between Armies Karpaty and Kraków.

During the next three days the main thrust of Rundstedt's German Army Group South was aimed at the juncture of the Polish Armies Łódź and Kraków. They reached the main defensive positions of Army Łódź on 2 September and seized the city of Wieluń, but the Polish defensive line was not yet breached, although to the south the situation was worsening by the hour: the 7th Polish Infantry Division, facing overwhelming pressure from the 1st Panzer Division and two German infantry divisions, was forced to retreat towards Częstochowa. In the haste and chaos of the retreat the Poles failed to destroy the last bridge over the Warta, and German Panzers were able to race across it. The danger now was that massed units of German armour would be able to break through to Piotrków and from there to Warsaw. Rapidly the other bridges (which the Poles had blown up) were repaired sufficiently to allow German troops and equipment to pass over them. On 3 September Krey wrote in his diary:

The German Army and a Culture of Violence

The implementation of severe retaliatory measures against the civilian population had a negative impact on the discipline of the German Army by encouraging random acts of violence. The Polish campaign witnessed escalating violence against both Jews and Poles. German brutality can partly be explained by the fact that the involvement of civilians in the fighting intensified the nervousness of inexperienced young German soldiers, exposed for the first time to the stress of combat. It was this age group, too, who were the most influenced by National Socialist ideology, which dismissed both Jews and Poles as racially inferior people whose fate was ultimately annihilation at the hands of the German master race. The entry in Willi Krey's diary for 11 September illustrates this all too clearly. His unit had stopped near a small village, which was populated mainly by *Volksdeutsche*, not far from Łódź. On being told that the Jewish owner of the village shop had often denounced the local Germans to the Polish authorities, Krey and his friend, Alfred, decided to murder him. The following chilling account is translated from Krey's diary:

> I told him that he must go into the kitchen. We followed him, Alfred kicked Isidor* into it [. . .] the cry that he gave still echoes in my ears. The flap was shut, and now we had to move quickly to push a heavy piece of furniture over it. We fetched two civilians to help and with combined effort we shoved a heavy chest of drawers and two large bags of clothes over the flap. [Source: Krey, IWM 94/26/1.]

On the way back to their unit they ran into the wife of the unfortunate shop owner and warned her that if she tried to save her husband, they would return and throw her in the cellar too.

* A name frequently used by Nazis for any Jewish male.

Poland Betrayed

This afternoon we crossed the Warthe [Warta]. The bridge had been completely shot apart by the artillery. But it had been for the second time rebuilt by German sappers. There were big delays in crossing the bridge for the troops because a whole division was involved in crossing the river. Once we crossed we again witnessed that same bleak picture. Women and children stood before their burnt-out houses and collected together their last precious belongings, which to a great extent had already been carbonized – artillery and planes had done their utmost to leave no stone on another in the little towns on the Warthe. [Source: Krey, IWM K94/26/1 (translated by the author).]

Ultimately, to stop this threat, the Reserve Army Prusy would have to be thrown into battle, but it still had not completed mobilization, which was originally planned to take a further three weeks. However, early on 2 September one of its cavalry regiments, the 23rd Grodno Ułan Regiment, was unloaded at Koluszki station and was able to take up position at the southern edge of the forest 3 kilometres from Piotrków. Its first task was to send out a reconnaissance party, under the command of Wiktor Jackiewicz, consisting of a half-squadron, a troop of machine-gunners, an anti-tank gun and a radio subsection to find out where the Germans were. Reconnaissance was to be conducted in the area of Rozprza–Kamiensk–Radomsko. They first rode through Piotrków, which had been heavily bombed the previous night. Jackiewicz noted that there was not a living soul in the streets, 'only stray dogs'. When they reached open ground outside the city they were attacked by Stukas:

Nine Stukas flew over from the south. I realized pretty quickly that our one hope was to disperse in the subsection line as far apart as possible and carry on at a jog trot forward. Here I had an opportunity to admire the perfect training of the 4th Squadron. Just like in the training field – a subsection in loose shooting line, without any wild galloping. Even the horrific howl of the diving Stukas created no confusion, though the horses held their ears flat. [Source: W. Jackiewicz, IWM 01/4/1.]

Campaign Chronicle

Fortunately, they were saved by the intervention of six Polish fighter planes, and were able to resume their mission. Some 5 kilometres to the north of Kamiensk their vanguard patrol reported a column of motorcyclists on the highway. A few hours later Jackiewicz found an ideal defence point in a small woodland copse 'with a perfect view on to the Piotrków road'. With field glasses it was also possible to 'partly observe' the Radomsko– Przedborz road:

> What a view spread out before my eyes. Tanks, lorries with infantry and mechanized artillery were roaring down the Piotrków road full steam ahead. Another column was marching from Radomsko to Przedborz, which I estimated to be a division of motorized infantry. The column heading for Piotrków consisted without the slightest doubt of at least one armoured division. I appointed NCOs from my group to take a separate count of the tanks and cars with infantry and artillery guns. I sent the appropriate radio report and instructed the telegraph operator to give an unofficial account of what he had seen. I was incredibly excited; the Ułans, as though bewitched, gazed admiringly at this mass of armoured cars. [Source: W. Jackiewicz, IWM 01/4/1.]

As a result of Jackiewicz's reports the armoured columns were attacked by Polish bombers, and he witnessed the 'blast of bombs, flames of burning vehicles, infantry scattering in panic'. Later, he observed: 'I don't know if any other officer in the September Campaign had as much satisfaction as I did at that moment. I was convinced that the raid was a result of my reports.'

The problem now was how Jackiewicz's reconnaissance group could find its way back to rejoin its regiment. The Germans managed to switch onto their radio wavelength and offered them an honourable surrender, but this was abruptly rejected. The Germans responded by sending a force of nine light tanks and twelve lorryloads of troops to take them prisoner, but under cover of darkness the Poles managed to escape, only to stray into an area already occupied by the Germans. Eventually, with the help of a twelve-year-old boy, who gave accurate directions, they managed to ford a small river, the Luciaza. Once across, Jackiewicz could see through his field glasses several small groups of German soldiers. These were too surprised by the sight of the Polish cavalry to provide much resistance, but then the patrol ran into a whole infantry battalion. Fortunately it was dispersed rather than entrenched, and short of surrender, they had no option but to charge straight through them. Later Jackiewicz recalled:

> The Germans dispersed before us, tried to set up their machine guns, loose shots were fired and strangest of all, there was total panic among the Germans. In this first phase I hardly had any losses, in the second phase several horses were rolled over, some men wounded or killed, unfortunately some way back. The party had forged its way through and before us the ground was clear as far as the Lubień forests. [Source: W. Jackiewicz, IWM 01/4/1.]

The success of this patrol showed that cavalry, when backed up by anti-tank guns, could evade German armour and at times demoralize German troops; but as the Battle of Piotrków was to show, the Polish Army was no match for the Wehrmacht when its full might was effectively deployed.

Army Prusy hoped to meet the German advance with a counter-attack late on 5 September but the German 1st Panzer Division pre-empted this by moving quickly against Piotrków. Initially, this advance was repulsed, and the Polish 2nd Light Tank Battalion actually managed to destroy seventeen German tanks, two self-propelled guns and fourteen armoured cars at the cost of only two Polish tanks, but in the afternoon the 1st Panzer Division managed to outflank Piotrków, and the Piotrków–Warsaw road was now open to German armour. The danger of a Polish counter-attack was averted when the 4th Panzer Division defeated the 2nd Polish Infantry Regiment at Borowa Góra. By the evening of 5 September Army Łódź was cut off from Army Prusy and Army Kraków, and in the north, its sector was threatened by encirclement by the 30th German Infantry Division.

Caught up in the fighting some 70 kilometres to the north-west of Piotrków was a young artillery Lieutenant of the Reserve, Piotr Tarczyński. On 5 September he was ordered with a corporal and four telephonists to lay a cable from the battery to a designated hilltop and then to prepare a dugout from where they could observe the German advance. They were rapidly pinned down by heavy German fire. After calling back to the battery Tarczyński was told in no uncertain terms that if he did not get a move on he would be court-martialled, but lacking the daredevil spirit of the cavalry, he remained cautious:

> However, I still did not feel quite happy that any useful purpose would be served by the men and myself walking straight into a hell where whole tree trunks were being torn to splinters by exploding shells [. . .] I suppose telling the men of the conversation and asking their opinion was contrary to the principles of good leadership, but I felt that our lives were worth at least some consideration before throwing them away in a reckless manner and that the men should have some say in the matter. In the end the consensus of opinion was 'let us wait a bit and see what happens', which we did. [Source: *Life File: reminiscences of a Polish D.P.* (unpublished), Peter Fleming (formerly Piotr Zygmunt Tarczyński), IWM 86/17/1.]

Shortly after the shelling stopped, they were able to take up a position near a sandpit overlooking the flood plain of the Warta:

> Some 2 or 3 miles away on the other side of the river I could see through my binoculars well scattered figures walking towards us across open fields. These I took to be German infantry. They were in one of my target areas but with the telephone dead, I could do nothing. Further in the distance were some woods behind which, most probably, were the positions of the German artillery, whose shells were now whistling high above our heads and exploding some distance behind our backs. They too were within the range of our guns but we were powerless. [Source: Fleming, IWM 86/17/1.]

Soon the German artillery began to shell their hill. Being on the edge of a sandpit, they faced the very real danger of eventually being buried alive by a landslide, and, once the firing stopped again, they set off individually to rejoin the battery. Tarczyński

> started to retrace the way we came. I walked through the bracken and the junipers down the slope towards the ploughed field and the woods beyond [. . .] I was still 100 yards from the first trees when the silence was suddenly torn by a burst of machine-gun fire [. . .] As the bullets hit the ground around me, I instinctively threw myself down between the furrows [. . .] After a while I decided to crawl along the furrows towards the trees. I moved no further than a yard when another burst from the machine gun barred my progress [. . .] I was rather tired and I cannot tell how long it was before I heard footsteps coming towards me [. . .] I slowly raised my head to look and saw men in unfamiliar uniforms coming towards me. They all had their rifles or pistols at the ready and pointed at me [. . .] As they made a circle round me, one of them snorted: 'Auf! Hände hoch!' [. . .] I got up gingerly and raised my hand. For a moment they did not seem quite certain what to do with me next. Then two of them were ordered to search me. If they expected to find an arsenal of weapons under my greatcoat, they were disappointed. My binoculars were taken from me and they seemed surprised that I had no pistol. As a matter of fact I myself felt a bit embarrassed about it. [Source: Fleming, IWM 86/17/1.]

As a consequence of the German pressure on Army Łódź, Marshal Rydz-Śmigły ordered the Armies Kraków, Prusy, Poznań and Łódź to start pulling back to defensive positions east of the Vistula. Throughout 5 and 6 September, Army Kraków's position continued to deteriorate. On the evening of 6 September it was ordered to withdraw over the Dunajec. Its northern components, the Jagmin Operational Group, the Krakowska Cavalry Brigade and the 22nd Infantry Division were to retire over the Nida river by the following day. Its southern forces, Operational Group Borota, were to come under the command of Army Karpaty (shortly afterwards renamed Army Małopolska), which was subjected to increasing pressure from the German 4th Light Division attacking through the Carpathians.

Britain and France Declare War

Three days after the invasion Britain and France at last declared war on Germany. The news was received with joy in Poland and with considerable alarm in Germany. Even the bumptious Willi Krey confided in his diary that he was pessimistic about the future, but Hitler was to be proved right that the Allied declaration of war was more of a formal gesture than the preliminary to direct action against Germany. As Captain Kleb caustically observed in his Berlin lecture to the Air Attachés of the neutral powers in November (see p. 69), Britain and France were ready 'to fight to the last Pole'! The British and French Military Missions did give the hard-pressed Poles advice, but precious little else. For instance, on 9 September, General Carton de Wiart, Head of the British Military Mission, 'impressed on the Marshal and Chief of Staff the primary necessity of establishing a firm line on the Vistula and San covering Lublin and Lwów, so as to maintain communications with Romania and form a pivot on which his right wing could swing back', but this was not backed up with firm promises of military assistance in the west.

As soon as Britain and France declared war, General Norwid Neugebauer, who was about to travel to London as Head of the Polish Military Mission, came to see Carton de Wiart, and stressed that the Polish Government needed to know what planes and war material the British Government would actually supply, so that they could plan accordingly. Wiart informed London that any information on this would 'have a considerable effect here in every way, moral and material'. Over the next two weeks this was to be a constant refrain from British military and civil officials in Poland. On 5 September the British Ambassador echoed Carton de Wiart by stressing that the arrival of even a 'limited number of forces, particularly fighters, in Poland, would achieve moral results on the population disproportionate to strength'. The War Cabinet was rather optimistically told by the Chief of Air Staff on 13 September that 'it would be a tremendous advantage to us' if the Poles could establish a strong but shortened eastern front:

Poland Betrayed

Provided Poland fights on in her new shortened line, the Germans will have tremendous supply difficulties, especially when the rain comes, owing to the length of their communications, and a Polish Army, which is not broken and which has not only the moral but also the material support of expectations of a regular stream of deliveries from us, might be a very unpleasant thorn in their sides. [Source: NA WO 550, Note by Chief of Air Staff, 13 September 1939.]

What, then, could Britain and France do to assist Poland? On 4 September yet another detailed list of requirements was forwarded to London. As Poland's main armament factories had been heavily bombed, there was an urgent demand for both equipment and ammunition. Out of a shopping list of thirty-seven items, the British Army was asked to supply machine guns, gas masks, ammunition for machine, Bren and Bofors guns, as well as a quantity of lorries. The Chiefs of Staff Subcommittee of the Committee of Imperial Defence reached the conclusion that 'the supply of these armaments could not be effected without serious interference with our programmes'. They could only offer 5,000 Hotchkiss guns, for which there was no ammunition, and 5,000 civilian gas masks.

It was, above all, planes that the Poles needed to blunt the murderous German attack on their armies and industries. As soon as General Neugebauer arrived in London he bombarded General Ironside – now the Chief of the Imperial General Staff – with demands for action and immediate supplies of planes. The British Government did manage to dispatch three ships, the SS *Clan Menzies*, the SS *Robur VIII* and the SS *Lassell*, which were to unload at Istanbul or Constanza. They contained thirty-five Fairey Battle aircraft, fourteen Hurricanes and one Spitfire, as well as gas masks, 5,000 Hotchkiss machine guns and some 500,000 civilian gas masks. Air Marshal Sir Cyril Newall was adamant that no more modern fighters could be released.

Embarrassed by the lack of help given to the Poles, the Air Ministry drew up a memorandum to help Kennard defend Britain's inactivity. It was stressed that no planes operating from bases in France or England had the range to help the Poles and that British bases could not be set up in Poland 'without at least a nucleus [of]

98

ground echelons and a supply of bombs, ammunition, spare parts and essential equipment, all of which were not available'. As for attacking western Germany, Kennard was to point out that the French had requested the British to withhold action against German industrial centres, which had been planned for 8 September. The Poles were to be firmly informed:

> Since the immutable aim of the Allies is the ultimate defeat of Germany, without which the fate of Poland is permanently sealed, it would obviously be militarily unsound and to the disadvantage of all, including Poland, to undertake at any moment operations unlikely at that time to achieve effective results, merely for the sake of a gesture. When the opportunity offers, we shall strike with all our force, with the object of defeating Germany and thus restoring Polish freedom. [Source: NA AIR 8/260.]

The Poles were not impressed by this. Rapidly the British and French became objects of anger and derision. When, a week later, the journalist Claire Hollingworth attempted to cable her reports through to London in the post office in Łuck, in south-east Poland, the Post Office official cursed her in German. Nor was British prestige increased by the dropping of leaflets on German cities. As the GSOI of the British Military Mission in Poland reported on 14 September: 'the Polish General Staff cannot comprehend and actually resent apparent restriction of our air activities to dropping propaganda when they [the Germans] raid factories, communes, aerodromes, etc.' [NA AIR 8/274].

In the night of 3 September, the leaflet-dropping started when ten aircraft flew over the Ruhr dropping 13 tons of leaflets informing the Germans that 'Your rulers have condemned you to massacres, miseries and privations of a war they cannot ever hope to win'. Of slightly more help was an attack by ten Blenheim bombers on naval installations in Wilhelmshaven, although little damage was done and five British planes were shot down.

Daladier, the French Prime Minister, was anxious to assist the Poles, and decided to send fifty planes by ship from Dunkirk and Marseilles. He also put pressure on Chamberlain to consider sending planes by rail for the first leg of the journey to Marseilles, but this plan had to be abandoned when it turned out that the cases in which they were packed would be too big to pass under the bridges. As far as direct military help went, the French were as reticent as the British. There had been plans to supply French units to reinforce Polish troops but these were shelved once Czechoslovakia had been occupied by the Germans. To requests to initiate attacks in the west, the French reminded the Poles that German air strength was sufficient to operate simultaneously on both fronts and that all French fighters were needed to protect their own land forces. The most the French were able to do, on 7 September, was cross the German frontier at three points: Saarlouis, Saarbrücken and Zweibrücken, but no major clashes with German troops occurred!

8–17 September: Battle of the Bzura

On 6 September the British Military Mission informed London that

> the two most dangerous [German] attacks at present are those of the motorized groups from Silesia and the forces moving southwards on Warsaw from East Prussia. Should these two arms of the pincers succeed in effecting a junction, a large portion of the old Polish Army might be surrounded. [Source: NA WO 193/763.]

The situation was certainly dangerous. The Łódź and Pomorze Armies were retreating to the main Vistula defensive line in an attempt to regroup, but German troops attacking Polish forces around Tomaszów Mazowiecki were nearer to this defensive barrier than they themselves were, and threatened to encircle them. In an attempt to avert this, Marshal Rydz-Śmigły ordered the formation of a new force, Army Lublin, from the remaining reserve units.

On the afternoon of 7 September the German 4th Panzer Division approached Warsaw. Because of this threat, Rydz-Śmigły decided, on 7 September, to move the Polish High Command from Warsaw to Brześć. In practice, this disrupted communications with the field armies and ensured that the Polish High Command effectively lost control of its forces just as the new defence line on the Vistula was being prepared. Late in the afternoon of the same day, German motorized forces belonging to the 5th Panzer Division managed to break through an undefended gap in the mountainous territory to threaten the rear of Army Kraków. Further German units, the 4th and 45th Light Infantry Divisions, managed to cross the Vistula and seize Tarnów. Army Kraków's position was made worse by the withdrawal of Army Małopolska from the Nida–Dunajec line on 6 September. This opened a gap between the two armies, which the Germans were able to exploit. Armies Łódź, Prusy and Pomorze were also in full retreat. Only Army Poznań had been able to withdraw in good order, relatively little harassed by the enemy.

Increasingly, as the Germans rapidly pushed eastwards, General Kutrzeba's plan to strike southwards at the northern wing of the German Eighth Army became a viable option that could do real damage to the German campaign and delay the advance of the Wehrmacht. The forces available for this counter-attack were composed of the 25th, 17th and 14th Infantry Divisions in the centre and the Podolska and Wielkopolska Cavalry Brigades on each flank. However, the Polish High Command initially remained sceptical of such a plan, as it wanted Armies Pomorze and Poznań to regroup east of the Vistula to help defend Warsaw. Kutrzeba opposed this. Given that the roads were blocked with retreating refugees and open to constant air attack, he feared that German motorized units would be able to catch up with the retreating armies. On 6 September he managed to get through on the phone to Rydz-Śmigły in Warsaw and was ordered to march to the capital 'as quickly as possible'. But Kutrzeba had not totally abandoned his idea of striking at the German flank, as he could still decide how, and where, and with what force, he could take the offensive while moving towards Warsaw. In the meantime, he issued orders to his divisional commanders to begin the withdrawal to the capital. The troops were to use as many different march routes as possible and deploy the maximum number of anti-tank and anti-aircraft guns and:

> During the march destroy the following: factories, ration depots, which will come under enemy control, railway material and above all locomotives.

Poland Betrayed

> Take the following with you: police departments, AA batteries and railway troops. Persuade the population to remain put. This is a very important matter because baggage trains of civilians not only get in the way of our columns but during Panzer and fighter attacks can cause panic. [Source: R. Elble, p. 96 (translated by the author).]

After two days' march, Kutrzeba came to the conclusion that it was better to stand and fight rather than retreat. Later, in his memoirs, he observed:

> Further marches with their psychical and physical burdens would weaken us without bringing any tactical advantages. We left Great Poland voluntarily, apparently without any desire to fight. Now battle was generally desired. We had a real chance of success. Advancing from the Bzura line in the direction of Stryków we would initially probably only come into contact with the 30th [German] Infantry Division, which was stretched out over 25 kilometres. [Source: R. Elble, p. 100 (translated by the author).]

Optimistically, Kutrzeba believed the operation would be successful because it would take time for the Germans to bring up reinforcements, and consequently the Poles would, locally, with the 14th, 17th, and 25th Divisions, have a preponderance of force. He was rightly convinced that the Germans had underestimated the size of Polish forces, as he had as far as possible attempted to move the mass of the Army at night.

In short, as the German military historian, Rolf Elble, said 'Kutrzeba preferred action, which released the tension, to passivity.' He rang General Stachiewicz, Rydz-Śmigły's Chief of Staff, in Warsaw, once again to ask for permission to attack, but until Rydz-Śmigły, who was in the process of moving his Headquarters to Brześć, could be consulted Stachiewicz was reluctant to agree. It was not until the afternoon of 8 September that connections were established between Warsaw and Brześć, and the following night Rydz-Śmigły's consent to an offensive was at last given.

The aims of the offensive were to disrupt the Wehrmacht's

Campaign Chronicle

advance on Warsaw and seize Łęczyca and Piątek. The Chief of Staff had hoped to coordinate the attack with Armies Łódź, Pomorze and Polish forces to the west of Warsaw, but Army Pomorze was still three or four days' march away, while the reports from Army Łódź indicated that lack of food, chaotic conditions and roads blocked by refugees had created an atmosphere of panic. Captain Christian Kinder, in command of a company in the 26th (German) Infantry Regiment, remembered that 9 September,

> began like every other day since the invasion of Poland. Our feet were sore as a result of the long march in the heat and dust on the uneven roads [. . .] Around eleven o'clock the columns came to a halt near the Zagaya windmill as the leading column was fired at from some farmsteads. It was clear that a major action would unfold here. [Source: C. Kinder, p. 9 (translated by the author).]

The initial Polish attack in the direction of Kros began on the evening of 9 September. Here Polish infantry divisions were to take the south bank of the Bzura and then advance 8 kilometres to the east of Ozorków. Unfortunately, one of the Polish units attacked prematurely in the Łęczyca area, and so alerted the Germans. Nevertheless, the Germans were surprised by the scale of the attack. In Łęczyca the lot of the German infantry was made even more difficult when their supporting artillery ran out of ammunition, and no further supplies were possible because the Poles had severed their supply lines. Particularly bitter fighting took place in the streets of Łęczyca, and it took several attacks to seize Piątek.

Captain Kinder's company, which was defending the road to Piątek, suffered heavy casualties. It was fortunate for his troops that they were able to take cover in a set of trenches dating from the First World War, but just before the Poles launched their fourth attack

> in intervals of three to five minutes hand and rifle grenades landed in the company's trenches. This section was

103

methodically and with surprising accuracy from the right to the left wing bombarded [. . .] two men very near to the Company were riddled with fine fragments and were killed immediately [. . .] each man now literally felt the moment come when the next hand grenade would strike him. [Source: C. Kinder, p. 27 (translated by the author).]

By the following day both the German 46th and 30th Infantry Divisions were retreating in total disorder. It was not surprising that Generalmajor von Brieson, the Commander of the 30th Division, informed the Headquarters of X Army Corps in the night of 10/11 September that the situation was 'exceptionally serious' and in a further message 'urgently requested reinforcement', stressing again, for good measure, that the 'Situation [was] deadly serious'. Kinder noticed that some of his own troops, 'shaken by the superior power of the enemy, were beginning to be resigned to defeat'.

The morale of the Germans was also badly affected by the surprise attacks from Polish cavalry in their rear. The 6th Ułans (Lancers) captured Uniejów and destroyed the bridge over the river, while the 9th Ułans (Lancers), according to Klemens Rudnicki,

met more and more small German Army units, which we annihilated. We caught up with German cars with Staff Officers and also German supplies from which our lancers delighted in supplying themselves with cigars, tinned food and other provisions. [Source: Klemens Rudnicki, p. 27.]

The OKW responded rapidly to this worsening situation. The remaining units of the German Eighth Army were moved northwards, and the decision was taken to attempt to encircle Kutrzeba's forces so that the whole of Army Poznań would be destroyed. Reserve divisions of the Eighth Army, together with the remnants of the routed 30th and 26th Infantry Divisions, would move in from the west. The 3rd Light Division in action near Radom to the south of Warsaw was moved to the eastern flank together with the 1st and 4th Panzer Divisions, which had already reached the suburbs of Warsaw. The infantry divisions fighting the retreating Army Pomorze would continue to move in from the north.

Even while these measures were being taken, the Polish advance began to run into problems. Kutrzeba had hoped for a quick success, but despite promises from the PAF, he received no air support and the broad, wide, open flood plain of the Bzura helped the German defence. By dawn on 10 September Kutrzeba was disappointed that his troops had only advanced a couple of kilometres overnight. Further advances were to prove very bloody. Desperate for success, some Polish infantry units advanced without artillery support, but even when the artillery was available, communications were bad because telephone and wireless connections had been destroyed. German sources reported that the Polish infantry often mounted frontal attacks against villages or farmsteads, which inevitably led to heavy casualties. In general the Germans conceded that the Poles usually won in hand-to-hand fighting but lacked crucial artillery support.

Over the next two days the Polish advance continued, but the Germans were beginning to fight back. On 11 September a German attack between Stryków and Ozorków was successful, despite stubborn Polish opposition, and some several kilometres were regained. By the following day the Germans outnumbered the Poles in the Bzura region by 1.3 to 1 in infantry, 2.4 to 1 in artillery and 4 to 1 in armour. Kutrzeba now had no option but to regroup behind the Bzura and reorientate his attacks from the south to the east. Regrouping took time and gave the Wehrmacht a valuable chance to bring up further reinforcements. On 16 September the XVI Panzer Corps attacked from the east, and the 1st Panzer Division broke through the Polish 14th Infantry Division. By the end of the day, Kutrzeba had little option but to draw up plans to break out of the German encirclement in the gap north of Sochaczew, which was weakly held by the 4th Panzer Division.

Only the remnants of the Polish cavalry and the 15th and 25th Infantry Divisions managed to escape. They successfully threaded their way through the Kampinów forest to the main Modlin–Warsaw road. Potentially, the forest provided cover for the retreating troops. It was bisected by a 2-mile-wide stretch of marshy meadow with a few dykes connecting both sides. The Germans were expelled from the northern arm of the forest, but they nevertheless managed to surround the exits with tanks and infantry. Klemens Rudnicki was later to describe the situation:

we were in a trap! Our only chance was to hack our way through ahead, and to do it quickly before we were overrun from the rear [. . .] The whole squadron was fighting a dismounted action with the enemy, who occupied all the surrounding dunes and sandy bush land, covering with strong machine-gun fire all the exits from the forest; bullets buzzed like wasps; the artillery began to respond; it was quite impossible to emerge from the forest [. . .] I decided to do everything possible to remain and hold out as we were for the time being, and after dark to disengage from the enemy, to leave the roads and to drop out in the forest, then rest a little and before dawn, to cross the northern arm of the forest and link up with the main forces of the cavalry group. [Source: Rudnicki, p. 37.]

Rudnicki was able successfully to carry out this plan and to emerge from the forest at dawn:

only a fleecy mist still spun, like cobwebs over our heads when we emerged [. . .] and rode into a small hamlet. We had to water our horses quickly [. . .] As soon as the squadrons dispersed among the farmyards, as the water cranes began to shriek, an aeroplane appeared with a loud roar over the hamlet looking for us. Perhaps they would not spot us because of the mist? But no! In less than ten minutes a short but sharp artillery burst came over us – two bursts one after the other.

I could never have believed it would be possible to leave the hamlet so rapidly, with the regiment dispersed in scattered farms, but in a few minutes we had all met outside the village and were walking in an orderly file ahead. We again lost an anti-tank gun: the Germans had scored a direct hit in the middle of a team of horses, just when it was leaving a farmyard; this left us with only two.

Having ridden another few miles, we met the 15th Lancers and Captain Choloniewski from Colonel Abraham's Staff. We were to link up with the main forces where the battle for the entrance to Warsaw was raging. [Source: Rudnicki, p. 40.]

The unfortunate troops left behind were attacked ruthlessly by the Luftwaffe. By 18 September organized resistance finally collapsed and for the next three days the Germans conducted mopping-up operations. By 21 September the Germans had achieved a major victory: they had smashed Armies Poznań and Pomorze and taken over 100,000 prisoners of war.

Even in victory war is poignant. Kinder's company paid one last visit to the sector of the battlefield where they had fought in order to obtain information about fallen comrades before moving back to Kalisz. A local German farmer and a Bavarian sergeant managed to give them the identity tags of seventeen soldiers. The pay books of some more of the fallen were found on children playing in a farmhouse, while an NCO's hat was discovered and where the company made its last stand, a captain's truncheon was also discovered sticking out of the earth.

10–20 September: The Situation Elsewhere

On 5 September Rydz-Śmigły had ordered the Polish armies to retire and regroup behind the Vistula, Bug and San rivers. The problem with this was that German mechanized columns had already broken through and were advancing faster than the Polish forces could withdraw. Only the Vistula front remained intact because the counter-offensive on the Bzura forced the Germans to withdraw their tanks from the outskirts of Warsaw, and it was not until 15 September that the German Third Army began to approach the Warsaw suburb of Praga (see page 112).

On 10 September, in an attempt to bring some order into this chaotic situation, Rydz-Śmigły set up the Northern and Southern Fronts. The former, commanded by General S. Dąb-Biernacki, consisted of Army Modlin and the Narew Group, while the latter, under the command of General Sosnkowski, was composed of

Poland Betrayed

Armies Kraków and Małopolska. The position, however, continued to deteriorate. On 10 September the German Third Army breached the defences of the River Bug. The Northern Front was then ordered to withdraw to hold the Koch–Brześć line, but this was pre-empted by the German Fourth Army, which began to move much more quickly from East Prussia in the same direction. An orderly retreat of the Northern Front was made impossible by constant enemy attacks and by the 11th was on the verge of disintegration.

The rapid German advance over the Bug and the Vistula led Rydz-Śmigły, on 11 September, to order the retreat of what was left of the Polish forces to the Romanian bridgehead in the south-eastern tip of the country. There, it was optimistically hoped, they would be able to hold out against the Germans until the French offensive, which was expected in six days. As Zaloga and Madej observe, 'the order bore little resemblance to reality'. Armies Pomorze and Poznań, which were already bogged down in the Bzura offensive, were ordered to attack towards Radom and southwards over the Vistula. In reality, however, 'these armies were barely capable of holding back German forces concentrating against them, never mind breaking through'. The Germans were already beginning to encircle the disparate Polish units trapped in the area of Radom–Kielce, while in the north the way was open to Panzer attacks in the direction of Brześć. The only reserves available were in the Grodno area, but these were in transit to the Romanian bridgehead. On 12 September the Special Operational Group Narew was outflanked by German units advancing on Brześć and found its road to Białystok barred. Army Modlin was more successful in withdrawing but nevertheless suffered very heavy casualties.

The German advance on Brześć caused the High Command, on 12 September, to move to Młynow, near the Romanian border, which again almost totally disrupted its contact with the field armies. These increasingly disintegrated into isolated groups, which stubbornly fought to break through the encircling German pincers, or else set up defensive positions in such cities as Lwów or Brześć. At times they could still administer a short sharp shock to the advancing Germans. For instance, the small German-occupied town of Wałdowa, south of Brześć, was attacked by Polish troops on 14 September: the German garrison had to be rescued by a Panzer company. A member of a German tank crew recalled that:

> Crossing the river took longer than the section commander had expected. In the meantime the town's garrison was having a very uncomfortable time since the Poles with a remarkable dash had carried their attack right up to the edge of the town. The section commander immediately launched a counter-attack with the Panzers. Unfortunately, it was so dark that the infantry could not join in. However, the Panzers did manage to force the enemy back in[to] the wood and form a defensive line around the town [. . .] in the early hours of the night there was some shooting in the town. It only stopped when we seized part of the male population and locked the Christians in the cinema and the Jews in the synagogue. [Source: K. Bernhard, p. 79 (translated by the author).]

The southern front was also on the verge of collapse. Army Kraków was unable to fight its way through towards Lwów, which, since 12 September, had been under siege by the German 1st Mountain Division, and instead had to move eastwards to Zamość. The German 2nd Panzer and 4th Light Division had managed to drive a wedge of armour between Armies Kraków and Małopolska, which prevented a coordinated attempt to relieve Lwów. The 2nd Panzer Division, which was meeting weak opposition, was in the process of cutting Army Kraków off from the east and encircling it. To break out of the encirclement, Army Kraków launched a major attack on the 2nd Panzer and 4th Light Division on 18 September at Tomaszów Lubelski, but by the 20th it was surrounded and forced to surrender.

On 17 September came the devastating news of the intervention of the Red Army, which effectively sealed the fate of Poland and any plans the High Command had for the defence of the Romanian bridgehead, but before dealing with the Soviet invasion, it is necessary to look at the situation in Warsaw.

Poland Betrayed

7–27 September: The Siege of Warsaw

By the end of the first week of the war Warsaw was a city swollen with refugees and retreating soldiers and was regularly bombed both day and night. Ryszard Zolski, for example, who had at last managed to unload the fleet of ambulances, which had been shunted for days on loop lines around Łódź and elsewhere, was ordered to use them to transfer patients from a bombed hospital at Grodzisk Mazowiecki to the capital. As he drove, he found that

> all roads to Warsaw were cluttered up with refugees, making it almost impossible for our troops to move, at best a crawl with many halts between [. . .] Most of the people were walking, pushing anything on a wheel or wheels, handcarts or simply prams laden with bundles of clothes, pots and pans, babies and small toddlers. Some of them were more lucky, they had a horse to pull the heavily laden carts. Farmers were driving herds of cattle with a few calves between. Most of the refugees were peasants, but amongst them were townsfolk also, well-dressed men and women, girls in smart dresses and high-heeled shoes, and elderly [middle-class] folk [. . .] The day was sunny and hot. The wheels of the moving transport and the thousands of tramping feet were raising the dust of the roads in clouds, and was settling on clothes and faces. Some of them were unwashed for a day or longer, and the women's hair was tousled: they looked just awful, dirty and tired . . . [Source: R. Zolski, IWM 83/24/1.]

Inevitably, this mass convergence of retreating soldiers and frightened refugees, frequently strafed by German fighters, created a febrile atmosphere in the city. The announcement by the High Command of their move to Brześć on the 6th, the departure of most government and diplomatic personnel to Lublin, together with a message on the radio that all men eligible for conscription should leave the city and report to mobilization centres in the east, understandably caused panic, as it seemed that the city was about to be abandoned. In the event, this latter order was countermanded by General Czuma, commander of the Warsaw defences.

Campaign Chronicle

The Lord Mayor, Stefan Starzyński, in a radio broadcast, assured the population that the city would be defended and asked for volunteers to dig trenches and erect barricades. Within half an hour 150,000 men and women had volunteered.

The advanced units of the 4th Panzer Division reached Warsaw on the afternoon of 7 September, and artillery began to shell the city from the west. Panzers, using the railway lines and roads that traversed the outer suburbs, reached the south-western suburb of Ochota with a force of about 1,700 tanks in the early evening of the 8th, but were driven back by point-blank artillery fire. Further attacks the next day in the Wola district ran into streets blocked with tramcars and well protected and concealed 37mm anti-tank guns and 75mm field guns, supported by troops. General von Rundstedt, Commander of Army Group South, commenting on this, observed that 'the fortress of Warsaw was very stiffly defended, not only in the city but also in the outer suburbs. At the very first time our Panzers penetrated into the city, the inhabitants had shot from cellars and thrown bottles of gasoline onto the tanks from houses'.

These Panzer attacks were supported by prolonged and heavy air raids. On 8 September units of Luftflotte 1 attempted to destroy the Vistula bridges and assisted von Reichenau's Panzers in the southern suburbs with over 140 Stuka sorties. Next day, the Praga suburb on the east bank of the Vistula was pounded by German bombers for six hours, while during the night a successful precision bombing mission was carried out using the X-Gerät navigation system on a munitions dump. One observer, a Colonel in the Warsaw defence command assigned to the Praga sector, commented in his diary on the 10th:

> The nerves of the people are still frayed from yesterday's shelling. All about us buildings lie in ruins. The fire at the Transfiguration hospital with its several hundred wounded, was a ghastly business. I saw a soldier with both legs amputated crawling from the building on his elbows; other wounded jumped out of the windows on the pavement. Five doctors and several nurses perished in the fire . . .
> [Source: F.B. Czarnomski, ed., p. 91.]

Poland Betrayed

After these initial failures, most of the Panzers were withdrawn to the Bzura theatre, although heavy bombing continued. The brief interlude of five days enabled the defences to be strengthened: holes were knocked in buildings for machine-gun emplacements. Life, too, returned to some semblance of normality. Public transport began to run regularly again and shops, restaurants, cinemas and theatres all reopened, and the city's inhabitants attempted to repair their houses as best they could. More troops, too, began to arrive, including the remains of the divisions that had fought at Mława and Ciechanów. The lull in the fighting also enabled masses of refugees to leave the city and flee eastwards.

On the 12th, the German Third Army managed to cut the railway lines to the north-east of the city and, turning in a great arc, completed the encirclement of Warsaw, which, to quote the words of one military historian, J. Bowyer Bell, was 'now almost the last island in a German sea'. The German plan was essentially to starve the inhabitants of Warsaw into submission. On the 15th, General Halder, the German Chief of Staff, when informed that complete encirclement of the city in the west was 'progressing', confided in his diary that he was 'against an attack into the city. Starvation! We are in no hurry and don't need the forces now outside Warsaw anywhere else'. In fact, the advancing Third and Eighth Armies did attempt to break into the city, but ultimately it was starvation that forced its capitulation. To exacerbate this, Hitler specifically ordered the Eighth Army not to let any refugees escape the city. Already, by the 15th, food shortages were serious, even though the water supply was restored. About 700 horses, including thoroughbreds, were being slaughtered daily for meat.

On the 15th, troops from the German Third Army began to advance on the eastern suburb of Praga. They were temporarily halted by the Polish 36th Infantry and 21st Infantry Regiments, but once the Germans brought up tanks and heavy artillery they were able to resume their advance, and it was only in the evening that the attack ground to a halt in Szembeka Square.

The Germans continued to bombard Warsaw both with artillery and planes and launch heavy infantry probes, but it was not until the fighting on the Bzura had ended that the Germans were able to amass about 1,000 pieces of artillery and thirteen divisions of troops. In the meantime, they managed to isolate Warsaw both from the Modlin garrison, which was still holding out, and also from the vital ammunition dumps at Palmiry. On 19 and 20 September some cavalry units, which included Rudnicki's 9th Ułan Regiment, did eventually manage to break through to Warsaw. Ironically, General Juliusz Rómmel, Commander of the newly constituted Warsaw Army, was not happy to see them, as he had no fodder for their horses. They were ordered to move out of the city, back into the open country, to harass the Germans there: but they were quickly sucked into the defence of the city and the order was ignored.

The advancing Germans encountered refugees and prisoners of war along the roads. Willi Krey's battery reached the edge of Warsaw on the 20th. He was confident of victory and arrogantly dismissive of the Poles, but nevertheless, he found the Polish resistance in Warsaw was very threatening indeed. He was part of a group that had to lay a 6-kilometre communications line to a German battery. They had only gone about a kilometre when 'they were on the receiving end of heavy Polish flanking fire', which both deafened them and made them speechless. Later, when he was on duty as artillery telephonist in a house previously occupied by a Polish Air Force family, his peace was disturbed not only by hostile artillery salvos but, on Saturday the 23rd, 'in the dawn a couple of hand grenades whizzed in the closest vicinity of our house, and the next two were only 75 metres away'.

None of this stopped Krey and his comrades from systematically looting whatever they could. He candidly confided to his diary that 'requisitioning continues undisturbed despite artillery fire because here outside it's our nicest and most varied occupation. Naturally every spare moment is used for it'. He then went on to recount how he and his comrades looted a parsonage from where the priests had fled, but which was occupied by several women, some of them elderly: 'I began to search all the rooms of the house, and as I opened the cupboards my eyes grew rounder and rounder. Peach kirsch in bottles, marvellous shirts, a nightshirt, a top Piłsudski medal and several bottles of wine were collected.'

Poland Betrayed

With victory on the Bzura, Army Group South was once more able to close in on the southern and western boundaries of the city. There were particularly heavy attacks on Saturday, 23 September, and on the 25th – 'Black Monday'. On that day about 1,200 aircraft attacked Warsaw. Amongst them were Ju 52 transports, which had been used in the Spanish Civil War as bombers. The Polish Army, however, still held out. One Polish colonel was entirely correct when he noted in his diary on the 23rd that the 'German infantry supported by artillery fire was repulsed as usual. Our soldiers hold their ground very well. They cannot easily be beaten'.

The population survived largely through the black market. According to Klemens Rudnicki's initial impressions after his regiment had arrived in Warsaw:

> The poor city, although in ruins was pulsating with life. Food was very difficult to acquire, however. Windows in undemolished houses were usually plugged up with planks or cardboard: it was impossible to procure glass. Everybody was trying to hoard food: everybody was trading. There were plenty of tradesmen in the streets selling goods. Nobody knew to whom these goods belonged or where they had come from: probably they came from bombed shops or those destroyed by fire. Nobody inquired into this, and nobody was surprised [. . .] It was most difficult to obtain food, as official supplies had not been resumed; but the enterprising spirit of individual tradesmen, or of self-styled 'wholesalers' was fabulous – they knew just how to smuggle in goods from the country. In spite of German orders and various misadventures, food was supplied more plentifully (and could be obtained at excessive prices) on the black market. Without it, I think Warsaw would have perished of starvation. The frenzy for trading completely took possession of the inhabitants, awakened their ingenuity, and saved the town. [Source: Rudnicki, p. 69.]

The constant bombing inevitably took its toll. Foreign observers in Warsaw all agreed that the Fire Brigade, in the words of a

Campaign Chronicle

Greek diplomat, 'worked superhumanly during the whole of the siege', but it was defeated by the sheer volume of attacks and could not quench all the fires that broke out. On 22 September there were, for example, about 500 fires burning simultaneously after a raid of 120 planes. The work of the Fire Brigade was made even more difficult by the bombing of the Warsaw waterworks, which destroyed its filters and pumps. Deprived of water for their hoses, firemen were reduced to throwing sand on the flames.

From 14 September onwards the raids succeeded each other continuously. One day the alarm was sounded thirty-seven times. The impact of heavy bombing is cumulative. Its disruptions, destruction of property, menace and constant threats of violent death naturally take their toll on morale. As Captain Kleb (see p. 69) was later to observe in his Berlin lecture, 'such continuous raids either paralyse all life and compel people to abandon their work or to scorn danger, or undervalue it, which results in many casualties in the case of heavy attacks' (NA AIR 2/9180). The impact of the raids on the civil population was also heightened by the poor quality of the temporarily organized air raid shelters, many of which received direct hits. By 18 September there were more civilian than military personnel in the hospitals, and the following day the parks had to be opened for burials. There were, however, many examples of courage and determination to lead life as normally as possible. For instance, St John's Cathedral was hit during Mass, but despite the death of many of the congregation, services continued as normal.

On 26 September, with water and electrical power cut, ammunition running out and vital medical supplies becoming increasingly scarce, a civilian delegation called on General Juliusz Rómmel and begged him to surrender because of the unbearable hardships inflicted on the population. Rómmel sent envoys to the German Eighth Army Headquarters and it was agreed that hostilities would officially end at 14:00 hours on 27 September. The armistice would last only twenty-four hours and within that time the surrender negotiations would have to be completed. Polish troops would have to withdraw behind a demarcation line, although 36,000 wounded still remained behind. Officers would then be sent into captivity while the other ranks were free to return home.

115

Poland Betrayed

A few isolated units attempted unsuccessfully to break through the German lines and so escape captivity. The 9th Ułans paraded for the last time on 29 September and hid their colours in St Anthony's Church in Senatorska Street. They were consoled with vintage wine from the departed President's cellars in the castle, but nothing could remove the bitter taste of defeat. Symbolic of this was the death of a cavalry horse, which had fallen into a deep well:

> We could only hear the growing muffled horrifying groans of a faithful companion in arms [. . .] It was almost human. We could not rescue it. The horse would not capitulate to the Germans. It had found another solution . . . [Source: Rudnicki, p. 53.]

17 September: The Soviets Intervene

When Britain and France declared war, Ribbentrop, fearful of possible attacks on a relatively undefended western Germany, hoped that Soviet troops would intervene sooner rather than later in the east, but Stalin was initially in no hurry. He reacted to Ribbentrop's enquiry on 3 September by stressing the importance of avoiding excessive haste, but he did, nevertheless, observe that at a 'suitable time it would be absolutely necessary for us [. . .] to start concrete action'. By mid-September, when the Polish command system was disorganized and their defensive front shattered, it was clear that the moment had come. Both British and German diplomatic and intelligence sources reported signs of military preparations in the USSR: 1½ million men were called up and the demobilization of conscripts stationed in the western provinces, which was due on 20 September, was delayed for another month. This was accompanied by a virulently anti-Polish propaganda campaign in the press, in which the Polish Government was made responsible for its own military failures. According to an article in *Pravda*, the Poles, who made up some 60 per cent of the population of Poland, could only maintain their dominant position through a 'white terror' carried out against the Ukrainians, Germans and the other 'subject' races.

A demilitarized Free City since 1920, the Baltic seaport of Danzig remained a bone of contention between Germany and Poland. The shelling of Polish positions by the old German battleship, *Schleswig-Holstein*, berthed in Danzig harbour, signalled the outbreak of the Second World War.

Ribbentrop and Molotov sign the Nazi-Soviet pact in August 1939. By agreeing on respective spheres of interest, Hitler and Stalin effectively sealed Poland's fate. Centre (seated): Molotov. Standing (right to left): Stalin, Ribbentrop, Marshal Voroshilov.

Marshal Edward Rydz-Śmigły succeeded Piłsudski in 1935 as de facto ruler of Poland.

Rydz-Śmigły's leadership during the September Campaign has been criticized, but no European power was capable of halting the German Blitzkrieg of 1939–40.

General Kazimierz Sosnkowski was one of Poland's ablest commanders. The multi-lingual, philosophical and art-loving Sosnkowski succeeded Sikorski as Chief of Poland's Armed Forces in the West, following the latter's death i 1943.

General Władysław Sikorski was refused a top job during the September Campaign but, following Poland's collapse, became leader of th Government-in-Exile and Commander-in-Chief of Polish Forces fighting for the Allies.

rman soldiers remove the frontier barrier with Poland – a posed photo for the Nazi propaganda achine.

rmans troops trot into Poland the old-fashioned way – horse-drawn transport was utilized by all mbatants in the September Campaign . . .

... But motorized infantry facilitated the rapid German advance.

German troops take cover – despite air superiority, the Wehrmacht met stubborn resistance in Poland.

German troops in Tarnów.

Polish cavalrymen amid the ruins of Sochaczew.

German motorized column muscles through a devastated Polish town.

German mounted reconnaissance unit passing through the village of Lubochnia.

Adolf Hitler (left), accompanied by SS Chief Heinrich Himmler (looking to the right), is presented with the captured banner of a Polish cavalry regiment.

eft: A group of Polish PoWs following the battle for Westerplatte. Right: Resigned to defeat – Polish officer of the vanquished Westerplatte garrison.

Polish PoWs at Kutno.

Capitulation – a pile of discarded Polish helmets and weapons symbolizes defeat.

Dotting the Is and crossing the Ts – German and Soviet top brass meet at Białystok.

'What did you do in the war, Comrade?' German and Russian troops fraternize at Brześć on 19 September 1939.

Heinz Guderian (left) discusses the Nazi–Soviet demarcation line.

Germans in action at Płta Oksywska – the Poles here fought till their ammunition was exhausted. Colonel Dąbek, the garrison commander, shot himself with the last bullet.

Hitler picks his way
through the rubble of
Westerplatte.

German trenches before
Warsaw.

SS Colonel Sepp Dietrich welcomes Hitler to Poland.

German troops in action before Warsaw.

Time out – German troops enjoy a
smoke during a break in the fighting.

Warsaw resists – Polish fighters defiant.

Warsaw falters – refugees seem oblivious to their protectors.

Warsaw falls – bombed and starved into submission.

Capitulation – on 1 October after Warsaw and Modlin had fallen, Vice-Admiral Unrug decided that further defence of the Hel Peninsula was impossible. The following day he surrendered all units under his control to the Germans at Sopot. However, isolated fighting continued elsewhere.

Hitler Salute – the Führer's motorcade passes the Saski Palace in Warsaw.

German victory parade in Warsaw – a planned assassination of Hitler by the 'Polish Victory' movement failed to materialize.

The victors – German troops goose-step across Warsaw.

Inside a German PoW camp – Polish soldiers were deported to the Reich as slaves, while officers were imprisoned in *Oflags*. The Soviets also deported Poles for slave labour but opted to murder officers and intelligentsia.

Massacre at Bochnia, December 1939 – for Poles, occupation meant unbridled brutality. (Jupiter Images)

Beaten but not broken – volunteers of the Polish Home Army continued to fight for freedom. Their Warsaw Uprising of 1944 was savagely crushed by the Germans while Soviet forces merely looked on from the east bank of the Vistula.

Campaign Chronicle

Ideally, the Soviets needed another two or three weeks to complete their mobilization, but the problem was that, by then, the Germans would already have reached the Soviet frontier. Consequently, on 16 September, Molotov was authorized to announce that Soviet intervention was 'imminent'. An armistice was quickly signed with the Japanese, ending the fighting in Mongolia. The status of the two military districts of Byelorussia and Kiev were changed to 'fronts' and their commanders ordered to draw up plans for an invasion of Poland. The defensive positions that were to be taken up were to be along the Wilno–Łomża–western Bug line. Boris Shaposhnikov, the Chief of the General Staff, cautioned strongly that 'Just see to it that in driving to the Bug you don't provoke war with Germany.'

There was also to be a complete news blackout. According to historian John Erickson, General Sandalov, Chief of Staff of the Byelorussian Military District, 'so terrified the typist with injunctions about secrecy over the orders that she fainted' and he had to 'two-finger type the orders himself'. The justification of the invasion was that the collapse of Poland made it imperative to protect Russian minorities in the Ukraine. The soldiers were to be given an intensive course of propaganda, which emphasized that they were liberating their class brothers from brutal exploitation at the hands of the Polish landlords and capitalists.

The two Front commanders, Kovalev in Byelorussia and Timoshenko in the Ukraine, both stressed the supreme need for speed and set up large mobile groups. Kovalev created a joint cavalry-mechanized group formed from a cavalry and mechanized corps, a motorized division and a heavy tank brigade. Timoshenko ordered each of his individual armies to form their own mobile detachments from tank and cavalry units. Altogether, when both groups were mobilized, they could deploy 7 field armies, 17 corps, 25 rifle divisions, 16 cavalry divisions and 12 tank brigades, which amounted, together with support troops and service personnel, to about 1 million men. Inevitably, attached to the Staffs of both commands were political commissars. Nikita Khrushchev, the later First Secretary of the Communist Party, kept an especially watchful eye on the key Ukrainian front.

On the Northern Front, General Kovalev set up three mobile

117

groups, the Polotsk, Minsk and Dzerzhinsk groups, each of which had specific targets and missions. Polotsk had to reach Wilno by late on 18 September, the Minsk group had to advance rapidly on Grodno, while the third group had to reach the River Szczaro and then Wołkowysk. Undoubtedly, the best route of advance lay in the south. Here Timoshenko ordered his troops to reach the Kowel–Włodzimierz Wołyński–Sokal line by the evening of 20 September, and then to advance up to the River San line. It was by no means clear what would happen once the Red Army encountered the Wehrmacht. Orders to the two groups stressed that any contact with the Germans must not lead to any military provocation whatsoever on the part of the Russians. Soviet troops were to stand firm on the demarcation line and only if the Germans advanced, would they have to show 'Soviet strength'.

At 3 a.m. on 17 September the Polish Ambassador was summoned to the Commissariat for Foreign Affairs in Moscow and read Molotov's note announcing the Soviet invasion of Poland. He refused to accept it, and according to the British Ambassador

> it was returned by hand to the People's Commissariat of Foreign Affairs, where it was sent back to him and he then readdressed it to the [. . .] Commissariat by post. [Source: NA FO 371/23103.]

A copy of the note was given to all neutral ambassadors:

> The Polish-German war has shown the internal bankruptcy of the Polish state. During the course of ten days hostilities, Poland has lost all her industrial areas and cultural centres. Warsaw as the capital of Poland no longer exists. The Polish Government has disintegrated and no longer shows any sign of life. This means that the Polish state and its Government have, in point of fact, ceased to exist. In the same way the agreement concluded between the USSR and Poland has ceased to operate. Left to her own devices and bereft of leadership Poland has become a suitable field for all manner of hazards and surprises which may consti-

The Fate of the Polish Diplomatic Staff in the USSR

According to the British Ambassador, Sir William Seeds, in a dispatch to the Foreign Office dated 18 October 1940, the Polish diplomatic and consular staff in the USSR 'in the course of the three weeks which had elapsed since the Soviet invasion of Poland [. . .] had suffered all those gradations of persecution ranging from petty annoyances to mental agony and even worse to which are exposed all the countless victims of Stalinist tyranny'. Through the Italian Ambassador he managed to persuade the doyen of the diplomatic corps, the German Ambassador Count von der Schulenberg, to intervene. Schulenberg, who, according to Seeds, was 'that comparatively *rara avis* – a German and a Gentleman – acted with the greatest goodwill in the world' and managed to secure an assurance from Molotov that the Polish Ambassador and his staff and their personal effects would be granted diplomatic immunity.

The fate of the Polish Consul of Kiev was more traumatic. Again, according to Seeds, he was 'summoned in the middle of the night personally by telephone by the local officials who represented the People's Commissariat for Foreign Affairs and with whose voice he was familiar'. The Polish Consul immediately drove over and was arrested with his two chauffeurs and had not been seen since. Schulenberg was unable to do anything to help. The unfortunate Consul suffered from a weak heart, and, as Seeds observed, 'the "third degree" to which he must have been subjected (in what was a resolute attempt to probe into the Polish Secret Service and so forth) may well have had fatal results.' [Source: NA FO 371/23149.]

tute a threat to the USSR. For these reasons the Soviet Government, which has hitherto been neutral, cannot any longer preserve a neutral attitude towards these facts.

Poland Betrayed

The Soviet Government also cannot view with indifference the fact that kindred Ukrainian White Russian people, who live on Polish territory and who are at the mercy of fate, should be left defenceless . . . [Source: NA FO 371/23103.]

17–30 September: The Russo-Polish War

Until the pioneering work of Ryszard Szawłowski, which was printed in 1986 and circulated 'illegally' in Communist Poland, little was known in the West about what can be called the Second Polish-Soviet War (the first being 1919–20, see page 5). In the following account I have drawn heavily on Szawłowski's account.

The Soviet advance was launched along the whole Polish border of over 1,400 kilometres. It was not well synchronized and began in different sectors between 02:00 and 04:00 hours on 17 September. The Germans appeared to be equally as surprised as the Poles. When the news reached Hitler's mobile Headquarters, one intelligence officer initially asked against whom the attack was directed. For the Poles, who were engaged in a bitter fight to the end with the Germans, it was a 'stab in the back'. At first, some Polish units and civilians believed that the Russians were coming as allies, but this rapidly proved to be an illusion.

When the Red Army attacked, both the Polish Government and the High Command were located in south-east Poland near to the Romanian border. The plan was to make a last stand here at a point where Allied aid could eventually be funnelled through the Romanian port of Galati. All available reserves of Polish troops had orders to move towards the south-east, but these plans, if indeed they were realizable, were now destroyed by the Soviet advance.

By 16 September there were between 100,000 and 150,000 Polish troops positioned along the eastern frontier zones. These comprised one brigade and seven regiments of the KOP, who were for the most part weakly armed. There were also a few regular troops, but the great majority were reservists, who were still in the process of an accelerated military training. When first confronted by Soviet troops the local commanders asked Headquarters what action they should take. Marshal Rydz-Śmigły initially ordered them to fight, but then, realizing how hopeless the situation was, he issued, at 16:00 hours on 17 September, a fresh General Directive, ordering units to negotiate with the Soviets a safe passage to Romania or Hungary. They were only to fight if the Bolsheviks actually opened fire on them or tried to take their weapons. Sadly, the Poles had little option but to fight, as it soon became quite clear that the Russians viewed the Polish Army as a hostile force and rapidly attempted to seal off the Romanian border. There then ensued a number of actions and skirmishes all along the eastern frontier with Soviet Russia.

In the far north, not far from the Latvian frontier and in the small town of Dzisna, there were several sharp clashes between Soviet troops and KOP units, local police and volunteers. The ferocity of these encounters can be judged from the fact that one battalion in the KOP Głębokie Regiment lost over 50 per cent of its numbers, while the rest were taken prisoner.

It took twenty-four hours for the Soviets to reach Wilno. Walery Choroszewski, who was a sixth form student at one of the local grammar schools, first heard the sound of Russian gunfire on the evening of 18 September. He and a group of fellow students attempted to volunteer for military service and went to the commandant's office, but found it in the process of evacuation. They were firmly told by the officer in charge that, while their offer was appreciated, they were in fact not required, and that it would be best to return to school and, 'for the sake of Poland, to study diligently'. The Wilno garrison consisted of some 10,000 men, as well as thousands of volunteers, who, like Walery, were ready to enlist. There was, however, a great shortage of ammunition and arms, but nevertheless, until the morning of the 18th, some sort of defence in the city was envisaged. Then the garrison was to make for the border and cross into Lithuania.

Walery and his friends did not return immediately to their books but went to see the film *Springtime*, in which Nelson Eddy and Jeanette MacDonald were playing. He recalled, sixty-eight years later, that, much to his surprise, 'all the city's lights were still

Poland Betrayed

on, the streets full of people and people behaving normally'. The next morning, however, all had changed. He woke up, as he later said, 'in a different world'. The main streets were full of Russians, and circling round the centre was a large, 2-kilometre column of Russian armoured vehicles, giving an impression of overwhelming strength. 'The city itself had changed: people in normal clothing disappeared. People wore the oldest rags they could find. The shops were shut and all goods were hoarded.'

It was, however, at Grodno where the fiercest fighting took place. On the 19th a revolt by the local Communist Fifth Column was defeated. In the early hours of the 20th the first Soviet attack was repelled with the loss of ten tanks, most of which were destroyed by gasoline bottles. The city was defended by some local troops, policemen, firemen and a considerable number of volunteers. These were joined by some of the troops retreating from Wilno and two reserve cavalry regiments. By 21 September it was clear that Soviet strength was so overwhelming that retreat was the only option and the order to evacuate towards the Lithuanian frontier was given.

The fate of those left behind was grim. Large numbers of PoWs – especially students and young volunteers – were shot by the NKVD. One of the cavalry regiments, the 101st Reserve, was again attacked on the border near Kodziowce. At considerable loss to itself it managed to beat the attacks off. Some twelve tanks were destroyed by bundles of grenades and gasoline bottles thrown at the tracks. The cavalrymen managed to cross the border into Lithuania on the afternoon of 23 September.

In the central sector of the frontier it was again the KOP who provided the first resistance to the advancing Soviets. To the east of Sarny, a proper system of concrete bunkers had been constructed. These were manned by several men belonging to the Regiment Sarny and the Polesie Brigade, which had been trained in bunker defence. Their number was further supplemented by units en route by rail for the south, but who were unloaded when news of the Russian invasion was announced. These actually possessed a number of anti-tank guns and even a small number of reconnaissance planes. Crucial to their efforts was the armoured train, *Bartosz Głowacki*, which shot down several Soviet planes

122

and destroyed a convoy of twenty trucks and carriers escorted by armoured cars.

Together, these disparate forces managed to hold off the Russians until 20 September, but then, to avoid encirclement, most of the troops withdrew westwards and joined with Orlik-Rückemann, the Commander of the KOP, who acted as a magnet for fleeing troops, forest guards, police, etc. His forces fought several battles with the Polish Communist Fifth Column and the Red Army. His capture of the town of Szack from Soviet troops helped his forces cross the River Bug without serious losses. Orlik-Rückemann managed to avoid capitulation either to the Germans or Russians. He dispersed his forces on 1 October, only when he heard that Warsaw had fallen. Some of these joined General Franciszek Kleeberg and continued to fight the Germans.

Elsewhere in the central section, as in the other sectors, it was often small groups of police and the KOP who took the initial brunt of the Soviet invasion. Inevitably they were rapidly brushed aside. For instance, Zbigniew Kwiatowski recalled the experiences of his father in Volynia, who had been called up to join the police on 27 August. In the night of 16 September he was manning the telephone at the Bystrzyce police station, but had nodded off, as he had been on the move all day, and without food: 'he came awake to hear the deputy commandant say "you can go on sleeping, they are still a long way off".' This puzzled him and fully woke him up. He heard the sound of gunfire to the south-east and was told that Soviet forces were attacking Ludwipol in the south-east about 8 kilometres away.

By the late morning of the 17th the space before Bystrzyce police station was congested with refugees and the first Soviet planes were sighted. Kwiatowski's men were reinforced by a squadron of cavalrymen from KOP Bystrzyce, bringing the total force up to 150 men. A cavalry patrol reported that four Soviet tanks supported by cavalry were less than 4 kilometres away. There was a short discussion on what should be done. Although they were prepared to make a stand against the tanks, it was not possible without heavier guns. The KOP Bystrzyce squadron was consequently ordered to retreat westwards and the police to disperse, taking with them as many small arms as possible. It joined the KOP Małynsk and became part of the Orlik-Rückemann group. Kwiatowski himself took a rifle, two revolvers, hand grenades and a shotgun plus ammunition. He crossed the Słucz river to the north bank shortly after midday and headed for home, where he discovered an apprehensive family, which had been listening to the sounds of distant gunfire coming from the Tynne bunkers, a part of the Sarny fortified area.

To the north of Ludwipol, at Lachwa, on the Russian frontier, Arnold Rymaszewski remembered a similar story. His father commanded a detachment of frontier guards. They opened fire on the Russians, and when ammunition was getting low, Rymaszewski sent his men home, while he covered their retreat. He was taken prisoner and eventually sent to Kazakhstan to work in the iron ore mines.

His family, like so many others, could only wait apprehensively for the arrival of the Russians. In the interval before they took control, local Russians and Byelorussians – led by 'a well-known Ruffian' – formed a committee to run the town. When the occupiers at last arrived, Arnold was struck by the way they went round

> like programmed robots [. . .] telling everybody [. . .] 'we have everything, finest quality in sufficient amounts.' And all using the same wording. But in the meantime they were grabbing what they could and sending it to Russia. [Source: M.A. Rymaszewski, IWM 02/28/1.]

As Soviet troops advanced westwards, they intercepted a considerable number of units which were in transit by train to the Romanian bridgehead. The 3rd KOP Infantry Regiment, for instance, first heard of news of the Soviet invasion at Rowne. The troops were immediately unloaded and started moving westwards, where they hoped to join up with larger Polish forces. They seized the small town of Kołki, which was occupied by Fifth Columnists and then fought a bitter two-day encounter with Soviet troops in the triangle formed by the villages Borowicze–Hruziatyń–Nawóz. In one sector alone there were nearly 200 Russian casualties. Only on 23 September, when the

Campaign Chronicle

Regiment was surrounded by Soviet tanks, did it surrender.

In the south the main defensive line lay along the River Dniester. Stefan Kurylak, who lived in a village on the western banks of the river, remembers

> the Russian tanks [. . .] thundering across our beautiful bridges crossing the River Dniester and [. . .] rumbling heavily down village streets and through our well-cared-for gardens and yards – and they shot at anything that moved. The panic and horror were indescribable, people ran in all directions, unable to find time or places in which to hide. I stood aghast as one small boy, frightened and confused, stopped to stare at an approaching tank. They simply machine-gunned him down.

Taking cover from the fighting, Kurylak hid in a potato pit, but could hear all too clearly the terrifying sounds of battle:

> the thundering tanks, gunfire, shouts and screaming went on all afternoon, and well into the night. By the morning things had quietened down and I ventured to poke my head out. [Source: Kurylak, IWM 78/52/1.]

The Soviet Occupation of Lwów

When the Red Army crossed the frontier, Lwów, the main city in south-eastern Poland, was already under attack by the Germans. Like Warsaw it acted as a magnet for retreating Polish units cut off from their armies. Altogether in the city there were some 30,000 troops equipped with some artillery, anti-tank guns and anti-aircraft guns, who were further strengthened by the arrival of two armoured trains. The city would have been a formidable nut to crack. Soviet troops reached Lwów on 19 September. The Polish commander, General Langner, rejected a German demand for surrender, and decided, instead, despite considerable opposition from many of the junior officers – who even attempted to mount a mutiny against him – to hand the city over to the Russians. Langner and his Chief of Staff managed to negotiate an agreement with the Russians that all Polish troops would surrender in Lwów at 15:00 hours on 22 September. After the initial formalities, the soldiers would be allowed to find their way home, while the officers could cross the border to Romania or Hungary. It appeared that Langner had successfully carried out Rydz-Śmigły's orders, but he was cruelly deceived. As one Polish colonel lamented in 1941:

> In accordance with the agreement made, all the officers assembled on the spacious square. Hardly had they laid down their arms when they were surrounded by Russian troops [. . .] and marched off. For four days they travelled without supplies, and for some unknown reason, they were left even without water. They were transported from station to station, sent this way and that. At the country rail stations, they jumped out of the trucks and tore up roots from the unharvested gardens. Unknown hands thrust food at them at the halts, but how could such charity meet the needs of so many men?
>
> My father, an insurgent of 1863, used to tell how the strings of prisoners on the march to Siberia, lived on the alms given to them by kind souls 'in Christ's name'. But seventy-five years have passed since then, and we had known twenty years of independence in our own beautiful country. Now once more the defenders of Poland were being driven eastwards. Beyond Husiatyn they were lost to us. What are they doing now? Where are they? How many of them are still alive? [Source: F.B. Czarnomski, pp. 54–5.]

These unfortunate men ended up in the prison camp at Starobielsk and were ultimately to be murdered at Katyń on Stalin's orders. General Langner was taken first to Tarnopol to be questioned by Timoshenko and Khrushchev about the tactics the Poles used against the Germans. Then, two days later, he was flown to Moscow, where he was questioned further about German operational methods, military organization and particularly the role of the Luftwaffe, as well as the best methods for combating German armour. Langner's attempts to discuss the implementation of the Soviet-Polish agreement at Lwów sadly got nowhere beyond the formal acknowledgement that it existed. By the time he returned to Lwów the NKVD were already busy with interrogations, mass arrests and deportments.

Some officers, however, were, for a time, able to avoid captivity. Christopher Muszkowski and four other cadet officers, who were some 8 kilometres west of Lwów, were first informed of the terms of the surrender by a Soviet officer using a megaphone. To avoid capture they decided to move into the city disguised as civilians. Christopher managed to 'borrow' the trousers of a head waiter. They then went to the Polish Radio Station, where they were welcomed and hidden in the cellars. Eventually, Madame Teodezja Lisiewicz, who was in charge of the station, managed to hide them in her flat for a month. In early October, when they were told that Lithuania had annexed Wilno, they managed, by hopping goods trains, to reach the frontier and cross it.

As a cadet officer Christopher was, of course, in great danger of arrest and deportation by the NKVD. At first the civil population was spared this. Władzia Pogoda, who lived south of Lwów, remembers that the Russians initially stressed that they were the protectors of the Poles and were Poland's 'friendly Slavonic neighbour'! To prove their point they actually took down the garlands which the local Ukrainians had put up to welcome the Soviet troops. This of course did not stop them rounding up Polish officers and NCOs.

In Lwów city itself, Ludwika Bombas, who was then aged six, was decidedly unimpressed by the first Russian soldier she saw: 'he wore a shabby uniform and a cap with a shiny red star. Suddenly he stood among us, a group of curious children, with a broad grin on his face. I didn't find him scary, although he had a machine gun and spoke in a strange language, which, as another kid explained, was Russian.' On the other hand, the more threatening side of the Soviet occupation quickly became visible when Soviet soldiers destroyed a small Skoda belonging to the Bombas' neighbours, which they were probably hoping to drive to Romania:

It was parked in the yard of their block of flats next door. We were told that three Russian soldiers appeared, surrounded the car and demanded the keys. One soldier switched on, struggled with the gears, went into reverse, accelerated and crashed into the wall which surrounded the yard. The poor little car fell apart, the boot was demolished, oil dripped from the back axle and the engine died. The driver got out, examined the destroyed vehicle and sniggered: 'That's what one should do with capitalist property.' Then they left and overnight the car was completely looted and taken apart, leaving a sorry wreck . . .

21–28 September: Germany and Russia Decide Poland's Fate

According to the secret protocol signed as part of the Nazi-Soviet Pact, the demarcation line between the future Soviet and Nazi spheres of interest lay along a line based on the Rivers Narew, Vistula and San. However, by 17 September twenty-one German divisions, which included four Panzer divisions, three motorized divisions and fourteen infantry divisions were only 100–150 miles from the Soviet-Polish frontier and advancing on a broad front at the rate of some 15 to 20 miles a day. Clearly, then, it would be a matter of days before the advancing Soviet and German armies joined up. On 21 September four German officers arrived at Moscow to arrange the military details of the boundary line, which were announced two days later.

Encounters between the two armies and then the subsequent withdrawal of the Germans took place without serious incident. However, in places there was some friction. Soviet troops managed to cross the Bug on 23 September, only to be ordered by their Headquarters to retire again to the east bank. This took five days, as the Germans had destroyed the bridges. In a sharp exchange with senior Wehrmacht officers, the Corps Commander, Yeremenko, accused the Germans of speaking to him as if he were a representative of 'landlords' Poland'. On the Ukrainian front, at Drohobycz, as the Germans withdrew behind the San, a large fire broke out in one of the refineries, which might have been a case of sabotage by German personnel. At Brześć, General Guderian was informed that he would have to evacuate the city by 22 September. This left him so little time that he could hardly collect his division's equipment before withdrawal. He had to leave behind all the war material he had seized from the Poles, but nevertheless his relations with the Red Army Commander, Krivoshin, remained good. They agreed on a military ceremony to mark the handing over of the city.

Hardly had the military demarcation lines been confirmed, when the whole future of Poland was reopened. Ribbentrop was interested in claiming the oilfields south of Lublin for the Reich. Stalin was furious at these claims and was not, initially, ready to make any concessions; but then, on reflection, he was ready to concede Lublin provided the USSR eventually gained Lithuania. Stalin also decided to abandon the idea of leaving a territorially greatly reduced but semi-independent Poland. Instead, he proposed that Poland should be partitioned between the two powers. Ribbentrop flew into Moscow on 27 September to discuss these questions. The following day he accepted Stalin's proposals: the new frontier between the USSR and German-controlled Poland lay along the East Prussian border to the River Narew and then down the River Bug to the Ruthenian border, leaving Drohobycz and Lwów on the Soviet side of the frontier. This left over 4½ million Poles east of the new frontier.

22 September–6 October: Mopping Up

Poland's fate was finally sealed with the invasion of the Red Army, but pockets of resistance continued to hold out until early October. On 22 September remnants of the Northern Front, under General Dąb-Biernacki, launched a desperate but unsuccessful southwards attack on the German 27th Infantry Division and the 4th Light Division around Zamość. When the Red Army reached the River Bug behind the Polish positions next day, Dąb-Biernacki had no option but to surrender. Nevertheless, small groups tried to escape and make their way southwards, but with little success. On 26 September 2,000 troops were captured near Bilgoraj, some 90 miles south of Lublin, and on the next day remnants of the Polish 7th, 39th (Reserve) and 41st (Reserve) were surrounded and forced to surrender. General Anders, with one cavalry group, managed to penetrate to the south of Przemyśl in an effort to reach the Hungarian border, but was intercepted by Soviet armour near Sambor, south-west of Lwów. After heavy fighting, in which several Soviet tanks were destroyed, the group was surrounded. Anders ordered the troops to disperse and make their way as best they could to the Hungarian frontier. Anders himself was wounded and captured by the Soviets. He was taken to General Tyulenev, who introduced himself as 'one of the few kind-hearted men' in the Soviet officers' corps, but this did not stop Anders from being imprisoned in Lwów and later the Lubyanka, from which he was released in July 1941.

To escape the Russians, several isolated units retreated westwards. The Special Operational Polesie Group, under General Kleeberg, which initially numbered some 17,000 men, fought a series of defensive actions against the Russians up to 30 September. At Milanów it inflicted over 100 casualties on the Red Army. Once it crossed the demarcation line on the Bug, it was still capable of fighting the German 13th Motorized Division around Kock for four days. It was not until 6 October that Kleeberg finally ordered his troops to surrender, after they had run out of ammunition.

Just to the east of the San, a KOP group under Colonel Tadeusz Zieliński, continued to fight both the Germans and Russians until the end of the month. For two days, over the period 30 September–1 October, it engaged Soviet troops near the town of Janów Lubelski, even managing to drive the Soviets from the village of Krzemień. On 1 October, with all their ammunition used up, Zieliński had no option but to surrender to the Soviets: but he and many of his fellow officers managed to escape across the frontier to Hungary.

19 September–2 October: Modlin and the Hel Peninsula

Besides these shattered remnants, which were slowly being mopped up, the Germans were still besieging Polish garrisons in Modlin and the Hel Peninsula, both of which had been cut off as the tide of war moved eastwards. Hel, being a narrow peninsula 20 miles long and a mile or so wide, was garrisoned by some

Campaign Chronicle

3,000 Polish troops. Because of its narrow neck the peninsula was easy to defend, but by the same token, it was also an easy target for German artillery, aircraft and the battleships *Schleswig-Holstein* and *Schlesien*. On 19 September Hitler moved his Headquarters to the luxurious Casino Hotel overlooking the Gulf of Danzig. There, while taking breakfast on the terrace, his staff was able to view the daily ritual of the naval bombardment of Hel. Paul Schmidt, an interpreter from the German Foreign Office, recalled later:

> With their high funnels and superstructure they made the whole scene look like some old scene of a naval engagement, especially when the Polish artillery retaliated and waterspouts shot up around the ships. Our hotel was beyond the range of Polish guns, otherwise not much would have been left of that fine building. Punctually at noon 'the naval engagement' was broken off, the ships withdrew, and the whole performance was repeated at the same time next day. [Source: A. Read and D. Fisher, p. 343.]

On 21 September, after Hel had been 'softened up', the 207th Infantry Regiment launched a major assault by land. Little progress was made until 30 September, when the Poles were pushed back to Kuźnica. There they detonated a series of landmines, which nearly severed the peninsula from the mainland. The commander, Vice-Admiral Józef Unrug, was determined to continue fighting despite the surrender of Warsaw on 29 September, but two days later it was clear that the garrison's position was no longer tenable, and it surrendered on 2 October.

Three days earlier Modlin fell. It had been defended by four infantry divisions of the former Armies Łódź and Modlin. Once Warsaw was invested and Palmiry had fallen, the Modlin fortress was surrounded. On 24 September the Germans launched an attack on the city simultaneously from all sides. Although it was beaten back, the garrison suffered heavy casualties, but it managed to hold out another five days before surrender.

Poland Betrayed

17–30 September: Exodus of the Fortunate Few

The Polish Government, the military GHQ, civil servants and foreign diplomats started to evacuate Warsaw on 5 September. The one place that still seemed to be secure was south-eastern Poland, bordered by the still neutral Russia and Hungary and Romania, which were both sympathetic powers. As the Germans advanced into Poland, to quote Nicholas Bethel, 'thousands of people were now gravitating into this 100-mile-wide funnel: ministers, civil servants, diplomats, soldiers, indeed any one rich enough to have a car'. The Polish GHQ moved first to Brześć, and then to Kuty on the Romanian border, where it was joined by the Government and the diplomats. On the evening of the 17th, the Polish Government crossed into Romania to be followed next day by GHQ and the British and French Embassies. Beck informed the British Ambassador bitterly that it had been 'the Russian stab in the back [that] had rendered it necessary for Polish Government to give up the struggle and cross the frontier'.

For the soldiers and officials who were left behind, escape became more difficult. Not only did they have to deal with the Germans and Russians but also hostile bands of Ukrainians, who used the occasion of Poland's defeat to pay off old scores. Ryszard Zolski, who had traversed virtually the whole length and breadth of war-ravished Poland, came upon a terrible incident near Dubno in south-east Poland:

> Somewhere on the way in a field not far from us we could see two horses standing back-to-back, and between them three men engaged in a furious struggle. One of them was in uniform, and when he was knocked to the ground, the other two tied him to the horses. There were ropes tied to his hands and feet, the one from his hands attached to one horse, the other from his feet tied to the second horse. Holding the man to the ground they whipped up the two horses which galloped away in opposite directions. It was horrible – there was no time to investigate what it was all about, it was obviously persecution of the man in uniform. We stopped the car abruptly, opening fire, instantly killing one man and one horse. The other horse was dragging the

victim together with the dead horse and had to stop. The second man was limping and had to run away, but another bullet cut the ground beneath his feet. We ran to the 'execution spot' where we saw a Polish officer in cavalry uniform was the poor victim. The poor man must have died with the first jolt of the horse . . . [Source: Zolski, IWM 83/24/1.]

So angered and disgusted were they by this incident that in their turn they took their revenge by leaving primed hand grenades 'wrapped in a hanky' in some empty houses, whose inhabitants had temporarily fled to the forest. The corners were tied up 'nicely, the safety pin of the grenade having already been withdrawn, but the lever pressed in, then leaving it on the table for some curious Ukrainian to discover [. . .] and on opening it, would be blown to pieces'.

Zolski and his comrades were fortunate that they reached the Romanian border on 16 September, one day before the Russian invasion. As they neared the frontier, they 'drove slowly rather like a funeral procession'. The people in the last villages ran out to wave at them. Once across the frontier, Zolski began, as he later wrote, his 'many wanderings over many foreign lands with the full realization that everything was lost. In just 23 days I personally, had lost my home, family, friends and job'. On the other hand, unlike many left behind, he did at least have his life.

Air Force personnel were also well placed to escape the tightening noose. Since early September, selected technical crews had been ordered to the Romanian frontier to receive and assemble the British Fairey Battles and Hurricanes that were due to arrive by sea at Constanza. Also, with the reorganization of the bomber brigade a considerable number of both their pilots and planes had been sent to Łuck. As the front was pushed eastwards by the Germans, all the remnants of the fighter units and their ground crews were concentrated at Litiatyn near Lwów. Consequently, it was a relatively easy business to escape to Romania on 17 September.

One airman, Franciszek Kornicki, remembered being briefed about the Red Army's invasion on the afternoon of 17 September, and receiving subsequent instructions that he and his fellow pilots should make for Romania. Shortly after that, forty-seven P-11 and P-7 fighter planes took off and landed at Czeriowice airfield across the border. Much to his irritation, Franciszek found that his own RWD-8 (a training aircraft) had been taken 'by an enterprising pilot in a hurry'. However, one of his fellow cadets from Lublin was able to requisition 'an almost new Opel'. Compared to his colleagues who had flown, the drive to the frontier was not easy:

> Our progress was very slow. Soon after nightfall we met several vehicles moving in the opposite direction – people shouted that the Red Army was only a few miles ahead and the road to Zaleszczyki was in their hands. 'Turn back and aim for the border bridge at Kuty,' they advised. Long after midnight we joined an endless queue of stationary vehicles before the bridge. We waited there until the early hours of the morning, fell asleep, and didn't hear somebody unscrewing our spare wheel from the back of the car. Another driver's need was obviously greater than ours; fortunately our tyres never caused any problems. At last the vehicles in front of us began moving slowly, and we followed across the bridge. We were in Romania. [Source: Franciszek Kornicki, IWM 01/1/1.]

Flight Lieutenant Poloniecki only just managed to take off from an airstrip south-east of Lwów before the Russians came:

> We had no maps and, if I remember rightly, no compasses either [. . .] My orders were to take one of the mechanics with me as a passenger (he didn't even have a parachute) and follow the others. Mine was the last plane to taxi out when suddenly one of my undercarriage wheels went into a deep hole. I could not move, even on full power, as the wheel was below the axle. Here we were stuck, and the Soviet Army only some 10 kilometres away. But for the mechanic, blessed be his memory, we would never have escaped. He jumped out, put his back under the lower wing, and as I opened up, heaved with all his might. Miraculously

the plane rolled out, and as he leapt on board again, we were off. The rest of the squadron were by now well ahead of us, but navigating by the sun and later picking up a railway line, we headed south towards the frontier with Romania. [Source: B.M. Poloniecki, IWM 92/2.]

For others, of course, who could not whisk over the frontier in a car or plane, attempts to cross the Romanian frontier were far more difficult and often ended in failure. A. Golebiowski, a young conscript officer in an anti-aircraft detachment, found the border already closed by Soviet troops. The countryside was also infested with Ukrainian bands, who were 'hunting anyone in uniform' and demanding money, horses and equipment. Golebiowski consequently decided to catch the train to Lwów. He noticed on the station 'here and there' Russian soldiers 'smiling in a friendly manner' but at Tarnopol, which was full of Russian troops, the train then suddenly and unexpectedly veered to the east. Once over the frontier in the USSR there was 'a large welcoming party of Soviet troops and civilians in leather coats, undoubtedly KGB [a lapse of memory: NKVD is meant here – ed.] officials, ready to segregate and register us'. After spending the night in a farmyard, they were loaded on a freight train and told by the guards:

> you are the enemy of the working class and a bourgeois capitalist Army, you are the enemy of the Soviet Union. You deserve your fate and are being sent to us for a proper re-education. [Source: Golebiowski, IWM 95/6/1.]

Golebiowski's fate was, unfortunately, the norm for Polish officers, and in the end for most middle and upper-class Poles, but there were exceptions and unexpected gestures of magnanimity from the Soviet troops. Take for example the case of the Stankiewicz family. The father was a regional judge at Kielze, and he had been told on 1 September to take his family eastwards in case the Germans took him as a hostage. By 17 September the family had reached Tarnopol. Wojciech, who was eleven at the time, remembers that his first sight of a Russian was 'a huge tank with a Russian colonel sitting on it proclaiming that he had come as a liberator'. Then a hospital train pulled into the station full of wounded Polish soldiers. As the Russians had no medical staff with them, the Colonel allowed the train to proceed to Romania, and attached a couple of cattle trucks to it in which the Stankiewicz family was permitted to travel. Wojciech's mother desperately wanted to stay in Poland, but his father, who had been in the Tsarist Army in the Great War and had a deep distrust of the Russians, vehemently overruled her and the family were able to escape. Years later, in 2007, Wojciech was to describe the Russian colonel 'as the only human being with the Red Star'.

Altogether about 100,000 Polish troops and nearly 10,000 airmen together with 300 planes managed to escape into Romania, Hungary and the Baltic States. These later formed the basis for the Polish Army and Air Force in exile. A few civil planes managed to fly to Sweden, while the Polish Airline, Lot, successfully evacuated all their planes as well as their machine tools, plant and equipment together with 300 of their trained personnel to Bucharest.

31 August–14 October: The Polish Navy Escapes to Britain

The Polish Navy had a more difficult task if it were to escape surrender, as it had to brave the German-dominated Baltic and navigate its way through the Kattgut and thence to Scotland.

The Polish Destroyer Division, however, received orders to sail to Britain as early as 30 August. At 14:15 hours the three Polish destroyers weighed anchor. The island of Bornholm was passed at 21:40 and the Sund was entered at 00:10 on 31 August. They were tracked by a German plane for a time on the afternoon of 31 August, but by midday on 1 September they had met with two British destroyers and were escorted into Leith. Two training ships, the *Iskra* and *Wilia*, which been in western waters, had already set sail and arrived in British ports.

The Polish Submarine Division, consisting of five ships, initially carried out only very low-key operations, which essentially amounted merely to observing German naval activity. It was only on 7 September that they were ordered to return to the central Baltic region, but their poor state of maintenance ensured that only the *Wilk* was actually able to take up her station. The reason for this was that, normally, Polish submarines were docked in May and October, but as a result of the international situation the docking had been held over, and consequently they had gone nearly twelve months without an overhaul.

On 14 September the Commanding Officer of the Submarine Division sent the following message to the commanders of the five craft:

> Carry out patrols and interdict enemy shipping as long as possible. When unable to operate further break out for United Kingdom. If that is impossible seek internment in Sweden. When approaching Great Britain contact Rosyth on 133 kilocycles and rendezvous 30 miles off May Island in the Firth of Forth. [Source: Michael Peszke, p. 40.]

As a result of damage caused by enemy depth charges and aerial attacks, both the *Sęp* and *Ryś* decided that internment in a Swedish port was the only practical alternative facing them. They were joined on the 17th by the *Żbik*. Altogether, more than 200 Polish naval personnel were now interned in Sweden, including 160 naval cadets from a training ship. They were moved from Stockholm to Göteborg, and in the words of the British Military Attaché, were 'living each on a small Polish cargo ship [. . .] without any winter clothes [. . .] with no proper messing arrangements, with two latrines for each party, sleeping in passages and on decks' (NA FO 371/23154). It was no wonder that the Swedish press were 'insinuating' that Poland's allies were indifferent to the fate of these sailors and cadets.

Only two submarines, the *Wilk* and the *Orzeł* made it to Rosyth. Before leaving the Baltic, the *Wilk* was attacked from the air and some thirty-eight bombs dropped over her, plus depth charges set at three different depths. This severely damaged her hydrophones so they could only be worked by hand, and all the time she was submerged, the pumps had to be kept going. The *Wilk* arrived at Rosyth on 20 September. The Base Security Officer interviewed the crew and found 'the morale of both officers and men excellent'. He went on to report that they drank to victory in what they called their Polish vodka, though they were resigned to the break-up of their homes and the probable destruction of their families, as being inevitable. [Source: NA ADM 1/115/533.]

The history of the voyage to Britain of the fifth submarine, the *Orzel* is epic indeed. After a nine-day patrol in the Baltic, the Captain – who was suffering from stomach pains – insisted on having the *Orzel* taken into Tallinn, the main port and capital city of Estonia, rather than to Sweden as ordered. This country was nominally neutral, but in reality sympathetic to Germany. The Captain was taken to hospital and Lieutenant Commander Jan Grudzinski took over command. According to international law he had to set sail within twenty-four hours, but since a German freighter was due to leave port within that period the *Orzel*'s departure – again according to international law – was delayed. Then, to their surprise, the Poles were told that, as they had exceeded the twenty-four hours allowed by international law they were to be interned. The breach locks of the guns and all charts and small arms were removed, as well as fifteen out of the twenty torpedoes. Two guards were placed to keep the submarine under surveillance. This did not stop Grudzinski from partially cutting through the hawsers undetected, until, in the words of the British Admiralty Report, 'only a single strand held them to the jetty'.

In the night of 17/18 September two Polish sailors crawled ashore and cut the lead of the searchlights on the jetty, which illuminated the *Orzel*. The two Estonian guards were overpowered and detained in the submarine and the berthing hawser finally severed. The *Orzel* had considerable difficulty in turning and hit a rock just short of the harbour's exit. She managed to float herself free by the use of her trimming tanks and escaped from the harbour under furious volleys of rifle fire and artillery. As the British Admiralty report almost lyrically put it:

Out into the night and freedom. There is a fringe of small fortified islands outside Tallinn. In half an hour searchlights began to sweep the surface. They were seen and fired on by heavy artillery which drove them under the water, and presently they heard the propellers of the destroyers and motors in pursuit of them. All night they fled submerged, steering blindly with no chart to give them soundings, and at dawn they lay down at the bottom. During the ensuing day they heard the hunters passing to and fro over them. Depth charges burst around them, some near, some far, till they lost count of the explosions. About 9 P.M. there was a lull, and at midnight they rose cautiously and had a look round. They judged themselves to be at the entrance to the Gulf of Finland, and there was nothing in sight . . . [Source: NA ADM 171/9971.]

Grudzinski then decided not immediately to head for Britain but to cruise in the Baltic looking for Russian or German ships. He also needed to find a sanctuary, where he could lie undetected on the surface and recharge the *Orzel*'s batteries. Ideally, too, he hoped to board a German merchantman and seize its charts before it was sunk. He found no merchantman, but did manage to recharge the ship's batteries at the entrance of the Gulf of Bothnia.

In the meantime the ship's escape had become an international incident. The German wireless denounced the crew as murderers of innocent Estonian guards and the USSR accused the Estonian Government of conniving in her escape. By 20 September the British Consul in Tallinn informed the Foreign Office that two 6,000-ton Soviet cruisers and six destroyers were patrolling the Gulf of Finland looking for Polish submarines. The *Orzel*, however, managed to land the Estonians with money, cigarettes and a bottle of whisky off the island of Gotland.

The *Orzel* cruised the Baltic for two weeks, but then, when water was getting low and the cook was suffering from an infected finger, the Polish submariners decided at last to leave the Baltic and head for Scotland. As they sailed into the entrance of the Sund, they sighted a flotilla of German destroyers. Only by diving to the shallow bed were they able to escape detection. When it was dark they surfaced to periscope depth, but then ran aground. The flotilla, ceaselessly patrolling, always just missed them, but they were able to float themselves free and creep up the Sund until they came to deeper water. The *Orzel* managed to make the North

Sea, where it was vulnerable not only to German attack but also to 'friendly fire' from British patrols. At last, on 14 October at 6 a.m., a British shore W/T station picked up a faint transmission from the *Orzeł* and a few hours later a Royal Naval destroyer escorted the submarine into Rosyth. According to the Admiralty report the Polish crew 'had only three requests: to land the sick cook, to replenish their water supplies and be given breach blocks for their guns. They were then prepared to go to sea forthwith on whatever patrol it pleased the British Navy to employ them'.

It is not surprising that the commanding officers, the first lieutenants, the engineering officers, chief torpedo men and mechanician on both Polish submarines were awarded DSOs.

September–December 1939: Escape from Internment
Despite the best efforts of the Red Army and the Wehrmacht, about 100,000 Polish troops and airmen managed to escape into Romania, Hungary and the Baltic States. They were preceded by the Government, which was immediately interned because, briefly, it tried to function as a belligerent regime on Romanian territory. It arrived, as the British Ambassador, Sir Samuel Hoare informed the Foreign Office, 'in corpore', since Mościcki, the President, issued an official proclamation to the Polish people vowing to continue the war and proceed to France as soon as possible. This immediately drew strong German protests and the Romanians had strictly to observe international law in fear of German intervention, and enforce internment. Mościcki was consequently under virtual house arrest in a country shooting box, where he was reduced to sending his wife to Bucharest on shopping expeditions so that she could pick up the latest political information and gossip for her husband.

There was a real danger, in late September, that Poland would be left without a government and that the Germans might be tempted to set up their own puppet regime in Warsaw, which would be recognized by the neutral powers. However, amongst the Polish refugees in Romania and elsewhere, there was an overwhelming feeling that there needed to be a new government. In other words, they felt, as Kennard summed it up, that 'a bankrupt concern needed a new board of directors'. Initially, Mościcki wanted to resign in favour of the Polish Ambassador in Rome, who was, to quote one Foreign Office official, 'a swashbuckling and heavy drinking soldier', but this was vetoed by the French for fear that his appointment would simply perpetuate the power of the old elites. Instead, Mościcki nominated Raczkiewicz as President, who appointed Sikorski as his new Prime Minister. The first meeting of this Government-in-Exile was on 2 October in Paris, after both men had managed to escape from Romania. On the same day the ex-ministers in Romania were moved nearer to the Yugoslav frontier whence, according to Sir Samuel Hoare, 'an unostentatious departure can now [. . .] be more easily arranged'.

Bucharest and the surrounding countryside was full of Polish refugees. According to the *Daily Telegraph* correspondent, Claire Hollingworth:

> they slept in cars or in the open fields, the rich buying food in the villages, the poor begging their way through a poor country. In Bucharest they flooded into the legations and consulates of the Allied and neutral powers as well as into their own. They got drunk and quarrelled with the civilian population. [Source: Claire Hollingworth, p. 45.]

Polish service personnel were supposed to report to provisional holding camps, but it was not hard to avoid detention or to escape, provided that some Romanian currency, the *lei*, could be procured. Franciszek Kornicki, for example, was able to pay for a set of civilian clothes to be made for him so that he could move undetected to Bucharest. Most of the Romanian officials were well disposed to the Poles. The airman, B.J. Solak, for instance, was temporarily interned in a prison, but his guard deliberately left the keys in the lock when he went for lunch so that he could escape.

To leave Romania it was vital to obtain a passport. Consequently, in Bucharest, the Polish Embassy became the

> focus for thousands of service people as well as civilians – men women and children [. . .] Our Embassy staff worked

141

on relentlessly day and night. They were well informed and enterprising people, scheming, wheeling, dealing, bribing and doing everything they could to get everybody out of Romania before the Germans took over the country. [Source: Franciszek Kornicki, IWM 01/1/1.]

The great majority did manage to leave Romania, but it took four or five months before the exodus was complete. The main exit routes were over the Yugoslav frontier and thence into Italy, or to the ports of Constanza and Balcik on the Black Sea, where ships were chartered to take refugees to Greece, and from thence via Beirut to France. The Poles set up a transit camp in Salonika for troops and airmen waiting for dispatch to Beirut. Initially, the British Colonial Office was worried about the concentration of so many Polish service personnel in Beirut, as it feared that 'a large proportion' of these men might be Polish Jews, who would want to make their way into Palestine and so 'be a source of disquiet to the Arabs' (NA FO 23154). However, the Colonial Office dropped its objections when reassured by the Foreign Office that there was unlikely to be a large number of Jews in the Polish Air Force.

Some groups of airmen and soldiers managed to reach British and French possessions in the Middle East individually, others were later transported in conditions of acute overcrowding in ships from Piraeus or Salonika. On 24 October, for instance, a party of twenty airmen arrived at Alexandria on the Romanian steamship, *Dacia*. They had managed to escape individually from holding camps and to collect their passports at Constanza. A week earlier 700 Polish airmen were picked up by the SS *Agio*, which was originally illegally chartered to carry Jewish emigrants to Palestine.

By December there were a growing number of Poles in Beirut. On 22 December, when the SS *Patris* arrived with about 1,200 airmen, the French base commandant informed them that the barracks in the town were too full to take them. The Polish steamer *Pułaski* was supposed to be arriving to take them to Marseilles, but it never turned up. Consequently, according to the British Consul, the unfortunate 'Polish airmen were kept huddled in a ship which was really not capable of holding more than a half of the number on board' (NA FO 24463).

In many ways evacuating troops, airmen and civilian personnel was a race against time. On 25 October Hoare informed the British Government that the Allies had given up, for the time being at least, using Constanza as an embarkation port, since German agents were increasingly vigilant there. At the same time, Berlin pressurized the Hungarian Government to close its frontiers with Yugoslavia to Polish military personnel, and there were also persistent rumours that the Germans would shortly demand the surrender of all Polish officers and men in the country. However, the British Ambassador reported that the Government was continuing 'to grant exit visas to all Poles in civilian clothing without enquiring as to antecedents' (NA FO 23155), and a steady stream of Poles managed to cross the frontier and reach Athens over the next two months.

The Romanian Government interned all military aircraft, but initially seemed prepared to allow the planes belonging to the Polish Lot airways to be flown out of the country, but then changed their mind and demanded the right to purchase them. It appeared that the Chief of Civil Aviation in Romania had been advised by his lawyer, who was allegedly 'a Transylvanian German and pro-German in attitude', that legally civil aircraft had no different status from military aircraft. If a sale was not concluded successfully, the Lot directors and personnel were threatened with internment in a concentration camp. To neutralize this threat, the company managed to bribe the Commissar of Police to grant them exit visas, but a few days before departure they were forcibly sent to a camp near the Yugoslav frontier. Several weeks later, while negotiations were still in progress, forty-two of them were allowed to travel to Athens, where they were then taken by boat to Alexandria (see page 147).

Exodus for the 5,000 Polish military personnel from Latvia and Lithuania to Sweden was much more difficult because the Swedes could not grant any travelling facilities, since the Germans threatened to shoot down aircraft transporting Polish troops to Stockholm. In October, nine airmen did manage to escape from

Poland Betrayed

Latvia, but then, according to the British Consul, the Latvians were extremely irritated by a spectacular but unsuccessful attempt to escape en masse and clamped down on security.

October 1939–May 1940: The Poles Fight On

The new Polish Cabinet met on 2 October in Paris. On 5 October President Raczkiewicz sent the following message to the Polish people:

> It is not the first time in our history that the head of state and the National Government has had to take refuge from the motherland which has been overrun by the enemy [. . .] In the course of a thousand years we have defended more than once our existence and Christian civilization against the thirst for conquest and oppression by Germany and against her barbarous oriental ally . . .
>
> I believe profoundly that the heroic contribution of Poland to the Anglo-French coalition war will not be in vain [. . .] it will result in final victory. [Source: NA FO 371/23152 (translated from the French by the author).]

On 23 November 1939 the Polish Government made an official entry into Angers, the French city on the River Loire, and High Mass was celebrated in the cathedral. A few days later, on 6 December, Kennard reported:

> M. and Mme Raczkiewicz [. . .] arrived by special train from Paris at the station of Trelaze just outside Angers, where the Prefect of the Department of Maine et Loire, a few other French officials and the members of the local government and the members of the Diplomatic Corps were waiting to receive them. [Source: NA FO 371/23153.]

Ensuring the reorganization of the Polish Armed Forces and their relation with Poland's much larger allies was of course the main task of the Polish Government-in-Exile, but on Sikorski's advice the President also set up a court for trying officers on charges arising out of their conduct during the campaign of

Campaign Chronicle

September 1939. For fear of its divisive impact the French refused to allow it to convene in France. Sir Howard Kennard, too, was sceptical. He believed that Sikorski was exploiting the Poles' desire to find a scapegoat for their defeat to get his own back 'on persons who in his opinion behaved unfairly to him in the years after 1926' (NA FO 371/2315).

It was relatively easy to integrate the Polish Navy into the Anglo-French coalition forces. For a start, there was only a small number of ships involved, and, as they were to work with one power, Great Britain, bilateral negotiations could be kept relatively simple. It also helped that Britain desperately needed extra ships and that there was an immediate role for the Polish Navy. As soon as Britain declared war on Germany, the Polish Admiralty drafted an agreement regulating Anglo-Polish naval cooperation. Essentially, all ships would be operationally under the command of the British Admiralty, but the internal organization and the crews would remain under Polish command. Ammunition, supplies and repairs, and the salaries of personnel would all be paid for by the British Government, which would grant a loan to the Polish Government for the duration of the war. Initially, this covered just the operation of the Polish Destroyer Division, but in November the Polish authorities offered to place at the disposal of the Admiralty all available ships, including liners and merchantmen and Naval reserve personnel. The Admiralty also agreed that the SS *Kościuszko*, which was being repaired at Dartmouth, would be recommissioned in the Polish Navy as the *Gdynia* and serve as a Polish Naval Depot. In November a formal agreement was concluded between Britain and the Polish Government-in-Exile confirming that:

A detachment of the Polish Navy shall be attached to the British Navy for the duration of hostilities and so long thereafter as may be mutually agreed.

The units or groups of units of the Polish Naval Detachment under the Polish flag and under command of Polish officers and manned by Polish crews, shall cooperate with the British fleet and shall constitute a part of the Allied Naval forces. [Source: NA ADM 116/4098.]

145

Poland Betrayed

Unlike the Army and Air Force, the Polish Navy in exile saw service immediately. As early as 9 September the destroyer *Błyskawica* was ordered to escort the SS *Lassall*, which was carrying war materials bound for Poland via the Romanian ports. The mission was, however, aborted when the ships arrived at Gibraltar on 22 September, as a result of the imminent collapse of Poland.

In October, the Polish Destroyer Division was sent to patrol the remote western shores of Ireland. The British Government feared that the resurgent IRA might enable German submarines to enter the small bays and inlets to refuel and reprovision. Given that the Royal Navy would breach Irish neutrality, which could, if it was discovered, lead to a first-class row with the USA, where the Irish lobby exerted so much influence, it was thought that Polish naval units would be less objectionable.

The two submarines, the *Wilk* and the *Orzeł*, which had escaped from the Baltic in October (see pp. 138–9) both needed major refits on their arrival in Rosyth. By the end of December they were taking part in routine patrols in the area south of Norway and Heligoland. On 29 December the Director of Naval Intelligence informed the Polish Ambassador that

> a Polish submarine has returned to port from its first patrol for the British Navy and that reports have been received commenting most favourably on the ability and enthusiasm of the Polish personnel. [Source: NA FO 371/24463.]

Rebuilding the Polish Army and Air Force was a more complex task. Potentially, the numbers of men were much greater, and organizing, clothing, equipping and retraining them presented formidable challenges to the French and British authorities. Highly skilled technical personnel and trained soldiers and airmen who had managed to leave Romania and Hungary, sometimes after weeks in a detention camp, often faced long delays in Beirut before they could be transported to Marseilles, which inevitably caused some loss of morale. Even when they finally reached their destination there were problems in absorbing, training and equipping them.

Campaign Chronicle

A report on forty-two technicians sent to Alexandria to await the arrival of the Lot aircraft from Romania, illustrates the difficulty facing the British and French in making the best use of skilled personnel. They arrived as 'destitute refugees'. They slept and were fed at the Fleet Club, while the British Imperial Airways paid them and attempted to find them productive work. This was not easy, partly because of the language difficulty and partly because it took time to find out what they could do. At last, on 26 February, after it had become clear that Romania could not be persuaded to release the Lot planes, they left Alexandria for Marseilles on the SS *Providence*. In his report, the Regional Director of the BOAC observed that

> Throughout their stay, the behaviour of the party was excellent. This is noteworthy because there were many reasons it might have been difficult to control them. Firstly there was their destitute condition and the suffering and hardship which they had endured through the evacuation from their homes and country and the journey to Alexandria. Secondly in nearly all cases they had no news as to their families, their homes or possessions.
>
> During their stay a few letters were delivered and a certain amount of news came through from their comrades in Paris. It is difficult to realize how mentally distressed most of them have been. Thirdly, they were all extremely patriotic and their own temperament worked up to an increasing extent the feeling that they were living in comfort in Alexandria [. . .] whereas their country and their homes were in ruins . . . [Source: NA FO 371/24467.]

The Poles who reached France reasonably early faced long delays before they could be equipped and be organized into effective units. They were given no uniforms, equipment or pay. Discipline inevitably suffered, especially as there was a deep distrust of the senior officers who had led them to their defeat in September. In January 1940 the British Ambassador in Paris reported that the French [had] received Poles in France without making any proper arrangements for them with the result that [they] have suffered seriously in morale and health for the appalling conditions in which they have been kept. [Source: NA FO 371/24463.]

This was, however, rather disingenuous of the British, as they were only ready to accept a strictly limited number of airmen and technical staff, even though the vast majority of the surviving PAF had opted for Britain. In truth, both the French and the British were sceptical about the fighting skills of the Poles and unsure as to how they would integrate them into their armed forces.

As early as 14 September it was decided, in principle, that any PAF personnel coming to Britain should be 'concentrated and employed as a unit or units' and that civilian technical staff would be dealt with in a similar way. In October it was agreed that the British would take 2,300 airmen. When General Sikorski visited Britain in November the prospect of a future land force 'composed of Poles from other parts of the Commonwealth and from other countries' was discussed.

In January the Franco-Polish Air Agreement was negotiated. This led in February to the formation of two *Groupes de Chasse*, each composed of two squadrons, one *Groupe de Reconnaissance* and cadre reserve units, which would enable new squadrons to be formed when the men and equipment became available. In Britain the first contingent of Polish airmen arrived at Eastchurch on 8 December. The RAF sent a recruitment board together with a Polish-speaking officer, Flight Lieutenant Dobrée to Lyons to select their quota. Initially only 200 a month were released by the French but this was later increased to 250. Two operational bomber squadrons and two operational training units were to be formed within the framework of the RAF. When commissioned, 'an oath to His Majesty [was] be taken before the British Commanding Officer at the RAF station and an oath to the Polish Republic [. . .] taken subsequently before the Polish CO at the station'.

There was considerable squabbling between the British and French authorities. General Denain, the Polish-French liaison officer, whom Colonel Gubbins, a member of the former British Military Mission in Poland, described as the 'evil genius of the Polish Army', apparently used his influence to retain as many personnel in France as possible. As a consequence there were still in February a large number of airmen 'living in the worst possible conditions in a camp near Lyons, where they had no uniforms, slept in stalls and were not being trained at all'. There was, Gubbins believed, a real danger that the men would 'go to pieces unless the French change their methods'. Perhaps in these circumstances it was no wonder that many were anxious to come to Britain. For instance, seven highly trained young technicians wrote to the King to solicit his support to join the RAF. They informed him:

> after our escape from Poland we arrived in France to continue the fight against Germany. There we presented ourselves to the Polish Military Atorities [sic] and because there are many regularly [sic] soldiers from the Polish Air Force and not much aeroplanes after waiting of two months there are [no] possibilities that we could soon be employed. As we think we cannot be more without occupation to fight against our enemy, we are ready to work in any part of the British Empire in the RAF at any way so that our notions [sic] and our strength would help a little bit the allies case. [Source: NA FO 371/24463.]

The remnants of the Polish Army were collected together in Bessières, a northern suburb of Paris, and were regrouped as the Polish Army Legion. There were approximately 43,000 Polish officers and men under the command of General Sikorski. This force acted as a magnet for Poles all over western Europe. They were joined by a further 40,000 from the large Polish community in France, and in Britain, too, there were volunteers. As early as 21 September the Polish Ambassador requested permission to set up a temporary camp for 50–100 Polish students at London University in either Highgate School or Dulwich College, whose pupils had been evacuated into the country. However, not all Poles wanted to join up. In March there was some talk in the

Poland Betrayed

Foreign Office of threatening individual Poles with deportation unless they volunteered. Apparently this was caused by the reluctance of Polish merchant seamen in Newcastle and a few recalcitrant students, possibly Communists, to volunteer for service.

By the spring of 1940 the Polish Legion had emerged as an effective fighting force. It consisted of the following units:

- The 1st Grenadier Division
- The 2nd Infantry Rifles Division
- The 10th Armoured Cavalry Brigade
- The Light Mechanized Brigade

During the battle for France for a second time both pilots and soldiers fought bravely in a lost cause. Once again there were incidents of extraordinary bravery, but, as in September 1939, soldiers, government officials and civilians had again to escape the advancing Wehrmacht. On 17 June the President and General Sikorski made 'desperate appeals' to the British to evacuate the Polish Army. Altogether some 22,500 men were evacuated from the Channel ports; 13,000 escaped over the border to Switzerland, for whose upkeep Britain agreed to pay to prevent them being turned over to the Germans. 10,000 men were concentrated in the region of Toulouse. Some managed to escape to Casablanca and Tangier and thence to British territories in the Middle East.

Yet again, Polish forces faced reorganization and restructuring in Britain, which had now become the 'last hope island'. Instead of a quick victory over the Germans the Poles, together with their allies, faced a long war of attrition.

Aftermath

The German Zones

Poland was partitioned by the Russians and Germans on 28 September. Hitler momentarily played with the idea of setting up, at least temporarily, a small Polish satellite state, but once it became clear that Britain and France were not ready to accept the German *fait accompli* in Poland, he announced in two decrees dated 8 and 12 of October the annexation not only of the territories that Germany had lost in 1918–21, but also of a huge area of west and north-west Poland, which included the entire Pomeranian and Poznań Voivodships, as well as most of the Łódź Voivodship and the five northern counties of the Warsaw Voivodship. These territories amounted to 94,000 square kilometres with a population of about 10 million. The remainder of the territory under German control was administered by the General Government, which had its capital in Kraków. It was subdivided into four districts: Warsaw, Lublin, Radom and Kraków, and had a population of about 12 million, which steadily grew as Jews and Poles were deported to the General Government from the annexed areas.

Essentially, in both territories, Hitler intended to eliminate the Polish elites so that never again would an independent Poland emerge. Himmler made this clear on 8 September to the newly formed Reich Security Head Office, when he announced that 'the leading part of the population in Poland will be rendered harmless as effectively as possible. The remainder of the lower classes of the population will receive no education and will in one way or other be repressed.' Ultimately, in both territories, the Jews and the Poles would be 'ethnically cleansed'.

151

Poland Betrayed

The General Government area became as lawless as the American Wild West a hundred years earlier. The conquerors, fuelled by anti-Polish propaganda, which made much of the 'Bromberg massacre' (see pp. 83–5), were given a free hand to murder, persecute and torture both Jews and Poles. The General Government was literally 'beyond the pale'. The Reich, together with the newly annexed territories, would be defended by the construction of an *Ostwall* or East Wall, outside which, as Himmler succinctly but crudely put it, 'the foreign-speaking Gau [province – ed.] would in practice be a no man's land'.

Within this power vacuum there existed no rule of law, not even martial law as exercised by the German Army, since it was 'governed' by a civilian administration under Hans Frank, who sat in regal splendour at Wawel, the former palace of the Polish monarchy, in Kraków. In early 1940 the Foreign Office in London received a report on occupied Poland. In it was a letter 'from a gentleman from Warsaw', which was quoted extensively. It graphically summed up the lawless horror of Frank's General Government:

> We often observe strange, curious facts, a behaviour, which makes us think we are under the domination of people who are not normal, who suffer from a peculiar form of race obsession. How else could one explain the following: Three Jews were crossing a street quietly. From the other side approached a young German soldier. Suddenly with no visible reason, he insulted them, began to beat them, to spit and to shout with a fury which made him half mad. Here is another case: Some time ago a young student slipped in the street and as he fell down, was unfortunate enough to knock accidentally against a passing German officer, who also fell down. The boy apologized and went his way. But a little further on they met a group of armed soldiers. The officer called them and ordered them to arrest the boy. He was severely beaten and insulted . . . [Source: NA FO 898/223.]

Aftermath

The churches and higher education were particularly targets for the German administration. In both areas priests and teachers were arrested. In Kraków, for instance, the whole teaching staff of the Jagiellonian University was summoned to attend a lecture. When they arrived they were rounded up by the Gestapo and driven off. After being kept all night in the corridor of a barracks without any seats they were sent to Sachsenhausen concentration camp. According to reports reaching Angers, about twenty Jesuit priests, several landowners and 'a very large number of secondary schoolteachers' were also arrested in Kraków and deported. In one situation schoolboys attempted to defend their teachers, and for their pains were also arrested and deported. All real estate, industrial or commercial, in the annexed areas were confiscated and their owners interned in concentration camps or deported to Germany. One Polish journalist, Count Romer, reported in December that about 5,000 people had been shot in Silesia alone. In June 1940 3,500 intellectuals were executed by the Gestapo in Palmiry forest, outside Warsaw.

The campaign against the Poles, their culture and language was at its most vigorous in the annexed areas, where all skilled jobs were reserved for German speakers. One exile, who managed to get out of occupied Poland in November, was convinced that the German authorities were trying to turn Kraków into a German city as quickly as possible. All Polish names of streets or buildings in the annexed areas were Germanized. In Katowice, on each house, a German flag had to be hung, together with a large poster reading, 'we thank our Führer'. In Łódź, Ludwika Bombas, who was then just seven years old, remembered how Polish street names had all been changed: 'the main street, Piotrkowska – probably originating after a Russian tsar [Peter the Great] becoming Adolf Hitler Strasse, of course!' Despite her grandmother being Austrian, Ludwika was banned from enrolling in a local school and instead attended a tutorial group composed of eleven children run by two Russian brothers: 'We tended to meet in different flats, as this sort of activity was illegal – Polish children were meant to work [. . .] and not receive an education.' (See pp. 215–18.)

In Poland the Germans created a racial hierarchy and a society based on racial discrimination. At the top were *Reichsdeutsche* or

Poland Betrayed

Germans from the Reich and then the *Volksdeutsche*, the ethnic Germans from both within Poland and the Baltic territories. These groups enjoyed German citizenship. A third group was composed of 'state members', which included Germans married to ethnic Poles and people of 'intermediate nationality', such as the Kashubians, Mazurians and Silesians. The fourth group was made up of 'renegades' or, in other words, Poles who looked like Germans and could gradually be re-educated as such. At the bottom of the list came the Poles and then the Jews.

The Jews – as an American businessman told the British Ambassador in Denmark – 'were given hell'. They were expelled from the annexed areas and in the big cities forced into ghettos after their property had been confiscated. They were not allowed to walk on the pavement, and at shops had to wait until the last German and even Pole had been served. They were at the mercy of any rabid anti-Semite. Szmulek Goldberg, a professional comedian from Łódź, remembered the pogrom that broke out in the city in the night before Yom Kippur and how 'all night long we could hear the screaming on the streets and the shouting of the people being beaten up and their homes looted'.

On a visit to the General Government in December 1939, a Swedish diplomat witnessed a chilling sight that summed up the fate of the Jews during those first six months of the German occupation. He informed a British colleague in Stockholm that when out in the countryside

> he came upon a turnip cutter normally worked by a pair of horses walking in circles. Attached to the cutter was a gang of elderly Jews with a Nazi urging them on with a whip. At intervals they were told to stop and eat grass, which they promptly did. [Source: NA FO 371/24469.]

Reports coming from German-occupied Poland give an unrelentingly negative picture of the occupation, but there were exceptions or 'good Germans'. As Michael Burleigh, the historian, has observed: 'decency was at least within this grim context a barely audible counterpart to the major theme of massive brutality'. General Blaskowitz, the senior Commander in Poland in

154

Aftermath

1940, was appalled by the behaviour of the SS and Gestapo and actually complained to Hitler, who dismissed his objections with the comment that 'one can't fight a war with Salvation Army methods'. Some individual Germans also treated the Poles and, where possible, the Jews, with magnanimity. Ralph Smorczewski, who lived with his parents in a large estate some 70 miles south of Lublin, remembers, after the Russians pulled back to the final demarcation line, that one day 'a big army car arrived, the general got out and stood at the bottom of the steps and said that before entering a Polish house, he wanted to apologize for doing it in the German Army uniform, but unfortunately he had no civilian clothes with him'. Smorczewski added that 'he was an officer typical of the old German General Staff school with very precise and correct manners'. More importantly, Smorczewski remembered that Dr Rost, the German *Kreislandwirt* – the official in charge of the county's agriculture – was an exceptionally humane and efficient man. In the final year of the war Smorczewski was later told that the resistance actually issued him with a free pass!

There were, too, countless other small gestures and acts, which have gone unrecorded. To take just two examples, which were remembered: when Szmulek Goldberg's mother died in Łódź, his family had to bury her 'under the watchful eyes' of German soldiers in the Jewish cemetery, but one of these was compassionate and allowed prayers in Hebrew to be said. Richard Stern, a Jewish student from Kraków, was waiting with some friends at Kraków station for a train to Sanok, in order to cross the frontier into the Soviet Zone, when they were picked up by the SS and subjected to a terrifying night of abuse and beatings. They were released in the morning 'dazed and in fear' but were offered a lift in a German Army lorry all the way to Sanok, where, quite safely, they were duly dropped off in the market place.

The Russian Zone
In the Russian Zone it was primarily class rather than race that motivated purges and persecution. Initially, things were better than under the Germans, but within weeks the situation deteriorated. The Russians stripped the eastern zone of all stocks of clothing, pharmaceutical products, foodstuffs and even articles

like needles, thread and knives, and dispatched them into the USSR. Private traders were discouraged and shops closed. The introduction of the *rouble* on 23 December caused particular problems for the population. Polish *złoty* could only be exchanged at one-tenth of their value for the new currency.

On 22 October a plebiscite was held to endorse the integration of the eastern provinces into the USSR (see p. 204). This meant that eastern Poland was now to be subjected to the full rigour of Communism. The unemployed and the refugees were registered for work in the Soviet interior. Although they did this voluntarily, many were sent to the northern Urals or to God-forsaken collective farms. This was not a punishment as such, but, rather, the reality of labour direction in the USSR. When the new civilian government was set up in early 1940, Soviet officials, together with their families, descended like a plague of locusts on the Zone. This intensified the pressure on local housing and led to the accelerated eviction of those deemed bourgeois or anti-social from their houses and flats in the towns, cities and countryside.

In schools, universities and public life a re-education programme was introduced. Russian and Ukrainian became the main languages, and Polish children had no option but to learn them. Communist ideology inspired the new teaching. Stefan Kurylak remembered that, in order to emphasize the 'bogus' nature of God, the children in his school were told to ask God for sweets. When nothing happened 'a teacher put on a Stalin mask and entered with sweets after the children had asked our great leader'.

Many leading priests, including the head of the Ukrainian Church, were arrested and the theological college at Stanisławów was closed. In several areas efforts were made to close the churches but, according to one report received by the Foreign Office in London, 'the crowds showed great opposition. The women especially were ready to fight for their churches, even if it cost them their life'.

The new regime was determined to purge the Polish landowners or 'Pans', the officer class, the clergy and the intellectuals. In the early spring, reports smuggled out of the Soviet-occupied area gave a chilling picture:

Aftermath

Arrests are so common that men from the intellectual class do not sleep at home, but every night in a different friend's house. OGPU [*sic*] always comes during the night. One never knows what is the cause of the arrest. Anyone can denounce whom he likes by writing his name and leaving the card in a box at the OGPU's [NKVD's] office. [Source: NA FO 898/223.]

This process was highly visible. Irena Haniewicz, who had just started school in Dubno, boarded with a family who lived next door to the local prison. She remembers distinctly the chilling sound of people being tortured, while Stefan Kurylak recalled how the 'Siberian holiday specials' carrying whole families to Siberia or Kazakhstan steamed past the bottom of his garden:

The nights were made unbearable not only by the racket of the trains themselves but by the piteous cries of adults and children begging to be helped to be let out of locked compartments. Sometimes in the winter the villagers would discover a frozen body besides the tracks. [Source: Stefan Kurylak, IWM 78/52/1.]

The terrible story of the deportations has come to symbolize the fate of the Poles after September 1939. Between February and May about 1½ million people were seized, often in the middle of the night, loaded on cattle trucks and deported to Siberia or Kazakhstan (See Appendix V). The Polish-Soviet Agreement of July 1941, which led to the resumption of diplomatic relations between the Soviet and Polish Government-in-Exile, led to the release of the deportees, and eventually, in two large evacuations, some 114,000 soldiers and civilians were able to emerge from their prolonged period of hell and reach Iran, where a new Polish Army was built up (see p. 169).

Prisoners of War
With the collapse of the Polish Armed Forces the Germans took some 587,000 Polish troops into captivity, while the Soviets held about a quarter of a million men.

157

Poland Betrayed

They suffered, particularly in the early weeks, from food shortages, overcrowding and exhaustion. Willi Krey described how the endless columns of prisoners with emaciated faces, often carrying their wounded comrades, passed him after the fall of Warsaw. They were then quartered in appalling conditions in Błonie, in barns, cattle sheds, stables and haylofts. They were given only bread and an undrinkable coffee. Klemens Rudnicki was shut up in a match factory with his fellow officers, but was able to escape disguised as a medical orderly. He remembered that 'there for the first time I saw people at their worst; there were horrible displays of crass selfishness. From time to time quarrels arose about a supposedly better place on a straw bed or about priority in the queues for meals . . .'

Piotr Tarczyński, who was taken prisoner in the first week of the war (see page 96), was initially treated very well, and fed adequately, but just before transit to Germany he ended up in a camp where there was no provision for food at all. The local population were allowed to bring provisions to the camp and there was 'a mad scramble' as bread loaves were thrown over the wire.

By the late autumn, the great majority of those held in captivity by the Germans had been transferred to thirty-five PoW camps in Germany. They were divided into three categories: those employed on the land, those used for building roads or fortifications, and those confined to camp, most of whom were officers. Conditions were overcrowded and they were given the minimum rations. Many of the officers were dragged before courts and charged with violence against the German population during military operations and shot.

However, compared to their comrades who fell into Russian hands, they had the easier time. The Russians separated the men from officers, who were then transferred to camps in the interior. Some managed to save their lives by pretending that they were NCOs. The men themselves were then confined in ninety-nine camps established over the period September 1939–June 1941. When Latvia and Lithuania were taken over by the USSR in the summer of 1940 two further camps at Kozielsk and Juchnowo were set up. At first, prisoners were told that they would be

Aftermath

released on 15 December 1939, but instead they were retained to work on the construction of new roads or rail tracks (see pp. 210 and 213). From time to time, NKVD teams would visit in attempts to ferret out officers.

In June 1941, with the German invasion of the USSR, the camps were rapidly evacuated. As John T. Gross, the historian of the Soviet Zone, has written: 'for three weeks until they reached the embarkation point in the town of Złotonosze in the Soviet Ukraine, they were led on a death march' (see p. 211) on which thousands died. From there they were taken by train to the camp at Starobielsk, where, at the end of August 1941, they were found by Colonel Wiśnioski, who had come with a mandate from Stalin to organize the Polish Army in the East.

Katyń

In early October 1939 all the Polish officers, unless, of course, they had been able to merge into the anonymity of the other ranks, were sent to the camps at Kozielsk, Ostashkov and Starobielsk. There the NKVD initially attempted to find Communists or men sympathetic to Communism, who could be used in setting up a post-war Communist regime in Poland. After intensive day- and night-long interrogations, in which particular attention was paid to whether an officer had fought in the Soviet-Polish War of 1920, it was concluded that the vast majority were deeply unsympathetic to Communism and would be a major obstacle to the creation of a post-war Communist Poland. A mere 448 were identified as sympathetic.

On 5 March 1940 Stalin approved a proposal by Lavrenti Beria for executing 25,421 Polish PoWs. The interrogations ceased, the pro-Communist Poles were sent to a new camp at Pavlishchev-Bor, and in April–May the rest of the officers were shot at three secret locations. Those from Kozielsk were marched out in groups of 50 to 360 men and shot in the back of the head by NKVD guards in the Katyń Forest. Those from the two other camps were also shot and their bodies buried in mass graves in Miednoye and Kharkov. In the spring of 1943 the Germans discovered the mass graves at Katyń, but the USSR, tacitly supported by Britain and America, denied all knowledge of these crimes. It was only in 1990 that Gorbachev, the last General Secretary of the Communist Party of the Soviet Union, admitted that the NKVD was responsible for the massacre of nearly 15,000 Polish PoWs.

Resistance

Even before the fighting ended, preparations for clandestine resistance began to be organized. The SZP (Service for Poland's Victory) was set up to coordinate both the remnants of the political parties and the various resistance groups that were springing up throughout the country. In December the new Government-in-Exile replaced the SZP with the ZWZ (the Union of Armed Struggle). In German-occupied Poland its commander was Colonel Stefan Rowecki, while General Karaszewicz-Tokarzewski commanded the organization in the eastern zone. In the winter of 1939–40 its ultimate task was to plan for an insurrection once Germany had been weakened by the Western powers. The British Ambassador in Angers was shown by the Polish Ministry of Foreign Affairs a report, which came from a commander 'conducting guerrilla warfare in the forests of the Kielce district' (possibly from Major Dobrzański or 'Hubal'). The latter was optimistic that German power would eventually collapse, but feared that the USSR might well exploit the vacuum created by the retreat of the Germans:

> The conspiratorial organization in the country will be able to cope with the Germans there when their powers of resistance have been sapped by failure elsewhere. That is to say, he anticipates in this field, *mutatis mutandis*, a repetition of the events of 1918. He also considers that the Poles in Poland will be able to prevent banditism but he fears that, unless they are in the meantime forced to modify fundamentally the general lines of their foreign policy, the Bolsheviks will try to gain the mastery of Poland internally and will employ their military force to support the subversive elements in Poland. The Polish forces which are now being organized clandestinely in the country might in that case not be strong enough to resist successfully while the

160

Aftermath

Polish forces in France could not reach the spot quickly enough. [Source: NA FO 889/223.]

Resistance in the immediate aftermath of Poland's defeat consisted of distributing propaganda, reporting on German and Soviet military movements and occupation policies and, where possible, sabotage and assassination. Its aim was to construct a broad coalition of resistance to Soviet and German occupation. The backbone of the resistance came mainly from the younger generation, especially amongst the peasants, workers and professional classes such as the teachers. German brutality did indeed deter many from joining, but it could also act as a recruiting sergeant. For instance, Smulek Goldberg, having been tipped off by an ethnic German that the Germans were about to conscript 1,500 young Jews to work on defences in eastern Poland, decided to quit the ghetto at Łódź and make contact with the Resistance in Warsaw. He was successful and was used to deliver guns. For a time he had to be boarded in a brothel, but the extreme anti-Semitism of its *madam* persuaded him to return to the Warsaw ghetto to found a resistance cell there.

The ZWZ also issued orders to resistance cells in Wilno, despite the fact that it had been ceded to Lithuania in October 1939. Its Headquarters was in one of the university's chemical laboratories and Christopher Muszkowski, who joined it after he had managed to make his way there from Lwów, remembers that its main activity was clandestinely printing leaflets and newspapers, which schoolchildren, for the most part, distributed.

Even after the surrender there were still armed groups in the forests. The most well-known was led by Major Henryk Dobrzański, known as 'Hubal'. Together with fifty volunteers he initially attempted to cross the Hungarian frontier, but after encountering strong German forces he decided to stay in the deep forests in the Kielce area and wait until the Allies attacked western Germany, which he optimistically assumed would happen in the spring of 1940. With the help of the local population he avoided capture by the Germans. In March 1940 his unit eliminated an entire battalion of German infantry near the village of Huciska, but on 30 April 1940 the Germans managed

161

to ambush his Headquarters and kill both 'Hubal' and the majority of his troops. In an attempt to deter any further partisans, the Germans mutilated his corpse and displayed it publicly in the local villages. It was then taken to Tomaszów Mazowiecki, where it was either buried secretly or burnt to stop the development of a 'Hubal cult'.

In the Soviet Zone fighting conducted by guerrilla groups continued well into 1940 and in some cases, right up to June 1941. Already by October anti-Soviet groups were springing up. The Polish Consul in Cernauti, Romania, reported in early November that the 'Polish Movement' had set up several centres, and organized a secret bureau for the collection of military information, which boy scouts and other volunteers reported to them. They were also compiling a registry of officers and NCOs and training drivers for future operations. The same source reported that on 12 October 'a considerable number of recently wounded Soviet troops had been brought to a Lwów hospital; the men were forbidden to say how or where they had received their wounds'. It was assumed locally that they had been fighting a Polish resistance group.

To the north of Lwów, in the provinces of Wilno, Nowogródek and Białystok, as well as in the remote marshland of the Biebrza and Narew rivers, there were also several partisan groups. On 3 October the *London Times* reported that:

> Polish Colonel Dombrowski, at the head of a strong detachment of partisans, is causing annoyance to the Russian troops occupying the provinces of Białystok and Wilno. Near the Lithuanian frontier his men are burning bridges, cutting telegraph wires, raiding provincial centres of the local Russian administration, harassing the new police and officials, skirmishing with the Red Army outposts, but eluding pitched engagements. Russian cavalry and even tanks have been sent against Colonel Dombrowski, but have hitherto failed to suppress these guerrilla fighters. [Source: *Times*, 3 October, quoted by K. Sword, ed., p. 161.]

Aftermath

Most of these groups were liquidated by the Red Army in the course of 1940, but isolated bands did manage to survive until the German attack on the USSR in June 1941.

Assessment

Poland re-emerged as a state in the winter of 1918/1919 only because Germany, Russia and the Austrian Empire had been defeated. Determined to seize this unique chance, a Polish Government was set up in Warsaw and hastily-constituted bands of Polish troops established a core Polish state. The boundaries of this state were, however, still fluid. In the west, the German province of Posen was seized, but the final delineation of the frontiers was a protracted business. As a result of Anglo-French disagreements it was not until 1921 that the exact extent of Polish Upper Silesia was determined. This delay only encouraged Polish ambitions, and attempts to seize German territory by force, which inflamed relations both between the two states and the ethnically mixed populations on the borderlands, made the Germans all the more determined to seek revenge and crush Poland in the future. One British official, serving on the Marienwerder Plebiscite Commission, observed in 1920:

> We all came here sympathising with Poland, but since we have seen things at close quarters, we have without exception changed our views. Even Prussian militarism was gentle compared with what is going on all-round our frontiers. Our impression is that aggression is more likely from the side of Poland than Germany . . . [Source: DBFP, Ser. 1, vol. 10, p. 764.]

In the east, the Poles exploited the chaos caused by the Russian Civil War to seize as much territory as they could, and in early 1920 embarked on a full-scale invasion of the Ukraine. The subsequent Russo-Polish War did much to determine the future of the Polish state. The decisive defeat of the Red Army just outside Warsaw led to a false belief in the capacity of the Polish soldier and his excellence at hand-to-hand fighting, bayonet charges and, above all, in cavalry operations – the Polish 'furia', as Léon Noël, the French Ambassador, called it. Perhaps even more important was that the Treaty of Riga led to the annexation of considerable areas of Byelorussia and western Ukraine, in which ethnic Poles were a minority. In many ways, Noël was right that this was a 'disastrous anachronism', as 'their loss was a running sore to Russia', who would seize them back at the first opportunity. This victory led Poland to overrate her military abilities and fuelled unrealistic ambitions. It also led Warsaw to see the USSR as Poland's principal enemy, and until 1936 military preparations were directed primarily to defend Poland from an attack from the east.

Inter-war Poland was the creation of Versailles. She was vulnerable in the event of a renaissance of either Russian or German power. In 1921 the Franco-Polish treaty made political and military sense, as indeed did the defensive alliance with Romania against the USSR. With the advent of Hitler, Piłsudski agreed to the German-Polish non-aggression pact, which effectively neutralized the alliance with France. Two years later an attempt by the French Government to bring Poland into a framework of alliance linking France, the USSR and Czechoslovakia was rejected by Beck and Rydz-Śmigły. This potentially made Poland vulnerable to German pressure, whenever it should be applied, but on the other hand her deep distrust of the USSR was not irrational, and, as time was to show, was fully justified.

In his report on the Polish defeat of September 1939 the French Ambassador to Poland bitterly criticized Beck for backing the Reich 'in systematic destruction of the peace treaties, the League of Nations, the little Entente, the state of Czechoslovakia, and in a word, of all those barriers which Poland, the creation of the Versailles Treaty, ought to have been the first to strengthen and uphold' (NA WO 106/1677). Given the reluctance of both Britain and France to uphold the Treaty, this is arguably rather a sweeping condemnation, but Poland did make a grave error in not seeking an agreement with Czechoslovakia, which had a common border with Poland of 600 kilometres and a highly effective modern Army, as well as a considerable industrial capacity. Both were targets of German revisionism. In September 1938, during the Munich crisis, the Polish Government actually informed the French that Poland

164

Aftermath

had no obligations to come to the help of Czechoslovakia and seized the chance to demand the return of Teschen.

Can it be argued that Poland should have agreed to the incorporation of Danzig into the Reich and the construction of an extra-territorial *Autobahn* across the Corridor in return for the extension of the German-Polish non-aggression pact to twenty-five years? Conceivably this would have taken the heat off Poland, while Hitler attacked in the west, but the destruction of Czechoslovakia in March 1939 was a stark warning that Hitler could not be trusted to observe any negotiated agreement about Danzig and the Corridor.

The German seizure of Bohemia and Moravia also made Poland acutely vulnerable to a German attack from the west. In this situation the acceptance of the British guarantee and the Franco-Polish mutual aid pact seemed the better option. However, as neither the French nor the British could send troops to Poland, it did need to be supplemented by an agreement with Soviet Russia, which would be able to provide military assistance. Yet this was rejected by Beck, who feared – as it turned out, all too accurately – the consequences for Polish independence of Russian intervention. This rejection was one of the factors that persuaded Stalin to agree to the Soviet-Nazi non-aggression pact with its secret agreement on the partition of Poland.

Poland was now open to attack from the strongest military power in Europe. Her allies, Great Britain and France, only declared war on Germany on 3 September and did little to relieve the pressure on Poland by attacking in the west. All the French did was to occupy a few square miles of forest in the Saarland! In the five-week campaign the Poles certainly did make several serious errors. Rydz-Śmigły was not a very effective commander, although he cannot be blamed for the tardy mobilization of the Army, as this was delayed almost until the last moment under Allied pressure, for fear of provoking the Germans. He was not good at delegating power to his generals and attempted to make all the key decisions himself. Possibly, in the past, this might have worked, but in the conditions of early Blitz warfare, Army and front commanders needed greater independence. A French assessment of the lessons to be learnt from the fall of France pointed out that

Poland Betrayed

The frontline does not exist any more and is replaced by a three-dimensional space extending on all the territory occupied by the fighting armies. Consequently the linear disposition of the troops along the frontier seems to appear totally wrong [. . .] The vital forces of the enemy have to be gradually destroyed. Their blows have to be answered by blows [. . .] The fight should be carried by independent groups of great units. The supplies should be secured from a system of Army bases, liable to be rapidly removed, and insensible to raids of armoured units and air bombardment. [Source: NA WO 193/763.]

The report came to the conclusion that 'we had almost returned to the Napoleonic conception of war'.

The strategic disposition of the Polish Armies left much to be desired. The Armies Pomorze and Poznań were much too close to the frontier. If the latter had been concentrated further into the interior of Poland, the Bzura counter-offensive would have had a better chance of success. The Polish Army also suffered from poor communications. The command network was too dependent on existing telegraph and telephone lines, all of which were vulnerable to aerial bombardment. In its modernization programme the High Command had unfortunately neglected developing a modern system of radio links for key command posts. A system of liaison officers was used but was ineffective, largely due to frequent moves of General Headquarters, which, according to the British Military Mission, 'were shrouded in such secrecy that liaison officers were frequently unable to find them' (NA WO 106/1747).

Essentially, however, the Poles fought with great courage and tenacity. Had there been near equality in tanks and planes between them and the Wehrmacht, the story might have been very different. As Zaloga and Madej point out, 'it should not be forgotten that the Polish Army fought for nearly five weeks against the full weight of the Wehrmacht and later the Red Army, even though it was substantially outnumbered. In contrast, the British, French, Belgian and Dutch armies, which outnumbered the Wehrmacht in men, tanks and aircraft [. . .] held out for only

166

Aftermath

a few weeks more'. The Polish record in Warsaw, Modlin, Hel and Westerplatte was second to none.

The Poles managed to inflict considerable casualties on the Germans: 16,000 killed and 32,000 wounded, while they knocked out 674 tanks, 217 of which were destroyed. The small and outdated Air Force, combined with ground defences, also managed to destroy, at a conservative estimate, about 220 Luftwaffe planes. The cavalry, far from indulging in useless deeds of derring-do, were often used effectively. Armed with anti-tank rifles and dismounted, cavalrymen were able to surprise and destroy German armoured units.

Colonel Beck and the Chief of Staff, General Stachiewicz, were convinced that by 16 September the momentum of the German advance was slowing down. They pinned their hopes on the orderly retirement of Polish forces into the Dniester-Stryj bridge-head, where eventually a smaller but more effective Polish Army could be reconstructed. According to Ryszard Szawłowski there was a real chance 'of offering strong and effective resistance to the Germans, perhaps for many additional weeks, possibly until the end of October'. The Soviet invasion, however, was a 'stab in the back' that made any further large-scale resistance impossible. Without it how long could the Poles have lasted? Certainly the German supply lines were lengthening and the wear and tear on their motorized vehicles was exacting its toll. The weather, too, had broken and rain and mud would undoubtedly have assisted the Polish defence. However, as the bridgehead was so small and was only served by a single-track railway from Romania, it would have been at the mercy of the overwhelming German air superiority. Essentially, at the very most, it would only have delayed Polish defeat by a few weeks. As the head of the British Military Mission observed in his final report:

> Fundamentally [. . .] the struggle was one between on the one hand a country of enormous industrial capacity and ruthless energy directed towards one end, war, and on the other a country of very limited resources and wealth, gallant but poor, still handicapped by the tragic history of her last 150 years. There could in the circumstances be but

one result – speculation could only concern the length of war it would take to achieve. Aided by an unprecedented drought – un temps hitlérien [Hitlerian weather] – and by her possession of the initiative, which enabled her to attack before the Polish Army was even mobilized, Germany's armoured columns and crushing air superiority carried her to victory in less than three weeks. [Source: NA WO 106/1747.]

The Germans did enjoy overwhelming strength, but they also committed several serious errors, which at the time were not fully appreciated by their opponents. The Germans were slow to give up their original plan for destroying the Poles west of the Vistula, and consequently enabled considerable numbers of Polish troops to concentrate on the eastern bank of the river. The Germans also overlooked the concentration of Polish forces between the Vistula and the Bzura, from where General Kutrzeba's flank attack caused them a serious, if temporary, setback.

The Polish theatre also revealed a number of shortcomings in German organization. Armoured divisions lacked sufficient fire-power, as was shown when the tanks of the 4th Division were unable to break into Warsaw. The German light tanks, particularly, were lacking in armament and protection, and were vulnerable to the Polish Mauser 8mm anti-tank rifle, while the Polish 37mm Bofors gun could destroy any German tank. The speed of the German advance also meant that the consumption of fuel exceeded expectations and several times large armoured columns or motorized formations were halted for several hours due to lack of fuel. The conditions of the Polish roads also had a big impact on the condition of German motorized transport. As lorries broke down, replacements became difficult and there were long delays before vital spares could be delivered from Germany. In time this would significantly have impeded the German advance.

The German Army was not the battle-hardened force it was to become by late 1941. Only the senior officers and the reserve officers, called back to the colours in 1939, had fought in the Great War of 1914–18. The majority of its soldiers were young

Aftermath

conscripts who lacked battle experience. When the tide of battle turned against them, as it did briefly on the Bzura, there was a tendency to panic. A report from the German Army Headquarters in February 1940 was highly critical of the widespread looting that took place. In factories, even driving belts and filing cabinets were seized.

Publicly, the Nazis liked to give the impression that, in the words of the American Naval Attaché, 'the Poles' performance had been pitiable and inspired nothing but contempt in the German Army', but, as the Germans themselves knew, the reality was rather different. All in all, a French military report on the war was correct when it observed that 'with equality of material the Polish troops were always superior to the enemy'. The final praise to the Polish fighting man was given by no less a person than Marshal Pétain in June 1940, when he told Sikorski that he had witnessed the 1st Polish Division on the eastern front in France drive back four German divisions. He added that 'if there had only been ten Polish divisions, victory would have been certain'.

Despite a devastating defeat, Poland managed to organize the fifth largest allied force in the Second World War, which, as Andrzej Suchcitz has pointed out, 'was no mean feat in itself considering the lack of her natural economic and manpower base'. Throughout the Second World War Polish troops fought with great distinction. They saw service in North Africa, Italy, and North-West Europe, while Polish pilots in 302 and 303 Squadrons brought down 130 German pilots in the Battle of Britain. The German invasion of the USSR led to the Polish-Soviet Agreement of 30 July 1941. This enabled the evacuation of 114,000 soldiers and civilians to Iran, which was just under 10 per cent of all those deported by the Russians following their occupation of Poland's eastern provinces. The remainder, which numbered about 400,000, joined the Polish People's Army and fought their way across Eastern Europe.

Tragically, the defeat of Nazism did not lead to an independent Poland. The unique conditions of 1918–19 were not repeated. The vacuum left by the collapse of Nazi power in Eastern Europe was filled, as many had feared, by Soviet Russia, which in 1944–45 effectively occupied the whole of Poland. The Western powers had

Poland Betrayed

little option but to recognize this. In deference to Stalin's wishes, Polish units in Britain were excluded by the British Government from participation in the great Victory parade in London in 1946, despite all that they had suffered and contributed to victory. Poland only became free with the collapse of Communism in 1989–90.

Appendix I:
Chronology of Major Events

1772–95
Polish state ceases to exist after being partitioned between Prussia, Austria and Russia.

1807
Napoleon creates Grand Duchy of Warsaw.

1815
Congress of Vienna partitions Poland once more between Russia, Prussia and Austria.

1914–18
First World War (Polish Legion set up and Polish units created within French Foreign Legion).

1917
Russian revolutions.

1918
Defeat of Austria and Germany.

1919
Recreation of Polish Second Republic by Treaty of Versailles and Polish Defence Force set up.

1919–21
First Polish-Russian war.

1920–22
Bitter disagreements between Poland and Germany over control of Upper Silesia (settled by League of Nations).

Poland Betrayed

1922
Treaty of Rapallo paves way for Soviet-German military cooperation.

1924
Poland forms Frontier Defence Corps (KOP).

1926
Marshal Piłsudski seizes power in Poland.

1929
Work begins in Poland on reconstruction of German *Enigma* machines.

1929
Reduction of Polish cavalry in favour of tanks vetoed by Inspectorate-General.

1932
Soviet military mechanization programme begins.

1933
Hitler comes to power in January and German rearmament starts.

1934
Polish-German Non-Aggression Pact.

1935
Polish Government initiates Plan Z to counter possible German attack.

1936
Polish Four Year Industrial Plan launched and construction of industrial triangle begins. Polish Air Force (PAF) modernization plan announced.

1937
National Guard integrated into Polish Infantry Reserve.

1938

12 March:	German *Anschluss* with Austria.
September:	Crisis over German claims to Sudetenland ends in its cession to Germany at Munich Conference.
21 September:	Poland claims disputed Czech territory of Teschen.
29 September:	ARP instructions issued to Polish civil population.
1–8 October:	Polish troops occupy Teschen.

Appendix I: Chronology of Major Events

1939

January:	Beck-Ribbentrop talks.
February:	Civil Defence exercises in Warsaw.
March:	German occupation of Moravia and Bohemia.
21 March:	German-Polish talks on Danzig and trans-Corridor motorway.
23 March:	Lithuania hands over Memel to Germany. Partial Polish mobilization and Polish Armed Forces issued with orders for action in first stage of war with Germany should hostilities break out.
31 March:	Provisional British guarantee of Poland.
April:	Beck visits London and converts guarantee to alliance.
11 April:	Hitler issues directive for *Fall Weiss* (Operation White) – the invasion of Poland.
May:	British Military Delegation visits Poland.
19 May:	Franco-Polish Military Protocol.
27 May:	Franco-Polish Air Agreement.
June:	Governor of National Bank of Poland visits London to discuss financial credits and a loan.
15 June:	Germans complete their plan for *Fall Weiss*.
11 July:	Army Karpaty formed.
17–21 July:	British General Ironside visits Poland on fact-finding mission.
5 August:	Alfred Naujoks entrusted with planning the attack on Gleiwitz Radio Station by Germans disguised as Poles, with the intention of creating an incident that would give Hitler an excuse to invade.
23 August:	Nazi-Soviet Non-Aggression Pact signed by Ribbentrop and Molotov. Poles secretly begin to issue call-up papers.
25 August:	Britain ratifies Polish guarantee. Hitler delays attack on Poland for a week.
31 August:	Poles announce general mobilization. Polish destroyer flotilla sets sail for Leith in Scotland.

Poland Betrayed

31 August–
1 September:

German commandos attack Gleiwitz Radio Station and launch Operation 'Agathe' on targets in Hochlinden and Pitschau.

1 September:

War begins with German dive-bomber attack on the Tczew bridge at 14:15 hours. At 04:45 hours the German battleship *Schleswig-Holstein* begins bombardment of Westerplatte. Germans held at Mokra but 1st Panzer Division breaks through in Upper Silesia. In the north, Germans attack through the Tuchola Forest and cross the River Brda. German attack on Mława stronghold initially repulsed.

2 September:

General Busch of the German VIII Corps issues orders dealing with Polish guerrillas. Wieluń falls to German troops.

3 September:

5th Panzer Division breaks through near Oświęcim and occupies Katowice. Polish forces driven out of the Corridor. *Volksdeutsche* uprising in Bydgoszcz. Britain and France declare war on Germany. RAF drops leaflets on German cities.

4 September:

Army Modlin retires behind the Vistula. RAF attacks German fleet at Wilhelmshaven.

5 September:

Piotrków taken and road to Warsaw opened for German armour. Armies Kraków, Prusy and Poznań ordered to retire east of Vistula. General Kutrzeba urges attack on German Eighth Army. Polish Government and foreign diplomats begin to evacuate Warsaw.

6 September:

Germans break through in the Carpathians and at Tomaszów Mazowiecki. Army Lublin formed. General Kutrzeba ordered to retreat to Warsaw.

7 September:

Rydz-Śmigły moves HQ to Brześć. French make frontier incursions at Saarlouis, Saarbrücken and Zweibrücken.

8 September:

German Panzers driven out of the Warsaw suburb of Ochota.

Appendix I: Chronology of Major Events

9 September: Army Poznań launches counter-attack across the Bzura and forces German Panzers to withdraw from Warsaw.

10 September: German Third Army breaches the River Bug defences.

11 September: Germans counter-attack on the Bzura. Rydz-Śmigły orders general retreat of Polish forces to Romanian bridgehead.

12 September: All rail links to Warsaw cut by German air and land forces. Polish High Command moves to Młynów on Romanian border.

14 September: Polish submarine division ordered to sail to Scotland once operations in the Baltic became impossible to carry out.

15 September: Food shortages acute in Warsaw.

16 September: Kutrzeba, surrounded by German forces, tries to break out towards Warsaw. Molotov announces that Soviet intervention is imminent.

17 September: Soviet troops cross Polish border. Polish Government crosses border to Romania. Oksywie Peninsula taken by the Germans.

20 September: Sarny bunker complex surrenders to Russians. Polish submarine *Wilk* arrives at Rosyth in Scotland.

21 September: Germans complete destruction of Armies Pomorze and Poznań. Grodno falls to the Russians. German forces 100–150 miles from Soviet frontier.

22 September: Lwów surrenders to the Russians.

23 September: Soviet forces cross the Bug.

25 September: 'Black Monday' – 1,200 German planes attack Warsaw.

27 September: Warsaw surrenders.

28 September: Soviet-German Agreement on Poland's eastern frontiers.

29 September: Modlin garrison surrenders.

Poland Betrayed

2 October:	Garrison on Hel Peninsula surrenders. Polish Government-in-Exile meets in Paris.
6 October:	Polesie Group, under General Kleeberg, surrenders to Germans.
8–12 October:	Details of German annexations from Poland announced.
14 October:	Polish submarine *Orzeł* docks at Rosyth.
22 October:	'Plebiscite' held in Russian-occupied Poland to endorse full Sovietization. Polish Destroyer Division begins patrolling western shores of Ireland.
8 December:	First Polish ground crews arrive in Britain.

1940

4 January:	Franco-Polish Air Agreement.
5 March:	Stalin approves plan to execute 25,421 Polish officers and NCOs.
30 April:	Major Henryk Dobrzański's (alias 'Hubal') partisan group destroyed by the Germans.

Appendix II:
Biographies of Key Figures

Lieutenant General Władysław Anders (1892–1970) served as a cavalry officer in the Russian Army in the First World War. In 1939 he was Commander of the Nowogródzka Cavalry Brigade, which was attached to Army Modlin. On 11 September he was then given command of an independent operational unit, Group Anders. He was taken prisoner by Soviet forces near the Hungarian frontier at the end of September 1939 and imprisoned in Lwów, before being transferred to the Lubyanka jail in Moscow. He was released after the German attack on the USSR in 1941 and given responsibility for forming a new Polish Army composed of the thousands of Poles who had been imprisoned in the USSR. This force, known as Anders' Army, eventually regrouped in the Middle East as the 2nd Polish Corps under ultimate British control. It played a key role in capturing Monte Casino in 1944. Anders died in London in 1970.

Józef Beck (1894–1944) served in the First Brigade of the Polish Legions, 1914–17, which fought for the Austrians, and was also Piłsudski's aide. In 1926 he played a key role in the latter's coup. From 1926–30 Beck was Chief of Staff to the Defence Ministry. After two years as Deputy Prime Minister and Deputy Foreign Minister, he took over the Foreign Ministry. After Piłsudski's death, Poland was effectively ruled by a triumvirate composed of Beck, Rydz-Śmigły and President Mościcki. Beck continued Piłsudski's attempts to balance between the USSR and Germany until the spring of 1939, when he was able to secure a guarantee of support from Great Britain. After the collapse of Poland in September 1939, Beck escaped to Romania with the rest of the Government, where he was interned. He died there in Stanesti on 5 June 1944.

Poland Betrayed

General Johannes von Blaskowitz (1883–1948) served on both the eastern and western fronts in the First World War. In September 1939 he commanded the German Eighth Army, which was forced, temporarily, to retreat in the battle of the Bzura. As a result of this he was not promoted to the rank of field marshal. In October he was appointed Commander-in-Chief of German-occupied Poland, but he was sickened by the atrocities committed particularly by the SS. Hitler relieved him of his command in May 1940, but he was then made Military Governor of Northern France, and then, from October 1940 to May 1944, he was Commander-in-Chief of the First Army. In September 1944 Blaskowitz again protested about German atrocities in Poland and was promptly relieved of his command of Army Group G until he was reinstated on 24 December 1945. He was charged with war crimes before a US military court, but committed suicide during the trial.

Colonel General Fedor von Bock (1880–1945) served with great distinction with the Prussian Foot Guards in the First World War. In 1932 he was appointed Commander of the 2nd Infantry Division and by 1939 was a Corps Commander. In the Polish campaign Bock commanded Army Group North, and in the attack on Western Europe the following year commanded Army Group B. In the Russian campaign, as Commander of Army Group Centre, he failed to take Moscow in December 1941 and was relieved of his command. He was killed by Allied aircraft fire a few days before the end of the war.

Field Marshal Walther von Brauchitsch (1881–1948) served on the German General Staff during the First World War. He was appointed Commander-in-Chief of the German Army in February 1938. He was finally relieved of his command in December 1941 and died before he could be prosecuted for war crimes in 1948.

General Sir Adrian Carton de Wiart (1880–1963) was born in Brussels and ran away from Oxford University to fight in the Boer War. In the First World War he was wounded eight times. He led the British Military Mission to Poland, 1919–24. He then retired to the Pripyat Marshes, where his main hobby was duck-shooting. He was recalled to head the Mission in September 1939. In April 1941 he was made a PoW by the Italians but in 1943 was dispatched to Lisbon to nego-

Appendix II: Biographies of Key Figures

tiate an armistice with the Allies. His last mission was to represent Churchill on General Chiang Kai-shek's staff. He retired in 1946.

General Stefan Dąb-Biernacki (1890–1959) fought in the Polish Legions in the First World War and commanded a regiment in the first Polish-Soviet War in 1920. In 1930 he joined the GISZ (Polish General Inspectorate of the Armed Forces), and in December 1939 was Commander of Army Prusy and later of the Northern Front. After defeat at Tomaszów Lubelski by the Germans he managed to escape to France via Hungary. He was bitterly criticized for leaving his troops in the lurch and played no role in rebuilding Polish forces. He died in London.

Major Henryk Dobrzański ('Hubal') (1887–1940) fought in Piłsudski's legions in the First World War. He became a professional soldier and an Olympic equestrian rider. In September 1939 he was deputy commander of 110th Reserve Cavalry Regiment, which was to become involved in heavy fighting at Grodno with the Red Army. After the capitulation of Warsaw, with a band of about fifty men, he waged a guerrilla war in the Kielce area, but was captured and executed by the Germans on 30 April 1940.

Hans Frank (1900–1946) had been Nazi Minister of Justice in Bavaria, and then, in 1934, Reich Minister without Portfolio. He was Governor-General of German-occupied Poland, 1939–45 and sentenced to death by the Allies at the Nuremberg trials. He was executed on 1 October 1946.

Colonel Sir Colin Gubbins (1896–1976) became an expert on irregular warfare. His initial experience of this was gained as a member of General Ironside's staff in Russia in 1919 and then in Ireland, 1920–21. Gubbins served as the military member on the International Commission in the Sudetenland. From 1935–40 he was a staff officer at the War Office and wrote manuals on irregular warfare, which were later to sent to the Polish Underground movement. He was Chief of Staff to the British Military Mission to Poland in September 1939. In November 1940 Gubbins was seconded to the SOE (Special Operations Executive) department. He retired in 1946 and became managing director of a carpet and textile manufacturers.

General Heinz Guderian (1888–1954) served in the First World War as a Signals and Staff Officer. After the war, in 1927, he was made responsible for developing plans for mechanized warfare. He published *Achtung Panzer!* in 1936-37, which developed his theories on the role of tanks and aircraft in modern warfare. Guderian was in a position to test out his ideas in both Poland and France. In the Russian campaign he commanded Panzergruppe 2, but as a result of disagreement with Hitler, was relieved of his command in December 1941. In 1943 he became Inspector General of the Armoured troops and then, in 1944, Chief of Staff of the Army. Guderian surrendered to the Americans but was not charged with war crimes, despite the Poles insisting that he had threatened to shoot Polish PoWs at the battle of Wizna unless their Polish commander ordered an immediate capitulation.

General Franz Halder (1884–1972) was an artilleryman who served as a staff officer for most of the First World War and the subsequent Weimar Republic. In 1931 he served in the Training Staff in the *Reichswehr* Ministry. As a result of his reputation as a brilliant staff officer and operations planner, he became Chief of the German General Staff from 1938–1942. In this role he drew up plans for *Fall Weiss*, and then for the invasion of France and the Low Countries, the Balkans and eventually Russia. As a result of disagreements with Hitler he was retired into the 'Führer Reserve' in 1942. He was arrested and imprisoned a day after the failed coup against Hitler on 20 July 1944. After the war he worked as historical advisor to the US Army Historical Division.

Field Marshal Sir William Edmund Ironside (1880–1959) had commanded troops in Russia, Persia and India and was Governor of Gibraltar, 1938–39. In his role as Inspector-General of Overseas Forces he visited Poland in July 1939 to assess the country's military capacity and advise on tactics. In September 1939 he became Chief of the Imperial Staff. After a year as Commander-in-Chief of Home forces, he retired.

Sir Howard Kennard (1878–1955) had served as a diplomat in various positions in Teheran, Washington, Havana and Tangier. He was Minister Plenipotentiary in Yugoslavia, and, before moving to Warsaw, Ambassador first in Stockholm and then in Berne. He represented the British Government in Warsaw from 1935–39, where he proved a highly effective ambassador, whose dispatches have become important historical documents. He was highly critical

Appendix II: Biographies of Key Figures

of the Polish occupation of Teschen but as supportive of the Polish Government as London permitted during the period March–September 1939. He accompanied the Polish Government to Romania and then on to Angers and London with Sikorski's Government-in-Exile. He retired in 1941.

General Franciszek Kleeberg (1888–1941) served in the Austrian Army and the Polish Legions in the First World War. On 9 September 1939 he was given command of Group Polesie. He capitulated on 6 October, when he ran out of ammunition and supplies. He was imprisoned in Germany and died in hospital in April 1941.

General Tadeusz Kutrzeba (1885–1947) fought as a second lieutenant in the Austro-Hungarian Army in the First World War. In September 1939 he commanded Army Poznań and planned and commanded the counter-attack across the Bzura. After the siege of Warsaw he was taken prisoner by the Germans. In 1945 he was appointed chairman of the September Campaign Historical Committee in London, but died in January 1947.

General Władysław Langner (1897–1972) served in the Polish Legions in Austrian service in the First World War. In 1928 he was moved to the War Office and in 1931 became Vice Minister of War. When war broke out he was commander of the Lwów garrison. Langner surrendered the city to the Russians, and after being taken to Moscow for interrogation, returned and managed to cross the frontier to Romania. After the fall of France he was put in command of the 3rd Carpathian Rifle Brigade in Scotland.

Léon Noël (1888–1987) was appointed French High Commissioner in the Rhineland in 1927 and then Secretary-General to the French Ministry of the Interior. From 1932 to 1935 he was French Plenipotentiary in Czechoslovakia. Then, from 1935 to 1940, he served as Ambassador in Warsaw and then Angers. He remained in occupied France but in 1943 rallied to General de Gaulle. From 1951–55 Noël was elected Deputy for Yonne.

Józef Klemens Piłsudski (1867–1935) was born in Russian Poland and studied medicine at the University of Kharkov where he became involved in the Narodniki revolutionary movement. He was sent to Siberia for five years. When he returned, he joined the Polish Socialist Party, of which he became one of the key leaders. Essentially he was a Polish Nationalist and worked towards the destruction of the Russian Empire. In Austria he set up the para-military Sporting Associations. These formed the basis of the Polish Legions, which fought with the Central Powers against Russia in the First World War. In 1916 Piłsudski agreed to serve in the Regency Kingdom of Poland created by the Central Powers and was appointed Minister of War in the newly formed Polish Regency government, but in 1917 he withdrew his support from the Central Powers and was imprisoned by the Germans.

With the defeat of Germany Piłsudski became Poland's Chief of State until 1922. In 1919–21 he led Poland's forces to victory in the Polish-Soviet War, but in 1923, as the National Democrats were in power, he withdrew from active politics. However, he returned to power by *coup d'état* in 1926, and effectively became dictator of Poland. Until his death in 1935, he was interested mainly in military and foreign affairs.

Joachim von Ribbentrop (1893–1946) joined the Nazi Party in 1932 and acted as Hitler's foreign affairs advisor in 1933. In 1936 he was sent to Britain as German Ambassador, and in 1938 was promoted to the post of Foreign Minister. His main success was the Nazi-Soviet Non-Aggression Treaty of August 1939. He was sentenced to death and hanged at Nuremberg in October 1946.

Colonel General Gerd von Rundstedt (1875–1953) fought in the First World War, and by 1918 was a divisional chief of staff. In 1932 he was appointed Commander of the 3rd Infantry Division. In 1938 he retired in protest after Werner von Fritsch, the Commander-in-Chief of the German Army, had been falsely accused of homosexuality by the Gestapo and forced to resign. In September Rundstedt was recalled and led Army Group South in the invasion of Poland. He commanded an army group in the invasion of France and the Low Countries and went on to command Army Group South in Operation Barbarossa in June 1941. In March 1942 Rundstedt was placed in command of German forces in western Europe. When he was captured in May 1945 he was charged with war crimes, but released by the British in July 1948.

Marshal Edward Rydz-Śmigły (1886–1941) grew up in relatively humble circumstances as the son of an NCO in the regular Austro-Hungarian Army. He studied both at the Jagiellonian University at Kraków and then at the Kraków Academy of Art. In 1912 he was one of the

Appendix II: Biographies of Key Figures

founders of the Polish paramilitary organization, the Rifleman's Association. In August 1914 he joined the Polish Legions and fought for Austria. By 1916 he was already a colonel. In the first Polish-Russian War of 1920 he played a key role and commanded the central front during the Battle of Warsaw. He was then appointed Inspector-General of the Polish Army, first in the Wilno District and then in Warsaw. He supported Piłsudski in the coup of 1926. In 1935, after Piłsudski's death, he was appointed Inspector-General of all the Polish Armed Forces. From this position he emerged as the effective leader of Poland and a year later was made a Marshal of Poland. As a result of his influence the regime developed increasingly authoritarian characteristics. On 1 September 1939 Rydz-Śmigły became Commander-in-Chief of Polish forces, but on 18 September fled to Romania where he was interned, but escaped to Hungary in December. Refusing to obey Sikorski's orders to join Polish forces in the British Empire, he went back secretly to Warsaw and joined the Resistance as a private soldier in the autumn of 1941. He died of a heart attack on 2 December.

General Władysław Sikorski (1881–1943) fought in the Polish Legions in the First World War. In 1922–23 he was Prime Minister and then, in 1922–24, Minister of Military Affairs. After Piłsudski's coup Sikorski fell from favour and it was only after the defeat of Poland that he became Prime Minister of the Government-in-Exile and Commander-in-Chief of the Armed Forces. In April 1943 Stalin broke off relations with his government because Sikorski demanded that the International Red Cross should investigate the Katyń massacre. In July Sikorski was killed in a plane crash at Gibraltar.

General Wacław Stachiewicz (1894–1973) joined the Polish Legions in 1914 on the side of Austria. In March 1918 he deserted the Austro-Hungarian Army and took command of the Warsaw branch of the Polish Military Organization. He became a staff officer in the new Polish Army, and in 1921 was sent to study at the French École de Guerre. In 1923 he returned to staff duties. In 1933 he commanded the 7th Infantry Division and on the death of Piłsudski was promoted Chief of Staff of the Polish Army. He was responsible for drawing up both Plans W and Z (Wschód and Zachód). On 1 September he became Chief of Staff at Marshal Rydz-Śmigły's headquarters and accompanied him over the Romanian frontier on 18

September. He was interned, but in January 1940 he managed to escape to Algiers. However, as a result of pressure from Sikorski, the French, too, interned him. It was only in 1943 that he reached London. He died in Canada.

Lieutenant Colonel Edward Sword (1899–1983) served briefly as an artilleryman in the First World War in 1918. After serving in India and studying at the Staff College, he joined the Military Intelligence Directorate at the War Office. In June 1938 he was appointed British Military Attaché in Warsaw and in September 1939 a staff officer on the British Military Mission. He returned with General Carton de Wiart to Britain, where he spent the war first as a staff officer and then in the Interservice Topographical Department. In 1946 he joined the War Ministry, and did not retire from government service until 1977.

General Semyon Timoshenko (1895–1970) fought as a cavalryman for the Imperial Russian Army until the Revolution and then joined the Red Army. By the end of 1920 he commanded the Red Army's cavalry and, thanks to Stalin's backing, was Commander, in succession, of Belarus, Kiev, the Northern Caucasus and then, in 1939, of the whole western border region. In September he was in charge of the Ukrainian front when the Red Army invaded eastern Poland. In January 1940 Timoshenko took over command of Soviet troops in Finland and managed successfully to conclude the war. During the Great Patriotic War Timoshenko lost favour with Stalin for initially failing to drive German forces back from Stalingrad, and was removed from front-line command.

Vice-Admiral Józef Unrug (1884–1973) was born in Germany and served in the German Navy during the First World War. In 1919 he transferred to the infant Polish Navy and became commanding officer of a submarine flotilla and, in 1925, of the whole Polish Navy. On 2 October 1939, after the fall of Warsaw and Modlin, he surrendered all the land units under his command, having ordered his ships to make for British ports. He was imprisoned in Germany, where his former German naval colleagues tried to persuade him to defect, but he refused to speak in German and struck no deals with the Germans. In 1973 he died in a Polish veterans' hospital in France.

Appendix III:
Glossary and Abbreviations

AA	Anti-aircraft Artillery.
ARP	Air Raid Precautions.
Blitzkrieg	A war of movement in which tanks, backed by motorized infantry would, to quote Hitler, defeat 'the enemy as quick as lightning'.
CIGS	Chief of the Imperial General Staff.
Einsatzgruppe	Special task force of German Security Police.
GISZ	Polish General Inspectorate of the Armed Forces.
GSO1	General Staff Officer First Grade.
Heimwehr	German paramilitary defence force (Home Guard).
kolkhoz	Soviet-run collective farm.
KOP	Polish Frontier Protection Corps.
Luftflotte	German air fleet.
Luftwaffe	German Air Force.
NA	National Archives (at Kew).
NKVD	The Soviet People's Commissariat of Internal Affairs. It was a political police responsible for security, intelligence and prisons.
OKW	German *Oberkommando der Wehrmacht* (High Command of the Armed Forces).
PAF	Polish Air Force.
Panzer	German term for armoured vehicles, especially tanks.
Plan Wschód	Plan 'East' for a Russian attack on Poland.
Plan Zachód	Plan 'West' for defence against a German attack on Poland.
PoW	Prisoner of War.

Poland Betrayed

PSZ	Polskie Siły Zbrojne (Polish Armed Forces).
PZL	Polish State Aviation Works. The planes it produced all had the prefix PZL. Hence the fighters, PZL P-7 and PZL P-11.
Reichswehr	The German Army. The name was used until 1935 when it was replaced by 'Wehrmacht'.
Sejm	The Polish Parliament.
SS	The Nazi 'Schutzstaffel' or 'defence unit'. Its initial role was to protect Hitler's person but by 1939 under Himmler it controlled the German police and had a paramilitary arm, the Waffen SS, which fought in Poland.
Ułans	Polish lancers.
Voivodship (*województwa*)	Province.
Volksdeutsche	Ethnic Germans who lived in Poland and eastern Europe.
Wehrmacht	In 1935 the German *Reichswehr* changed its name to Wehrmacht, which also included the Navy and Luftwaffe.
X-Gerät	A German system for using radio navigation for bombing.

Appendix IV:
Orders of Battle

————⋙•⋘————

Polish Order of Battle 1 September 1939

Based on information provided by Zaloga, S.J., and Madej, V., *The Polish Campaign 1939*, Hippocrene, 1985, pp. 41–44.

Army Pomorze (General W. Bortnowski)
Group East
4th Infantry Division
16th Infantry Division

Group Czersk
9th Infantry Division
15th Infantry Division
27th Infantry Division
Pomorska Cavalry Brigade
Chojnice Local Defence Regiment
Kościerzyna Local Defence Battalion

Support Units
46th Motorized Engineer Battalion
Vistula Local Defence Regiment
Toruń Local Defence Regiment
Chełmno National Guard Regiment
River Flotilla (7 boats)

Air Command
141 Fighter Squadron
142 Fighter Squadron
42 Attack Squadron
43 Recon. Squadron
46 Recon. Squadron

Poland Betrayed

Army Modlin (Brigadier-General E. Krukowicz-Przedrzymirski)
8th Infantry Division
20th Infantry Division
Nowogródzka Cavalry Brigade
Mazowiecka Cavalry Brigade

Support Units
Modlin Regiment
Kazan Regiment
Płock Local Defence Regiment
Pułtusk Local Defence Regiment
Zegreze Local Defence Regiment
60th Motorized Engineer Battalion
Armoured Trains 13, 14, 15
1st Heavy Artillery Regiment
98th Heavy Artillery Detachment

Air Command
152 Fighter Squadron
41 Attack Squadron
53rd Recon. Squadron

Operational Group Wyszków (Brigadier-General W. Kowalski)
1st Legion Infantry Division
41st Reserve Infantry Division
Armoured Train 55

**Special Operational Group Narew
(Brigadier-General C. Młot-Fijałkowski)**
18th Infantry Division
33rd Reserve Infantry Division
Podlaska Cavalry Brigade
Suwalska Cavalry Brigade

Support Units
Osowiec Local Defence Unit
Wizna Local Defence Unit
34th Fortress Group

Air Command
151 Fighter Squadron
5 Attack Squadron
13 Recon. Squadron

Appendix IV: Orders of Battle

Army Poznań (General T. Kutrzeba)
14th Infantry Division
17th Infantry Division
25th Infantry Division
26th Infantry Division
Wielkopolska Cavalry Brigade
Podolska Cavalry Brigade

Support Units
47th Motorized Engineer Battalion
Armoured Trains 11, 12
7th Heavy Artillery Regiment
5th Machine-gun Battalion

Air Command
131 Fighter Squadron
132 Fighter Squadron
34 Attack Squadron
33 Recon. Squadron

Army Łódź (General J.K. Rómmel)
2nd Legion Infantry Division
10th Infantry Division
28th Infantry Division
Kresowa Cavalry Brigade

Group Piotrków
30th Infantry Division
Wołyńska Cavalry Brigade

Support Units
2nd Battalion, 4th Heavy Artillery Regiment
7th Heavy Machine-gun Battalion

Air Command
161 Fighter Squadron
162 Fighter Squadron
32 Attack Squadron
62 Recon. Squadron
66 Recon. Squadron

Army Prusy (General S. Dąb-Biernacki)
3rd Infantry Division
12th Infantry Division

13th Infantry Division
29th Infantry Division

Cavalry Operational Group
19th Infantry Division
Wileńska Cavalry Brigade

Support Units
81st Motorized Engineer Battalion
1st Company, 2nd Engineer Battalion
Armoured Train 55
1st Heavy Artillery Regiment
3rd Heavy Artillery Regiment
50th Heavy Artillery Regiment
1st Light Tank Battalion
9 AA Sections

Army Kraków (General A. Szylling)
Group Śląsk (on 3 Sept. renamed Operational Group Jagmin)
23rd Infantry Division
55th Reserve Infantry Division
Katów Fortress Brigade
95th Heavy Artillery Detachment
1 AA Section

Group Bielsko (on 3 Sept. renamed Operational Group Boruta)
1st Mountain Brigade
21st Mountain Infantry Division

Group Misianga
6th Infantry Division
7th Infantry Division
10th Mechanical Brigade
Krakowska Cavalry Brigade
22nd Mountain Infantry Division

Support Units
64th Light Artillery Detachment
65th Motorized Engineer Battalion
5th Heavy Artillery Regiment
Armoured Trains 51, 52, 54
1st Motorized AA Battalion
Kraków Local Defence Regiment
12 AA Sections

Appendix IV: Orders of Battle

Air Command
121 Fighter Squadron
122 Fighter Squadron
24 Attack Squadron
23 Recon. Squadron
26 Recon. Squadron

Army Karpaty (General K. Fabrycy)
2nd Mountain Brigade
3rd Mountain Brigade
Karpaty National Guard Brigade
Warsaw Mechanical Brigade
46th Light Artillery Detachment
47th Light Artillery Detachment
22nd Infantry Division
38th Infantry Division
1st Motorized Artillery Regiment
9th Heavy Artillery Regiment
12 AA Sections

Air Command
31 Fighter Squadron
56 Recon. Squadron

Group Grodno (Brigadier-General Olsyna-Wilczyński)
Grodno Local Defence Regiment
Wilno Local Defence Regiment, HQ
Baranowicze KOP Regiment
Kleck Light Artillery Battalion
9 AA Sections

Group Kutno (never mobilized as a group)
5th Infantry Division
24th Infantry Division
9th Heavy Artillery Regiment
71st Light Artillery Detachment

Coastal Defence
Morska (Naval) National Guard Brigade
1st Naval Rifle Regiment
2nd Naval Rifle Regiment
4th National Guard Battalion
Naval Light Artillery Detachment

Krakus Detachment
83rd Fortress Group
Hel Fortified Region

Naval Assets
Minesweepers: *Czajka*, *Czapla* (not completed), *Jaskółka*, *Mewa*, *Rybitwa*, *Żuraw* (not completed)
Sloops: *Haller* and *Piłsudski*
Submarines: *Orzeł*, *Ryś*, *Sęp*, *Wilk*, *Żbik*
1st Torpedo Squadron
1st Training Squadron
Support Ships plus Coastal Air Defence

German Order of Battle 1 September 1939

Based on information provided by Zaloga, S.J., and Madej, V., *The Polish Campaign 1939*, Hippocrene, 1985, pp. 188–190.

Army Group North (Colonel-General F. von Bock)
Fourth Army (General G. von Kluge)
I Frontier Guard Command
207th Infantry Division

II Corps
3rd Infantry Division
32nd Infantry Division

III Corps
Netze Division
50th Infantry Division

XIX Motorized Corps
2nd Motorized Infantry Division
3rd Panzer Division
20th Motorized Division

Reserve
II Frontier Guard Corps
XII Frontier Guard Corps

Third Army (General G. von Küchler)
I Corps
11th Infantry Division
61st Infantry Division
Kempf Panzer Division

Appendix IV: Orders of Battle

XXI Corps
21st Infantry Division
228th Infantry Division

Brand Corps
Lötzen Brigade
Goldap Brigade

Wodrig Corps
1st Infantry Division
12th Infantry Division

Reserve
217th Infantry Division
1st Cavalry Brigade

Army Group Reserve
73rd Infantry Division
206th Infantry Division
208th Infantry Division
10th Panzer Division

Army Group South (Colonel-General G. von Rundstedt)
Eighth Army (General J. Blaskowitz)
X Corps
24th Infantry Division
30th Infantry Division

XIII Corps
10th Infantry Division
17th Infantry Division
1st SS Division *Adolf Hitler*

Reserve
XII Frontier Guard Corps
XIV Frontier Guard Corps

Tenth Army (General W. von Reichenau)
IV Corps
4th Infantry Division
46th Infantry Division

XI Corps
18th Infantry Division
19th Infantry Division

XV Motorized Corps
2nd Light Division
3rd Light Division

XVI Panzer Corps
14th Infantry Division
31st Infantry Division
1st Panzer Division
4th Panzer Division

Reserve
XIV Motorized Corps

Fourteenth Army (General W. List)
VIII Corps
8th Infantry Division
28th Infantry Division
5th Panzer Division
2nd SS Division *Germania*

XVII Corps
7th Infantry Division
44th Infantry Division
45th Infantry Division

XVIII Corps
3rd Motorized Infantry Division
4th Light Division
2nd Panzer Division

Reserve
XXII Corps

Army Group Reserve
VII Corps
27th Infantry Division
56th Infantry Division
57th Infantry Division
62nd Infantry Division
68th Infantry Division
213th Infantry Division
221st Infantry Division
239th Infantry Division

Appendix IV: Orders of Battle

Luftwaffe Units
Luftflotte 1 (General A. von Kesselring) – supporting Army Group North
Luftflotte 4 (General A. Löhr) – supporting Army Group South

Soviet Order of Battle 1 September 1939
Based on information provided by John Erickson, 'The Red Army's march into Poland, 1939', in K. Sword (ed.), *The Soviet Takeover of the Polish Eastern Provinces*, Macmillan and School of Slavonic and Eastern European Studies, 1991, pp. 14–15.

Byelorussian Front (Army Commander M.P. Kovalev)
Third Army (Commander V.I. Kuznetsov)
IV Rifle Corps
'Lepel Group'

Fourth Army (Commander V.I. Chuikov)
V Rifle Corps
XXIII Rifle Corps
29th Light Tank Brigade

Tenth Army (Commander I.G. Zakharin)
XVI Rifle Corps
III Cavalry Corps
VI Cavalry Corps
Mechanized Cavalry Brigade
6th Light Tank Brigade
21st Light Tank Brigade
XV Tank Corps

Eleventh Army (Commander N. Medvedev)
XVI Rifle Corps
VII Cavalry Corps
6th Tank Brigade
Mobile Groups
1st Cavalry Division
I Cavalry Corps
I Tank Corps
1st Tank Brigade
Air Support

Poland Betrayed

Ukrainian Front (Army Commander S.K. Timoshenko)
Fifth Army (Commander I. Sovetnikov)
VIII Rifle Corps
XV Rifle Corps
3rd Light Tank Brigade

Sixth Army (Commander F. Golikov)
XVII Rifle Corps
II Cavalry Corps
24th Light Tank Brigade

Twelfth Army (Commander I. Tyulenev)
IV Cavalry Corps
V Cavalry Corps
XXV Tank Corps
XXVI Tank Corps
23rd Light Tank Brigade
26th Light Tank Brigade
Air Support

Appendix V:
Survivors' Reminiscences

Teresa Glazer

The following is an extract from The Poles in India. *This is still in manuscript form, but Tereza Glazer and her co-authors hope to have it published soon.*

I was seven years old and living in Warsaw when the Second World War broke out. I was equipped with a gas mask and well used to the sound of air raid sirens announcing practice alarms. Yet when the Germans started their strategic bombing raids on the capital on 1 September without any warning, nobody made for the air raid shelters – people stopped in their tracks and looked up in disbelief at the clear September sky from which a shower of bombs fell.

We lived in the Żoliborz part of Warsaw, next to the Citadel, flanked by a railway bridge on the left and the Gdański railway station on the right. In the first days of the war we saw families evacuated from the west of the country in overcrowded trains which used to stop outside the station to make room for regular trains, and our mother passed on hot drinks and words of encouragement to them, but as the raids on Warsaw intensified our turn came to be evacuated from the city. Our train was hit by a passing plane a few miles outside Warsaw.

My father was in the Army and mother had to look after my two-year-old brother, Andrzej, my elderly granny and I, as well as a small suitcase with just a change of clothing, since nobody doubted that the war was going to end quickly in German defeat as our Allies, Great Britain and France declared war on Germany on 3 September.

Poland Betrayed

In the meantime we were moving away from the capital in a horse-drawn cart, driving through small towns like Ryki with all the houses along the main road burning as a result of German incendiary bombs, or other ones where human and horse corpses lay on both sides of the road. When German planes on the way to or from a specific bombing raid flew low, shooting at people thronging the road, my mother hid us in roadside ditches, sheltering our heads with her hands saying: 'If they get us, let's be together.' My Gran, however, never descended from the cart but waved her umbrella fiercely at the planes, muttering awesome curses. Somehow we got safely to the country house of the Parysiewicz family near Kowel, where it looked as if the war had not reached. But after a few days, on 17 September, the Bolshevik armies marched in, occupying the whole of eastern Poland. Our friends' country estate was confiscated and we all moved to the nearby town of Kowel, where my father, in civilian clothing after the fall of Warsaw, managed to join us. We tried to return to Warsaw but that was not easy, as it meant crossing the new Russo-German border. We tried to do it openly and applied for permission to travel from the new authorities.

But the third wave of mass deportations of the Polish population into Russia was on its way. It consisted mainly of people who had been evacuated from western Poland at the start of the war and of refugees. They came for us at 2 a.m. on 29 June 1940 and told us to pack our belongings within half an hour. The NKVD man in charge said sarcastically, 'You wanted to travel to Warsaw, didn't you?' We were packed into cattle wagons without any windows. The train rushed without any stops till it crossed the Russian-Polish border. Later, on Russian territory, it would often stop in the middle of nowhere, outside railway stations, and people would get out to stretch their legs, try to boil some water on a primus stove, boil eggs, etc. It was rather hazardous because without any warning the train would start moving slowly and it was necessary to get back on in a hurry. After crossing the Polish border nobody tried to run away. From time to time we were herded to communal baths to wash and have our clothes 'deloused'. Lice were the first of the plagues visited upon us. Later came others, namely hunger, frost [. . .] and bedbugs.

We left the train in a small town called Teguldet, in the district of Novosibirsk. From there we were taken by a steamboat along a river

Appendix V: Survivors' Reminiscences

to a settlement in the midst of huge forests. In the autumn these forests provided us with edible mushrooms and all kinds of berries, but in the winter there was only the daily ration of black, clay-like – yet the best-in-the-world-tasting – bread. Andrzej and I just talked about food non-stop [. . .] I used to describe cakes, butter, cocoa, chocolate to him like objects beyond one's reach in a fairy tale. My grandmother often gave him her ration saying, 'I can't eat this clay!' She soon died and we buried her in the hard frozen earth in a primitive box made of a few rough boards.

After amnesty was declared in 1941 my father wanted to join the Polish Army being formed in southern Russia. We started our journey down the river on a raft, trying to reach the nearest town with a railway station. Unfortunately our primitive raft was tossed from one bank of the river to the next and we had to stop at the nearest settlement of Polish deportees. My father got a job looking after the horses working for the local *kolkhoz* (collective farm). My mother had to chop wood, clean, and generally look after the dormitory for thirty single young working women.

Next door to us lived a family with four children, whose father tried to commit suicide several times until he succeeded. All the neighbours tried to help, since the prevailing philosophy at that time in Russia was: 'he who does not work does not eat'. My father told the eldest boy to come to the stables and he gave him a small bag of oats meant for the horses. Unfortunately, the boy was apprehended and the marked bag identified. At night my parents talked long into the night that it was not safe for him to stay, since, in spite of the political amnesty, he might never be able to reach the Polish Army if they accused him of giving away fodder meant for working animals. Father disappeared that night and we had no contact with him for some time until a Polish Jew, who managed to conduct some commerce between the different settlements, brought the letter. It was decided that I would travel with this enterprising man on the next journey down the river in a steamboat to arrange a family reunion and the continuation of our interrupted journey to the Polish Army. Mother gave me some money for the ticket in a string bag, which I put round my neck and hid inside my jumper. After we boarded the boat my guardian placed me on the top berth and went about his business. I waited for him for a long time and then tried to buy the ticket myself. Since the woman selling the tickets could just about see the top of my head she told me that my mother should get the ticket: I stretched my hands up, pressing my fare on her and explained that my mother was not with me, but it was no use.

When we arrived at our destination people were leaving the boat via a wobbly plank thrown onto the land and handing their tickets to a big woman standing by the exit. I took my money out and tried to explain why I did not have a ticket but the woman pushed me aside like a tiresome insect [. . .] What was going to happen to me? This was the worst experience in my eight-year-old existence because for the first time I found myself without any grown-ups in charge. I took advantage of some important woman carrying a baby being made a fuss of and scarpered onto dry land. I found my guardian talking to a group of people, and he dismissed my concern with a simple statement that I saved my ticket money, so what was there to talk about? Later we found my father, who had managed to contact some Polish authorities and arrange our journey to southern Russia.

After we reached Jangiyul, where my father joined the Army, the last transport of civilians was organized to Persia through the mountains in army trucks. The list of people included in this transport was being read out in alphabetical order and since there were more people waiting to get out of Russia than it was possible to include in that transport, you could hear people crying when their letter was finished and the list went on to the next letter of the alphabet.

We travelled through dangerous mountain serpentines [sic] in army trucks, from Ashkhabad through Mashed to Teheran [. . .] We only stayed a short while in Teheran. Polish officials, together with the British authorities, prepared more permanent settlements in Africa and India, where we were to await the end of the war. We chose India. Having travelled through Ahwaz, where we lived in royal stables for a time, then a transit camp in Karachi, we reached Valivade.

Irena Haniewicz

The following is an extract from notes for a talk given by Mrs Irena Haniewicz.

22 JUNE 1939

I am coming home for summer holiday to my father's farm – to my beloved Bortnica (that is the village where I was born).

Appendix V: Survivors' Reminiscences

I am twelve years old and have just passed the examination to go to Gimnazjum [high school – ed.] [. . .] My father is driving me home in [a] horse carriage and looks at me with great pride. His only daughter is going to high school. I am bursting with happiness, everything is right in my small world [. . .] Before me, two months of utter bliss; walking in the woodland with my dog Finek, riding my horse and helping with harvesting.

But in my child's mind little did I know what black clouds were gathering on my horizons. On 1 September, as I was about to start high school, Germany invaded Poland from the West and on 16 [sic] September Russia entered Poland from the East [. . .] Even at that tender age I understood that something terrible had happened. Suddenly my parents were very serious, there was a lot of visiting from our neighbours and constant discussions about war [. . .] 'What was going to happen?' everybody was asking.

Then the high school opened and I was taken to the nearby town called Dubno to start my education – with a difference. It became compulsory to take Russian language and Ukrainian. Though I understood Ukrainian, I did not know how to write it as the letters are different, but somehow I overcame it and life sort of settled down.

In February 1940 my father came to visit me and told me that the Russians had taken all his horses away. I begged him to take me home, and, as I could twist my father round my little finger, he agreed to take me back home to our farm. And it was just as well that he had done so because the next day, about five o'clock in the morning, we heard knocking. Our servant came and told us that something bad was happening in the village, perhaps they are arresting the men. My father quickly dressed and ran out to hide in the barn.

Soon we heard dogs barking and [a] Russian officer knocked on our door and asked for my father. Mother told him that he was not at home. He said we have got to pack a few belongings, as we are being moved from our farm, not even telling us where we were going. My mother got hysterical, the servant girl was crying so he told me that I had to do the packing. At twelve years old I really did not know what to pack but I packed what I thought important – my brand-new, shining school uniform and books in my leather satchel.

When my father realized what was happening, he came out of hiding but was told to sit on the floor and the servant girl packed

201

some of our belongings into bags. In no time at all, we were told to get into [the] cart and we left our farm with father walking behind the cart, under escort. My last glance of our farm was [the] snow-covered orchard and the shining roof of the house. The sun just began to shine. My mother was crying and I was so afraid. Little did I know that it was the last glimpse of the beloved home where I had spent a blissful childhood.

We were taken to [the] railway station and put into cattle trains and driven to the north of Russia, near the White Sea – Archangel. The journey lasted three weeks – with no toilets. We were expected to squat down inside the train. I did not go for two weeks, as I was embarrassed. We were left in the deep forest with temperatures of minus 50 degrees.

My parents were sent to work in the forest, cutting trees. We lived in primitive wooden huts with no beds, just planks of wood to sleep on. The food was almost non-existent, just a slab of bread each day and watery porridge [. . .] As the summer approached we found some fruit and nuts in the forest [. . .] Later we found mushrooms. We received a parcel from my grandparents with precious food; also, my grand-mother sent me a dress, as at that time I had suddenly grown very tall.

Life was very hard and the cold was killing us, people were dying around us. We had no medicines or doctors. I remember a little girl of two years dying in the hut we were living in. I will never forget her lying there in a great fever and choking to death. We buried her behind the little hut and put [up] a wooden cross with her name inscribed.

Suddenly, in August 1941, the commandant of the camps called us together and told us we were free to go where we want[ed] and told us that Germany had invaded Russia so Poland is occupied by Germany, and we cannot go there. My father decided to go down [to the] south of Russia, at least he said we would be warmer. He [. . .] built [a] wooden raft and one sunny [day in] September 1941 we sailed on the river towards the nearest railway station, Kotlas. On the way our raft collapsed and we fell in the water, losing most of our belongings. We were drowning but my mother, who couldn't swim, was shouting, 'Save the photographs!' which we managed to [. . .] We managed to get to Kotlas by small boat and then started this scramble to get tickets down south.

Appendix V: Survivors' Reminiscences

Again we only managed to get [a] cattle train with planks of wood to sleep on. The journey down south took about two months, with constant stops, which sometimes lasted two to three days. We would get out and try to cook something or just boil some water. Also, occasionally, the train would stop in a small town and we would try to buy some food, which was a rare occurrence. After a long time we came to the end of the journey. We left the train in Uzbekistan and started looking for a place to live. About twelve of us managed to find one room and when we spread some blankets to sleep there was no room to move.

At that time we heard that [the] Polish General Anders [was] organizing [a] Polish army so my father decided to join. [It] was allowed to leave Russia through the Caspian Sea to Persia (Iran). My father somehow got us out of Russia as well [. . .] but thousands of Polish people did not manage to get out and spent all the war years living the most awful lives. Some never returned to Poland after the war.

In Pahlevi, in Iran, we were met by English soldiers [. . .] and for the first time since we left Poland real food entered our stomachs [. . .] People became ill eating real food.

In Teheran, Polish authorities organized Polish High School, where I [. . .] spent a year.

One year later we travelled to [. . .] Kolapur where, very kindly, the Maharaja of Kolapur let us have a piece of land on which we built small houses made [of] straw mats – but first we built the church.

Jan K. Siedlecki

The following is an extract from The Poles in India. *This is still in manuscript form, but Jan K. Siedlecki and his co-authors hope to have it published soon. This material was also written for Mr. Siedlecki's children.*

We were billeted in the outbuildings of a local manor house when we encountered the Russian invasion of 17 September. Huddling together in our quarters were three families, the colonel's wife, Mrs Kiszkowka, and her two children, a boy and a girl, slightly older than us, and a lieutenant's wife, Mrs Palys, with her baby. Soon the butchery started. The Russian soldiers with their guns hung on strings, their grey coats in shreds at the hem, drunk on vodka, were killing pigs and sharpening their knives on the stone steps. Our terrified mothers were hiding their hands under aprons, frantically disposing of or cutting up photographs of their husbands, which might betray them for whom they were. The fear being that the soldiers would eventually come for us. But it seems the pigs and vodka was enough for them.

Sometime later, when our family was billeted at the vicarage, the Russians organized a plebiscite to legalize their occupation of eastern Poland. Our bedroom was next door to the room where the votes were being counted and although the door between the two rooms was closed, we could clearly hear what was going on. The avalanche of Russian swearing – *Kakiye ludie!* (What sort of people are they! Etc., etc.) It sounded as if quite a lot spoiled their voting cards by cursing the Russians or voting the opposite way. The next day the results were announced as being 98 per cent for the annexation. I learned my first lesson in Soviet democracy.

My grandmother also fled to eastern Poland and reached her 'family' house in Radzyń near Lublin. My mother was anxious to join her there but when Mrs Palys's brother-in-law turned up and invited us to join him in crossing the frozen River San, my mother was frightened and declined. She placed her faith in arranging the affairs in a formal way by registering with the Soviet authorities her desire to join her mother on the German side of the demarcation line. Thus when it came to the deportation next year they knew where to come for us. It was difficult to know on what basis these deportations were being conducted. Was it for the 'sins' of our fathers? Against the 'ruling classes'? The Polish 'intelligentsia'? But I believe they took people away who might give them trouble on the future of the country. Anybody who had some sort of standing in society, be it a teacher or a chairman of an archery club was fair game.

As usual they came for us in the early hours of the morning, looking for arms they said (the revolver of my father and his military insignia I buried in the garden sometime before) and their faces lit up when one of them got hold of a metal bar supporting my brother's mattress. Curse. Never mind [*sic* – the Russians had hoped that they had discovered a gun] . . . 'Pack all your things, we are going to take you to your grandmother,' they said. I did not believe a word of it, but my younger brother, Bronek was clapping his hands in joy. Soon

Appendix V: Survivors' Reminiscences

a peasant cart was taking us to an assembly point. Mother was morose, wrapped up in fur coats. I was particularly irritated when some younger children started singing a very inappropriate song of 'how happy we all are going on this journey and how amazed we are that the world is so wonderful'. Thus we reached our temporary destination of a convent in Sambor, converted into a prison [. . .] I had a problem with my teeth and as Mrs Z. Chrzaszczewska [a fellow prisoner] knew a dentist in her home town a number of times I 'escaped' to have these seen to. It occurred to me then that I could escape altogether. But then what? I could not face it.

On 15 May we began our journey east. In the cattle trucks (similar to those in the *Dr Zhigavo* film) with metal bars in the windows and a double storey at each end of the carriage with a hole in the floor in the middle as a toilet [. . .] At long last we arrived in the town of Aktiubinsk at the southern end of the Ural mountains.

I don't know how big our hut was but it certainly accommodated several families [. . .] and millions of bugs. Of course the slogan was 'kto nie rabotayet, ten nie kushayet' ('who does not work, does not eat'). So all the adults had to go out and work on the farm, digging potatoes or harvesting tomatoes and being paid in kind [. . .] There was not really much to eat and the evenings were spent discussing wonderful recipes and interpreting dreams on when and how we were going to be released from these 'slave labour camps'. In the meantime, the children were roaming the steppes gathering dry twigs to mix with cow dung to make fire for cooking the food, which consisted mainly of various potato or flour mixes . . .

At Christmas our hut was totally covered with snow, right up to the ridge of the roof, but we still sung our beautiful carols and the neighbours thought it was a miracle that they were hearing Polish carols [. . .] We were in the same hut when the spring came and the surrounding countryside was flooded. So the rescuing party of the dreaded NKVD made their HQ in our hut, treating us with lumps of sugar and tea (totally unobtainable then). This provoked some sarcastic comments from us in Polish, to which one of the gang warned us to be careful, as he understands Polish.

My mother then decided that we will not be able to survive another winter in these conditions and applied for permission to move into [the] nearby town of Aktiubinsk in October 1941. How she managed

Poland Betrayed

that, whom she had to bribe and how we were supposed to live there I have no idea. Except, in retrospect, the 'amnesty' must have helped. All I know, with the German invasion of the Soviet Union on 22 June of that year our spirits rose [. . .] Something was bound to change for us. Of the subsequent Sikorski–Maiski agreement we knew nothing yet. The aim was to survive – somehow. Queuing at the shops in case something would be brought in [. . .] Vodka was frequently available and it was a useful commodity to obtain as it could later be traded for something really needed, or even as a bribe.

It must have been at that time that we began to have the taste of a privileged class when we got a pass to a 'closed shop' accessible to people like the NKVD or other elite rulers and now us. At the same time we were aware that the Polish Army was being created out of recently released PoWs [. . .] Eventually a soldier arrived to escort some officer's family to Yangi-Yul in Tashkent, the last outpost of the Polish Army before evacuation to Persia [. . .] On 21 August some of us ended up on the roof of the train [. . .] as we moved farther south we began to enjoy ourselves, buying all sorts of fruit and water-melons . . .

The last Polish Army camp was being liquidated and the atmosphere was tense. Conflicting orders were flying about. One of the last stated that the number of civilians to leave with the departing Army was to be severely curtailed. The bulk of the Army and civilian refugees left by the Caspian Sea from Krasnovodsk to Pahlevi near Rasht. But we were going to travel by land to Ashkabad and then to Meshed in Persia. But who was actually going? Apparently, the night before our departure, it was decided that if the worst comes to the worst, some mothers will stay behind in order to let their children go . . .

All I remember was when we eventually crossed the highly deco-rated gate proclaiming the boundary of the Soviet paradise, we all fell on our knees with a prayer for the deliverance. But a few hundred feet later we froze, when the lorry stopped, the flap was lifted and the Russian voice barked a command counting us out. What we did not know was that Persia at that time was occupied by Americans, the British, and the Soviets to safeguard oil supplies. What a fantastic land journey then followed through the wild and bare mountains of Kopet Dog, which, unfortunately, we only had a

Appendix V: Survivors' Reminiscences

glimpse of, due to the tent-like tarpaulin cover (because of the ever-present clouds of dust), while the Persian drivers were hell-bent on overtaking each other with disastrous results, as we learned later of one army lorry (Dodge) tumbling into a ravine with a loss of life of the occupants . . .

We entered Tehran in September 1942 and ended up in the refugee camp no. 2, which must have been near a military airbase [. . .] Finally, at the end of April 1943, we set sail to Karachi [. . .] From there by boat to Bombay and then by train south to Valivade (just outside Kolapur).

Walery Choroszewski

This account of Mr Walery Choroszewski's experiences is based on interviews with him conducted by the author in London on 21 June 2007 and 16 August 2007, and on a manuscript e-mailed to the author in September 2008. Mr Choroszewski is hoping to have his memoirs published shortly in Poland.

Walery returned to his grammar school in Wilno (now Vilnius, the capital of Lithuania) on 3 September 1939, the third day of the Second World War, for the autumn term. At first, war seemed far away, but on 17 September Soviet forces invaded Poland and in the early morning of 19 September occupied the city. Overnight change was unbelievable. In the evening of the 18th he went to bed, listening to distant artillery guns but otherwise in a normal, Western-style city, with shop windows full of all sorts of goods, people well dressed, and transport operating normally. Next morning, hardly any civilians were to be seen in the streets and those who ventured out were dressed in the oldest and drabbest clothes they could find. The streets were filled with tanks, roaming aimlessly and endlessly around the main street. [There were] occasional bursts of gunfire from last pockets of Polish resistance, shops and offices closed and locked, and no public transport. At first the Soviets appeared to be friends of Lithuania and even allowed Lithuanians to incorporate Wilno and the district into Lithuania. A few days later a Lithuanian policeman called at Walery's digs and left an order for him to report the following day at a camp for Polish war prisoners and refugees.

Walery drafted a petition, which he delivered personally to the Lithuanian Military Commander of Wilno. He was received by him personally. Walery explained that he was not a refugee, as he had been born in Wilno, lived in the city with his parents for many years, and that his grandparents were even buried there. The Commander appeared to be a sympathetic, fatherly type, but explained that he could not rescind the order, although he could delay the date for going to the camp until 30 June 1940, which would give Walery a chance to sit his matriculation exams.

Walery was therefore able to complete his studies. He had a scholarship and earned a little money by helping students with 'learning difficulties', and joined the Underground movement in November. Unable to reach the Polish units in Narvik in June 1940, he managed on 30 June to catch a train to Estonia, where he worked initially as a seasonal farm labourer. At the end of August, after being refused any wages in advance to buy an overcoat, which was necessary to protect him against the increasingly cold weather, Walery moved on to Tallinn, where he made contact with a group of Poles and managed to rent a room in a private hostel. He got casual labouring jobs through the winter, and even managed to secure a job in a Russian naval base. He hoped that he would be able somehow to escape to Sweden, but was firmly told by the Soviet base commander that the authorities knew all about him and that he was not a free agent. Nevertheless he was allowed to return to Tallinn where he got a job as a junior store keeper.

When the Germans attacked the USSR in June 1941, Walery and his fellow Poles had a 'little conference' on what to do. The majority decided to stay put, but Walery reckoned that it was best to report to the Soviet authorities. The reason for this was that he was bilingual in Russian, and he also assumed that the Germans would put the Poles in labour camps or else conscript them. Another important reason was that Russia was in such chaos that he would probably have an opportunity to desert from the Russian Army and escape southwards to Iran where there were British troops stationed at the time.

He was ordered, with 8,000 young Estonian men, to embark on a Soviet ship, which took them to Leningrad. They were then transported by rail to a military camp south of Moscow, where, one day while eating lunch, Walery heard on the radio of the Sikorski-Maiski Pact [Polish-Soviet Agreement of 30 July 1941] and of the creation of

208

Appendix V: Survivors' Reminiscences

the Polish Army on Soviet soil. In the meantime, his military training went on in a base on the Volga near Kazan. After realizing that the Estonian marching songs were intensely anti-Russian, the Soviet authorities decided that the Estonians would be better deployed in pioneer and building units rather than in front line units. The work was exhausting, but one day Walery heard a military band giving a send-off to troops going to the front, and, as he could play the French horn, volunteered his services which were accepted. He figured out that he would survive longer in an orchestra than in a labour battalion! Years later, Walery reflected that he was 'not sure about the existence of God but that he had a guardian angel'.

In October 1941 Walery was sent to Czelabinsk in Siberia to work in a tank factory. When he arrived at the station he noticed a Polish petty officer on the station. Walery told him that he wished to join the Polish armed forces. He was told to stay put but given the address of a military unit whose job was to supply Poles moving south to join the new Polish Army with food and clothing. Once or twice when he was in town he visited this unit and was advised to make an official request to his Soviet commanding officer for release. When he did so, he was firmly told that he had joined the Red Army and had Soviet nationality. Again the Polish unit advised him to stay put until the Sikorski-Maiski negotiations had been concluded.

At Czelabinsk Walery worked virtually as a free agent, was reasonably well fed and could use the workers' clubs in the town. It was a 'reasonably happy period', except that he worked twelve hours a day with one hour's walk through the Siberian cold to the factory and one hour back to his billets. His 'guardian angel' continued to watch over him. For instance, he dared stop work in protest when for two consecutive days there were no lunches. His commanding officer told him, 'I know you are from the West where you strike but here in the USSR you are executed for that!' Still, on this occasion he was pardoned.

Walery was then moved from labouring to the foundry, where the rule was introduced that he must supply two machines at the same time. This involved physically lifting up tank sections. In order to avoid being worked to death he realized that he would have to do something. Again he was lucky. One day, while urinating outside in the snow, he stumbled on a whole stack of key parts for replacing

209

machines and realized that if they stayed there too long they would be useless. He went to the chief engineer and told him as a result of his store keeper experiences in Tallinn, that with an assistant he could create a spare store room and keep check on them. Walery's initiative was appreciated and he managed to escape being worked to death.

One day, when Walery was working as store keeper, somebody from the factory office came in and started taking down his particulars. He then asked where he was from. When he was told Vilna (Russian name of Wilno), he congratulated Walery on being liberated to which Walery retorted that Vilna had been occupied and not liberated at all. The official found this attitude 'interesting' and a frank exchange followed. Although they parted 'as the best of friends' the conversation was duly reported to the Party and Walery was accused of counter-revolutionary activity. Again he was lucky and able to escape to the Polish unit in town, and was smuggled onto a train going southwards. He reached a naval unit in the south and then in March 1942 was evacuated to Iran. From there, via Bombay and Cape Town, he reached Glasgow and, at last, joined the Polish Navy.

Adam Lasocki

This account of Mr Adam Lasocki's experiences is based on an interview with him conducted by the author in London on 7 July 2008.
Adam Lasocki finished his exams at his grammar school in July 1939, where he had had some preliminary military instruction. On 16 August he joined the Polish Youth Organization of Work, and was employed building fortifications along a quiet sector of the East Prussian border until 5 September, when he and his fellow workers were dismissed and left to make their own way to safety. Adam had been given his call-up papers but was never actually ordered to report to any regiment. By 17 September he managed to reach Kowel largely by cadging lifts from horse-drawn military transports. He remembers interestingly that his trek across country was 'absolutely free from any Luftwaffe attack'. He attempted to catch a train to Warsaw from Kowel, but ended up going in a lorry to Brody and then Złoczów, where he was eventually rounded up by the Russians and detained in a PoW camp in a derelict castle. He was employed on building a road from Lwów to Kiev. In early 1940 he nearly managed to escape. One evening, when he came out of the hut he was living in to urinate, it

Appendix V: Survivors' Reminiscences

was snowing heavily and pitch-black. He realized that the guards would be unable to see anything. He consequently dashed back and seized his coat and haversack. He managed to climb over two fences but by the time he reached the third, the snow stopped and the moon came out. Despite a guard shooting at him he managed to get over but then, as he tried to run for cover in a nearby village, Soviet troops caught up with him, shot at him again and one bullet entered his chest. He was, however, able to walk back to the camp, where he spent the night in the medical room. The following day he was taken to Złoczów, where the surgeon decided not to operate. Adam's life was probably saved when a fellow prisoner, W. Sypel, asked if he could speak Russian. When Adam answered in the affirmative, in an act of great generosity, Sypel offered to exchange his safe office job in the camp with him and to take up his place in the road-building gang.

For the next year Adam worked in the office, but when the Germans launched their attack against the USSR on 22 June, they were rapidly moved into the interior of the Soviet Union. They were force-marched for a period of four weeks. Adam was in the column of prisoners who were bombed by the Luftwaffe. Some 200 prisoners were wounded or killed. A Polish medic, Doctor Serota, volunteered to stay with them – they were never seen or heard of again. Eventually, Adam and the remaining PoWs arrived at a former monastery, where they were met by NKVD officials who informed them that 'for now, we are friends'. This was met with a chorus of wolf whistles! But they were informed that, as a result of the Sikorski–Maisky Pact, they would be able to catch a train southwards.

Adam caught the train. He remembers that, at one station where there was a buffet selling sausages and cheesecake, he queued with five other Poles only to miss the train. They then went to the station master, who put them on a goods train going in the same direction. At the next junction they went to the NKVD office to get their ration cards. Adam managed to find a red pencil and in front of the number 5, insert a 3. On the journey south they travelled on both goods and passenger trains. On one passenger train they stood on the coupling between two carriages. They met a gang of newly released Russian criminals, who accused Adam because of his foreign accent of being

211

Jewish, and threatened to throw him off the train unless he gave them visual proof that he was not a Jew, that is, by showing he had not been circumcised. From time to time, Adam managed to earn a few *kopeks* by helping wealthy Muscovites fleeing from Moscow to find places in the trains.

Eventually they arrived at a Soviet artillery exercise ground at Totskoye, where the original trainload of Poles had ended up. They were put under canvas and began military training. In the end they were sent to Iran, and Adam joined the 3rd Carpathian Rifle Division of the Polish Army which incorporated the former Carpathian Brigade, that had been formed in Syria in April 1940.

Władzia Tańska (née Pogoda)
This account of Mrs Tańska's experiences is based on an interview with her conducted by the author in Little Chalfont, Bucks on 3 December 2007.
Władzia lived near Lwów and Brody on a large farm owned by her parents. Her first experience of the war was when she heard the Germans bombing the town of Brody, where they hit an ammunition train. She was at her grandmother's and immediately wanted to go home; her house was very near but there were German planes 'flying all over the place' and bullets hitting the tin roof of her grandmother's home. Her granny told her 'to run and hide under the trees or they will kill you'. She remembers, too, the crowds of refugees, running from the Germans and asking for food and shelter. One day she witnessed the shooting down of a German plane. Her father insisted that the crew should be interred in the local cemetery as 'they were human beings too'.

Gradually the shooting eased and on 17 September 1939 the Russians moved in. She felt quite safe at home and her family was more frightened of the local Ukrainians than the Russians. She did, however, now have to attend a Ukrainian school, 'the Polish school was closed', where she was bullied and her buttons were cut off by the Ukrainian children. Shortly before Christmas her family were asked for food and refuge by a group of Polish soldiers attempting to make their way through to the 'green border' of Romania or Hungary. They stayed overnight but had to bury their rifles behind the barn and the children were encouraged to roll on the snow to hide

Appendix V: Survivors' Reminiscences

any traces from the Russians. One remained with them to work on the farm. Władzia does remember the internment of Polish PoWs and how her mother and cousins would take food for them to the camp while they were working, building the road nearby in very cold weather, with snow everywhere. One time a Russian guard kicked over a bucket of soup, which she had just brought them, and said 'They have to work, not eat.'

The family was able to celebrate Christmas at home, although at school she was told that there was no such thing as Father Christmas or God. In January their uncle heard from some local Ukrainians that the Poles were being deported. This did not surprise Wladzia's father, who realized that 'something will happen – either they kill us here or take us away.' On 10 February 1940, just as she was going to school, Russian soldiers and a local Ukrainian official appeared and told them to get ready and pack up some belongings. Her father was put facing the wall with his hands up – he was shouting in anger that this was their farm, and her mother was crying, telling him to stop because she feared they would kill him and she would be left alone with two children. The Polish 'uncle' or soldier, who had stayed to work on the farm, somehow managed to escape that fateful morning. The horse was harnessed to the sledge and all that could be taken was food and clothes. Her mother just had time to kill a few chickens for food on the way. Her daughter remarked poignantly that within a few hours they had 'lost everything' – their lovely home especially. Władzia remembers particularly how their dog barked all the time as they loaded up the sledge.

That evening they were taken to the station and the rest of the family were also picked up. They were all packed into the same wagon, but two cousins managed to escape and hide with local Poles. Why did they escape? It was because they were taken with their father, while their disabled mother and sister were left at home. Władzia's family spent some three weeks on the train. There was a stove in the middle of the wagon and a hole for the toilet. She still remembers the monotonous sound of the wheels and the puffing of the locomotive. There were many wagons on each train and there were hundreds of trains. They could see through a small window, and would shout to people asking where they were from. Eventually they reached Kotlas, where they at last got out of the train and were able to walk along the track to a smaller train and travel in an open truck to Kotowalsk. There they lived in a wooden hut. They could buy food in the canteen, if there was any left. In three or four months they were moved on to a camp at Privodino. Władzia went to a Russian school, and her mother had to work shifting timber to the river while her father was working in a wood yard. Each family was given a small room within the hut. Her parents, her mother's parents, her sister, a brother and herself all lived in this one room. The camp commandant was a zealot who banned prayer and kept saying that they would 'die like dogs' there. Parcels could be sent from Poland and she remembers one day some flour and dried bread arriving. The Commandant duly checked to see whether a gun was hidden in the flour and discovered a bottle of butter. Her father remarked that if it had been a gun he would have shot the Commandant dead. They were free to grow some vegetables in the summer and some of the camp inmates would steal food from the fields. She herself was sent to a nearby house to buy milk for her little sister with *roubles* earned by her parents (the camp was fenced with very high wooden planks, but someone had managed to take two panels away and one could get out, but the planks would always have to be replaced). At school Władzia and other Polish children were always told that they would never go back home to Poland. It was hard at school – different alphabet, different systems.

After the Polish-Soviet Agreement of July 1941 they were freed from the camp, but not everyone. Władzia's parents had received the correct papers to go, but her grandparents did not – they had to stay. She never saw her grandfather again – he died, although her grandmother did eventually get out of Russia. They returned to Kotlas and lived with a Russian family, to whom they gave some of their clothes as rent. They then travelled south by train. The train took four months to arrive at its destination at Guzor, since the engines were frequently detached and coupled onto Russian troop or ammunition trains. Her family survived by buying food from the surrounding villages. One day her father and friends jumped out of the wagon to find food, only to return to see the train beginning to move off. Her father managed to leap on the end of the last wagon and just had the strength to hold on until the train stopped again.

When they arrived at Guzor the Polish authorities sent them to a

Appendix V: Survivors' Reminiscences

collective farm some 30 kilometres into the mountains on the Afghan border. They travelled all day on donkeys and horses and arrived on Christmas Eve at Jaskro village, where, 'like the Holy Family' they were housed in a stable with straw on the ground. They stayed with the Uzbeck peasants until March 1942. Władzia remembers her father and another Pole killing a dog for food. Afterwards the remains were buried outside the hut and the children were told to use that spot as a lavatory to disguise it from the Uzbecks, who might well have killed her father if they had known that he had eaten one of their dogs. As she remarked, 'everything was put as a joke, as otherwise they would not have survived'.

When they returned to Guzor, the Polish military authorities housed the families in mud huts and the men were conscripted and put under canvas. Władzia's sister and both parents caught typhus. She remembers seeing soldiers taking bodies to be buried, and putting them on a lorry like logs. She was in the meantime put in an orphanage, where she developed malaria, but she did manage to see her uncle, who told her that her parents had survived. In due course she was transported to Iran, where she met up with her mother in Teheran. After five years in the Middle East, during which she was ill 'for much of the time', she landed in Liverpool in September 1948.

Louise McCall (née Ludwika Bombas)
The following is an extract from the unpublished memoirs of Louise McCall.
I was due to go to school at the age of six in September 1939 and was enrolled at a convent school in Lwów. The uniform was a navy-and-white sailor-suit-type dress with a lovely pleated skirt. It hung on my wardrobe door from May 1939 onwards but I never got to wear it, as the beginning of the war coincided with the start of term . . .

September 1939 was a terrible month with hourly bulletins announcing the ever worsening Polish situation until the capitulation on 21 September, when the announcer actually wept on air to the tune of Chopin's funeral march [. . .] The Germans occupied Lwów only briefly, keeping a low profile, and life continued, although abnormally, with a feeling of foreboding that worse things were to come.

Poland Betrayed

The first foreign soldier I saw did not come from Germany but from the USSR [. . .] (see p. 128) The Russians did not bother much with setting up camps but were billeted in Polish homes, apparently helping themselves to whatever took their fancy. We were quite lucky in that our 'lodger' was a young major, aged twenty-two, who was good looking and civilized. He told Tildi (Ludwika's mother) that he would go somewhere else to have a bath if she preferred he didn't use ours. So he didn't bother us too much and went in and out quietly, as did my father, who had joined some conspiratorial group from which one day he did not come back at all. Our lodger told us he had probably been deported to Siberia and that we must leave immediately, otherwise we would be the next to go . . .

We were being increasingly hassled by various commissars to show our sympathy to our masters. One day Tildi was presented with a huge poster of Stalin, which had to be displayed from our balcony during a military parade. Obviously, all balconies facing the parade area had similar requests. Poor Tildi spent ages sewing the thick paper onto a kilim [a pileless, woven carpet – ed.] and hung it from our balcony last thing at night, as instructed. Unfortunately a strong gale came up and in the morning our balcony had lost *batiushka* (little father – Russian pet name for Stalin). There was a loud banging on the door and a policeman admonished Tildi, threatening her with instant eviction as she had subversively removed the poster. Fortunately our 'lodger' stepped in, assured the official that the poster had been displayed and particularly as other balconies were also bare, no more was said of the matter.

There were severe food shortages and Tildi decided to pre-empt any possibility of deportation by throwing in her lot with her Austrian family, relatively easy at the time as the Russians and Germans were buddies and she had dual nationality anyway [. . .] Prompted by the option given to inhabitants of Lwów who were of Austrian nationality, my grandmother, Rosa Leeder persuaded Tildi to join the rest of the family on a resettlement programme to the German-occupied Zone. As already described, from 22 September 1939 Lwów was occupied by a motley band of Russian (Mongolian) soldiers, poor, pock-marked, smelly and dirty, compared to whom the German Wehrmacht looked like a chorus line from a Wagner opera. After my father's capture by the Russians in February 1940, we had no reason

216

Appendix V: Survivors' Reminiscences

to stay in Lwów, as we would probably have followed my father to Siberia, as did thousands of others. Tildi therefore registered for settlement and after being dragged round western Poland and eastern Germany (I only remember a camp in Chemnitz) for a few months, we were allocated flats in Łódź, then called Litzmannstadt, after a First World War general, who later became a Nazi. We lived in Schlageterstr. 9/22, a nice first-floor apartment with pleasant neighbours called Gerono, obviously of Italian origin. Polish street names had all been changed [. . .] Our papers were obviously not good enough for me to be enrolled in the German school, for, in spite of Tildi saying to the headmaster, who grilled her about her background, 'Sie ist ein uneheliches Kind' ('she is illegitimate' – amazing how that sort of thing sticks in a child's mind), I could not be enrolled and attended a 'komplet', or tutorial group, run by two Russian brothers in the company of eleven other kids, some of whom may have been Jewish, as they stopped coming after the first year. We tended to meet in different flats, as this sort of activity was illegal – Polish children were meant to work instead of receiving an education . . .

I don't remember how I met Christl Nazarwicz [. . .] Her family had become *Volksdeutsch* (given German nationality due to German parentage), although her father spoke hardly any German, but Opa – the mother's father – was German and on that basis the whole family had changed. Of course Christl attended school and I used to spend most afternoons at her house doing homework in German with Opa's help.

Unfortunately, most pleasant memories have something Germanic about them: Lunapark, lovely meals with the Feyerabendts (Reichsdeutsch – native settlers who were brought into central Poland to speed up Nazification) who once delighted in showing us photographs they had taken of a public hanging of Poles – and riotous parties with Hungarian officers in German uniforms.

Tildi worked in the benefits section of the local *Landratsamt* (town hall) dealing mainly with assistance to Polish/German folk who had not been absorbed by the system. Of course there were no beggars, so everyone had to have at least a basic subsistence level income. Due to this we could have a maid, Władzia, who looked after me [. . .] I wanted to go to her house, but she refused saying it would be too dangerous [. . .] One day, in September 1944, she rushed in crying,

Poland Betrayed

saying that she had received an 'Arbeitsauftrag' [job order] to go to work in a factory in Germany. There was no escaping this order as the penalty was death. We went to see her off at the Łódź 'Umsatzplatz' and I still see her climb into a lorry, wearing a purple coat and carrying a small brown suitcase with armed German soldiers [. . .] After that things went from bad to worse. We spent a long time in the country [. . .] on my father's stepmother's farm [. . .] I used to disappear for hours with my dog Molly [. . .] until I was told off and stopped going out alone, as there were soldiers and partisans [AK – Polish Home Army] roaming the countryside; the front was moving ever closer [. . .] We returned to town towards the end of 1944.

We struggled on for the rest of the year until the front moved to Łódź in 1945 and it was relatively easy to run away to the West with the panic-stricken Germans. We had received irregular communications from my father from abroad with veiled instructions to leave and this became imperative in January 1945, when one could actually hear the shooting in the outskirts, so once more Tildi obtained false documents and bribed a peasant to take us across the border into the German Reich, to be dumped at the first German railway station.

[*Ultimately, Ludwika Bombas and her family ended up on a farm in Bavaria, where they were rescued by their uncle in November 1945. Her father died in Cairo on 12 May 1945 without ever seeing the family again.*]

Sources

Manuscripts in the Imperial War Museum
Blaichmann, E.F., 02/23/1
Fleming, Peter (P.Z. Tarczyński), 86/17/1
Goldberg, S., 06/521
Golebiowski, A., 95/6/1
Jackiewicz, Wiktor, 01/4/1
Kornicki, F., 01/1/1
Krey, W., 94/26/1
Kurylak, S., 78/52/1
Parker, M. (née Pokorney), PP/MCR/378
Poloniecki, B.M., IWM 92/2/1
Rymaszewski, M.A., 12/28/1
Smorczewski, R., 03/41/1
Solak, B.J., 90/11/1
Wright, W., 06/108/1
Zolski, R., 83/24/1

The Imperial War Museum also has a collection of photostats of German documents captured by the Allies in 1945. The following series were useful:
Al 1053/11 Der Feldzug von Polen by Helmut Greiner
AL 1448 Absicht des Ob.d. und Aufträge
AL 1449 Arbeitsstab Rundstedt
AL 1494 Lagebericht Polen
AL 1887 RHSA Meldungen and Berichte
MI 14/912 Erfahrungsbericht

Memoirs Held Privately
Memoirs of Mrs Teresa Glazer (née Kurowska)
Memoirs of Mrs Irena Haniewicz
Correspondence from Mr Rolland Kwiatkowski
Memoirs of Louise McCall (née Ludwika Bombas)
Memoirs of Mr J. Siedlecki

Poland Betrayed

Interviews With Survivors
Mr Walery Choroszewski
Mr Zbigniew Kwiatowski
Mr Adam Lasocki
Mr Christopher Muszkowski
Mr Naharnowicz
Mr Wojciech Stankiewicz
Mrs Władzia Tańska

Records at the National Archives, Kew

The Foreign Office, the War Office, the Air Ministry and the Admiralty have a considerable number of files with relevant information on the Polish-German-Soviet conflict as viewed through British eyes. The following files were particularly useful to the author:

Foreign Office
FO 898/223; FO 371/23093, 23098, 23100, 23103–4, 23136, 23138, 23142–45, 23147, 23149, 23151–57, 24463, 24465, 24467–69, 24483.

War Office
WO 106/1677, 1747; WO 139/550; WO 178/68; WO 190/798, 843; WO 193/550, 763, 831; WO 216/47.

Air Ministry
AIR 2/9180; AIR 8/260, 274; AIR 14/116; AIR 40/1208, 1624, 2049; AIR 75/6.

Admiralty
ADM 1/ 115, 533, 1052; ADM 116/4098; 171/9971.

Published Sources, Diaries and Memoirs
Adamczyk, Wesley, *When God looked the Other Way*, University of Chicago Press, 2004.
Bernhard, K. (ed.), *Panzer Packen Polen*, Mitteler and Sohn, Berlin, 1940.
Cannistro, Philip, et al (ed.), *Poland and the Coming of the Second World War: The Diplomatic papers of A.J. Drexel Biddle, Jr.*, Ohio State University, 1976.
Czarnomski, F.B. (ed.), *They Fight for Poland*, Allen and Unwin, 1941.
De Lannoy, François. *Album Historique. La Campagne de Pologne, Septembre-Octobre, 1939*, Editions Heimdal, 1999.
Hollingworth, Claire, *Front Line*, Jonathan Cape, 1990.
Kinder, C., *Männer der Nordmark an der Bzura*, Mitteler and Sohn, 1941.

Sources

Kornicki, F., *The Struggle. Biography of a Fighter Pilot*, Stratus, Poland, 2008.

Pielalkiewicz, A., *Polenfeldzug*, Gustav Lübbe, 1982.

Rudnicki, Klemens, *The Last of the Warhorses*, Bachman and Turner, 1974.

Smorczewski, R., *Bridging the Gap: Reminiscences*, Troubadór Publishing, 2007.

Stern, Richard, *Via Cracow and Beirut: A Survivor's Saga*, Minerva Press, 1994.

Sword, Edward, *The Diary and Despatches of A Military Attaché in Warsaw, 1938–39* (eds. E. Turnbull and A. Suchcitz), Polish Cultural Foundation, 2001.

Secondary Sources

Aurich, Peter, *Der Deutsch-Polnische September 1939*, Westkreuzverlag, 1985.

Bethell, Nicholas, *The War Hitler Won*, London, Penguin, Allen Lane, 1972.

Bielecki, Zygmunt and Ryszard, Debowski, *In Defence of Independence*, Interpress Publishers, 1972.

Bowyer Bell, J., *Besieged: Seven Cities Under Siege*, Chilton, 1960.

Cienciala, A.M., *Poland and the Western Powers, 1938–39*, Routledge and Kegen Paul, 1968.

Citino, Robert, *The Evolution of the Blitzkrieg Tactics*, Greenwood Press, 1987.

Cooper, M., *The German Army 1933–45*, Macdonald and Jane's, 1978.

Cynk, Jerzy B., *History of the Polish Air Force, 1914–1968*, Osprey, Reading, 1972.

Davies, Norman, *God's Playground: A History of Poland*, Vol. 2, Columbia I.P., 1982.

De Lannoy, François, *La Campagne de Pologne*, Editions Heimdal, 1999.

Elble, R., *Die Schacht an der Bzura aus Deutscher and Polnischer Sicht*, Verlag Rombach, Freiburg.

Erickson, John, *The Soviet Command: A Military-Political History, 1918–1941*, (third edition), Frank Cass, 2001.

Fowler, Will, *Poland and Scandinavia, 1939–1940*, Ian Allen, 2002.

Garder, Michel, *A History of the Soviet Army*, Pall Mall Press, 1966.

Garlinski, Josef, *The September Campaign in Poland*, Macmillan, 1985.

Hooton, E.R., *Phoenix Triumphant: The Rise and Fall of the Luftwaffe*, Arms and Armour, 1994.

Janowicz, Krystof, *Luftflotte I*, Kagero, 2002.

Janowicz, Krystof, *Luftflotte IV*, Kagero, 2003.

Jurga, Tadeusz, 'Polish Strategy in the Defensive War of 1939' in *Military Technique, Policy and Strategy*, Defence Publishing House, Warsaw, 1976.

Poland Betrayed

Karski, J., *The Great Powers and Poland, 1919–1945*, University Press of America, 1985.

Kennedy, Robert, *The German Campaign in Poland*, US Army Pamphlet, 20–255, 1956 (first edition 1942).

Kimmich, Christopher, *The Free City: Danzig and German Foreign Policy, 1919–1934*, Yale University Press, 1968.

Kozaczuk, Władysław and Straszak, Jerzy, *Enigma: How the Poles Broke the Nazi Code*, Hippocrene, 2004.

Michaelis, R., *Die Geschichte der SS Heimwehr, Danzig*, Verlag fur Militarische Zeitgeschichte, 1990.

Norwid-Neugebauer, *The Defence of Poland, September 1939*, Kolin Ltd, 1940.

Peis, G., *The Man Who Started the War*, Odhams, 1960.

Piekalkiewicz, J., *Polenfeldzug*, Gustav Lübbe, 1982.

Preszke, Michael A., *Poland's Navy, 1939–1945*, Hippocrene, 1999.

Read, Anthony and Fisher, David, *The Deadly Embrace: Hitler, Stalin and the Nazi-Soviet Pact, 1939–41*, Michael Joseph, 1988.

Solarz, J., *SS Verfügungstruppen, 1939*, Militaria, 2004.

Spiedel, W., *The Luftwaffe in the Polish Campaign*, Parts I and II, MLRS Books (reprinted), 2006.

Spiess, A. and Lichtenstern, H., *Das Unternehmen, Tannenberg*, Limes, 1979.

Stachura, P.D., *Poland Between the Wars, 1918–1939*, Macmillan, 1998.

Stjernfelt, B. and Boehme, *Westerplatte 1939*, Rombach, 1978.

Strzetelski, Stanisław, *Where the Storm Broke*, Roy Slavonic Publications, 1942.

Suchcitz, A., *Poland's Contribution to the Allied Victory in the Second World War*, Caldra House, 1995.

Suchcitz, A., 'Poland's Defence Preparations in 1939' in *Poland between the Wars, 1918–1939*, Macmillan, 1998.

Sword, K. (ed.), *The Soviet Takeover of the Polish Eastern Provinces*, Macmillan and School of Slavonic and Eastern European Studies, 1991.

Szawłowski, Ryszard, 'The Polish-Soviet Wars of 1939', in K. Sword (ed.), *The Soviet Takeover of the Polish Eastern Provinces*, pp. 18–43.

Vorman, Nikolaus von, *So Began Der Zweite Weltkrieg*, Druffel Verlag, Leoni and Starnbergersee, 1988.

Zaloga, S.J., *Poland 1939: The Birth of Blitzkrieg*, Osprey, Oxford, 2002.

Zaloga, S.J., and Madej, V., *The Polish Campaign 1939*, Hippocrene, 1985.

Zuk, Bill and Zurakowski, Janusz, *Janusz Zurakowski, Legend in the Skies*, Crécy Publishing, 2004.

Index

Index

Poland Betrayed

Index